Susanna Wilhelmina Derks

Power and Pilgrimage

Nijmegen Studies in Development and Cultural Change

edited by

Prof. Dr. Frans Wijsen, Prof. Dr. Ruerd Ruben
and Dr. André van der Ven

Volume 47

The Nijmegen Studies
in Development and Cultural Change
are peer reviewed

LIT

Sanne Derks

POWER AND PILGRIMAGE

Dealing with Class, Gender and Ethnic Inequality at a Bolivian Marian Shrine

LIT

This publication has been realized with the financial support of the J.E. Jurriaanse Stichting and the Radboud University Nijmegen

Layout: Marije Rosing

Bibliographic information published by the Deutsche Nationalbibliothek
The Deutsche Nationalbibliothek lists this publication in the Deutsche Nationalbibliografie; detailed bibliographic data are available in the Internet at http://dnb.d-nb.de.

ISBN 978-3-643-90014-2

A catalogue record for this book is available from the British Library

Fresnostr. 2 D-48159 Münster
Tel. +49 (0) 2 51-620 32 22 Fax +49 (0) 2 51-922 60 99
e-Mail: lit@lit-verlag.de http://www.lit-verlag.de

Distribution:
In Germany: LIT Verlag Fresnostr. 2, D-48159 Münster
Tel. +49 (0) 2 51-620 32 22, Fax +49 (0) 2 51-922 60 99, e-Mail: vertrieb@lit-verlag.de

In Austria: Medienlogistik Pichler-ÖBZ GmbH & Co KG
IZ-NÖ, Süd, Straße 1, Objekt 34, A-2355 Wiener Neudorf
Tel. +43 (0) 22 36-63 53 52 90, Fax +43 (0) 22 36-63 53 52 43, e-Mail: mlo@medien-logistik.at

In Switzerland: B + M Buch- und Medienvertriebs AG
Hochstr. 357, CH-8200 Schaffhausen
Tel. +41 (0) 52-643 54 85, Fax +41 (0) 52-643 54 35, e-Mail: order@buch-medien.ch

Distributed in the UK by: Global Book Marketing, 99B Wallis Rd, London, E9 5LN
Phone: +44 (0) 20 8533 5800 – Fax: +44 (0) 1600 775 663
http://www.centralbooks.co.uk/html

Distributed in North America by:

Transaction Publishers
New Brunswick (U.S.A.) and London (U.K.)

Transaction Publishers
Rutgers University
35 Berrue Circle
Piscataway, NJ 08854

Phone: +1 (732) 445 - 2280
Fax: + 1 (732) 445 - 3138
for orders (U. S. only):
toll free (888) 999 - 6778
e-mail: orders@transactionpub.com

To Martha Condori Cruz
and my mother, to whom I promised to be a writer

CONTENTS

LIST OF MAPS AND PHOTOS

MAPS

PHOTOS

ACKNOWLEDGEMENTS

For five years I have dedicated myself entirely to this PhD project. I have experienced it as an intense pilgrimage, full of sacrifice and joy. Blood, sweat, and many tears have been invested, but there have also been lots of jokes, friendships, passion, and confidence. This thesis could not have been completed without the help and support of those that I mention here.

First of all, I want to thank my colleagues of the research program *The Power of Marian Pilgrimage: A Comparative Study*: Willy Jansen, Catrien Notermans, Anna-Karina Hermkens, and Ien Courtens for all the inspiration, girlpower, and fun. My study has been part of this research program that was carried out at the Institute for Gender Studies and the Department of Cultural Anthropology at the Radboud University Nijmegen. In the pilgrimage project, five pilgrimage places on four continents, in France, Jordan, Indonesia, Papua New Guinea and Bolivia, were studied and compared on the power dynamics that came into play at each particular shrine. I also want to thank the Dutch Organization for Scientific Research (NWO) for financing the program in the research line: 'The Future of the Religious Past' and for the yearly conferences.

I owe deep gratitude to all Bolivians who have opened up to me during fourteen months of fieldwork. For some people I have used pseudonyms, for others not, depending on their wishes. In particular, I want to thank the vendors of the Calvary Hill who accepted me in their midst, and who provided me with a wealth of information on all possible topics. I would like to mention here Virginia and Victoria Willca, the two self-willed, extravert, and sweet sisters with whom I established a profound and special friendship, as well as warm, sensitive, and beautiful Margarita who cared for me as for a daughter, and has contributed much to the intensity of my experiences. I also want to mention Natalia, Sylvia, Eli, Flora, Cecilia, Julia, Francisco, Rosa, and Mercedes for sharing numerous bottles of coca cola with me at the feet of our *Virgen*. I also owe a debt of gratitude to Angela, who always looked out for my visits, and who liked to answer all my questions extensively from her candle stand next to the church. Other Bolivians that I want to thank by name are Ezequil, the sacristan in church, and Alfredo Ramos, who was one of the priests in charge in 2007. Juana, Dora, Gregoria, and Santusa also deserve to be named in this thesis. In the city of Cochabamba I would like to give special thanks to Escarlent, Judy, and Yomar, for sharing so many details and also lots of joy with me. I am so lucky I met all of you overseas! Furthermore, a word of thanks to Arturo, for being my assistant in 2005 and letting me get closer to my data in 2007. In addition, Chrisco, thanks for always being there when I am in crises!

Next I want to thank all dancers from the *Tinkus San Simon* for being able to join you and learn about the complexity of this dance and its meanings. Furthermore, I want to thank all theologians, missionaries, historians, anthropologists, and others I interviewed in Bolivia, as well as all other people who have shared a conversation with me during my fieldwork. I want to thank Hans van den Berg, the director of the Universidad Católica Boliviana in Cochabamba for giving me permission to collect material at the Biblioteca Etnográfica and Roberto Tomichá and Cecilia Eróstegui for the opportunity of giving a few lectures at their university.

Many colleagues have supported me during this PhD-trajectory. The Institute for Gender Studies was an inspiring environment where I felt at ease. Thanks to all, and in particular to Ria Janssen, for being so helpful, enthusiastic, and interested, and Ria van Ooijen, Carla van Rooij and Claudia Krops. I also want to express my gratitude to several colleagues who commented on previous versions of chapters. I thank Marieke van den Brink, Azza Abdelmoneium, Louis van den Hengel, Anna-Karina Hermkens, Anke Tonnaer, Meike Heessels, David Morgan, Evelyn Hendriks, Judith Samson and all others that I forgot to mention. I want to thank all my fellow PhD colleagues for grousing with me about our tough and inspiring jobs.

Also my family and friends have been indispensable blessed rocks of support. My father and Diny for their pep talks, never-ending interest in all my research activities, and for being proud of me. I am grateful that you could come to Bolivia in 2005 to see what this 'anthropologist' was doing in her dangerous field. I also want to thank my sister Nienke and all of my friends for not having left me, their, at times neurotic, stressed out, and control freaked friend. Thank you for connecting me to your worlds and for sharing all the joys and sorrows along the road.

Several people have contributed to the final stage of this dissertation. I thank Jill Bradley for the accurate English corrections, my uncle Harry van Schijndel for the maps and drawings of the Calvary Hill, Elisa Ambrogio for translating the summary into Spanish, Janneke van der Aa and Marije Rosing for the lay out, and Louise Moors for designing the manuscript cover.

A special word of thanks to the two strong women that will stand next to me on the day of the defense. Relinde Moors, you learned to walk in my first shoes, and since then you followed every step I made in my life. You are the closest friend I have, and with your passion and energy you were always able to remind me why I was doing this for the past five years. Marieke van den Brink, I met you as a colleague at the Institute for Gender Studies. Your critical view and powerful drive helped me to understand this weird world of academics. During our PhD work we always went through the same stage together. Analyzing, winning prizes, a recovery holiday in Egypt, finishing, and submitting! It was 'very nice' that you were always there to share experiences.

Last I want to show my gratitude to the two persons to whom I am most indebted. The whole project would not have been possible without the patience and eternal support of my promoters, Catrien Notermans and Willy Jansen. Catrien, thanks for all the effort, the endless comments for improvement, and for being such a pragmatic and passionate woman. Willy, I want to thank you for giving me the space to negotiate my own pilgrimage through the academic world. Thanks for giving me the freedom to develop, for showing me the ability to believe in every idea, and for having faith in me.

Photo 1: Victoria praying from her heart for pilgrims at the Calvary Hill

1

INTRODUCTION

'The Calvary Hill is a calvary...'

- Virginia Willca, Quillacollo, 4-8-2005

These words were spoken by Virginia, a poor 59 year-old petty trader: every day she sells her prayers and blessings to pilgrims on the Calvary Hill at the Catholic pilgrimage site of the Virgin Mary of Urkupiña in Quillacollo, Bolivia. Many Latin American sanctuaries have their Calvary Hill to commemorate the suffering of Christ (Boero Rojo, 1993). Virginia was referring to her own suffering, because that day she had not sold any blessings and had been involved in a fight with the other vendors of blessings. Living in poverty, she is dependent on the precarious income she makes at the Calvary Hill. Poverty is not her only problem, as a Quechua migrant woman she also suffers from gender and ethnic inequality.

Her interpretation of the Calvary Hill as a place that represents suffering is shared by other pilgrims to the shrine, as most people go there to deal with problems they encounter in their daily lives. As a vendor of blessings, Virginia is confronted every day with people's suffering as they tell her their stories, and seek her assistance in putting their problems to Mary. It is the relation between religion and the suffering due to different inequalities of daily life, as seen at a pilgrimage site, that is the topic of this book. In particular, it is about the ways that devotees deal with different forms of social inequality at the pilgrimage shrine of the Virgin of Urkupiña.

Pilgrimage is seen as an arena where the power structures in society are articulated and mediated. Pilgrimage reveals much about the power structures in society as devotees come to the shrine to articulate their sufferings in a religious discourse, and to seek support in coping with or overcoming problems. As people come together with different goals and desires, pilgrimage can be seen as a product and manifestation of a social environment (Reader & Walter, 2001), and a reflection of the power structures in society. Places of pilgrimage, in general, act as platforms for recognition of personal distress because they provide space for public performances in which problems and suffering are made visible and can be discussed (e.g. Dubisch, 1995; Orsi, 1996, Notermans, 2008). In addition, pilgrimage often provides pilgrims with possibilities to deal with problems and suffering. This raises the central question: How do Bolivian devotees deal with class, gender and ethnic inequality at the pilgrimage shrine to the Virgin of Urkupiña?

The shrine of the Virgin of Urkupiña is located in Quillacollo, a market town in a valley in the Cochabamba department, only 13 kilometers from the city of Cochabamba. Due to its position in the middle of the country, between the highlands and lowlands, it is often called 'the heart of Bolivia'. It is only since the 1970s that the shrine has gained national popularity. Before it was just well-known locally, and attracted mostly Quechua people from the direct surroundings of Quillacollo. Nowadays people from all over the country and from different backgrounds come to the shrine. The pilgrimage to the Virgin of Urkupiña is a year-round pilgrimage, with pilgrims coming every day to visit Mary's shrine. Most pilgrims visit both the church in the town, where the image of the Virgin of Urkupiña is housed throughout the year, and the Calvary Hill, two kilometers out of town, where they make their requests and perform most of their rituals. However, her shrine receives the most visitors during the *fiesta* of Urkupiña, from the 13th until the 16th of August, when hundreds of thousands of pilgrims from all over Bolivia and even from abroad visit their *Virgencita* - the Spanish diminutive for Virgin that expresses an affective relation - in Quillacollo.

Given its increased importance in Bolivian society, I was interested to know why the Virgin of Urkupiña appeals to so many people, and with what kinds of social inequalities devotees dealt in this particular pilgrimage. When listening to people's stories three kinds of problems kept coming to the fore. These were related to class, gender, and ethnicity. Therefore, the research question will be answered by asking three interrelated sub-questions: How do Bolivian devotees deal with class inequality on a macro and micro level? What form of gender inequality is expressed, and how do women deal with it on this pilgrimage? Finally, how do pilgrims deal with ethnic inequality at the shrine?

At the present time, pilgrimage is receiving renewed anthropological interest as a result of the revival of religiosity at old places of pilgrimage, and the rise of new sanctuaries. Until the 1980s there had been little anthropological research on pilgrimage. This is remarkable, as anthropological studies are traditionally characterized by the study of religion and ritual, and people in every era and every society have gone on pilgrimage to saints or gods (Jansen & De Jonge, 1991). The study of pilgrimage offers special challenges to anthropologists, whose tradition has emphasized the notion of a field 'site', as it violates notions of limitation (Dubisch, 1995; Eade & Sallnow, 1991; Morinis, 1992). After all, pilgrims come from different places, and usually do not stay at the shrine for any length of time, nor do they necessarily form a definable group with an identifiable culture. After Victor and Edith Turner (1979) introduced their theory on pilgrimage, interest increased. For example, Eade & Sallnow (1991) reacted to Turner's idea of 'communitas', and proposed viewing pilgrimage as an 'arena for social conflict', as a heterogeneity of different people - and powers - coming together at the shrine. Based on Eade & Sallnow (1991) I consider the pilgrimage site as an arena where power relations between people are articulated and mediated.

Anthropologists have rarely studied pilgrimage from the perspective of the socially weak, and asked why marginalized persons are such important agents in pilgrimage: only more recent studies have taken this question into account (e.g. Orsi, 1996; Dubisch, 1995; Coleman & Eade, 2004; Hermkens, Notermans & Jansen, forthcoming). This project is in line with these earlier studies, and questions the power differentials. Following Foucault's (1977: 98) view on power, individuals are seen as 'always in the position of simultaneously undergoing and exercising power.' My study aims to show how the pilgrims and other actors at the site, such as priests or vendors, are actively negotiating for power within the social inequalities they experience, by approaching Mary. In addition I ask whether Marian devotion empowers them, and if so, how. The word 'negotiate' indicates the - llimited - agency of pilgrims to deal with these different forms of social inequality. They can look for solutions; they can contest and resist the inequalities in pilgrimage. Furthermore, the word 'to negotiate' indicates a trade relation that is established in the pilgrimage. In rituals and performances about their suffering of inequalities in daily life pilgrims negotiate with Mary. It is even more relevant because the pilgrimage to the Virgin of Urkupiña is an economic affair par excellence.

This study looks at the everyday lived experience of religion of Bolivians at the pilgrimage site, and how the problems of daily life are interwoven with pilgrimage, regarding religion as it is practiced in the context of daily life (e.g. Orsi, 1997; 2005; Hermkens et al., forthcoming). Pilgrimage is an exceptional practice, both out of the ordinary, as emphasized by Turner (1979), and part of daily life. It will be asked what everyday struggles the pilgrims bring to Mary, and what experiences and objects they bring home. The daily problems of different people that work at the shrine will also be discussed.

Lived religion does not necessarily correspond with official religion, as it consists of the actual practices and beliefs of people as they live their lives (Christian, 1972; Mcguire, 2003), and these beliefs and practices are not necessarily in line with what the church prescribes (Janssen, 2002: 16). Religion exists in a multiplicity of personal and remarkable variations (e.g. Janssen, 2009: 7). The focus will be on the personal interpretations of religion and religious experiences of Bolivians at the shrine of Urkupiña, that is, on the informal side of religion. This implies that individuals are studied in order to understand what is meaningful to them, and how they construct these meanings of what they perceive as religious behavior. The institutional side is addressed only to provide a contextual frame. Central is the personal creative, flexible and dynamic side of religion.

Throughout the world Mary, as a symbol, is susceptible to multiple interpretations and appropriations. The Virgin Mary and the multiple meanings she has for different people confirm the ambiguity of religious symbols (De Haardt, 1999: 25). In differing cultural contexts, devotees refer to Mary with different titles and representations. However, despite her plurality of representations, she is one, a single acknowledged figure. It is this that makes her so powerful: she is universally recognizable, but at the same time receptive to multiple appropriations (Jansen, 2005; Notermans, 2008). As an important and universal religious symbol, it is interesting to study the devotion to her in a specific context like Bolivia, since every context brings forth different forms of devotion and religious interpretations. The Virgin of Urkupiña is recognizable by her apple-red cheeks, her facial expressions, her long curly eyelashes, her colorful dresses full of glitter and embroidery, and her sparkling jewellery. Her appearance of wealth plays a role, in that she is particularly famous for her help in economic issues. However, she is universally recognizable as the Virgin Mary with Jesus on her arm. The meanings and interpretations that Bolivian devotees have of Mary, and of the Virgin of Urkupiña in particular, will be studied.

Insights into pilgrimage, lived religion, power, class, gender, and ethnicity have been gathered by analyzing the narratives, objects, and performances present at the pilgrimage site. These stories, objects, and rituals are seen as the tools to express religiosity, and studying the meanings invested in them can lead to an understanding of how social inequality is manifested, contested, and mediated at this Bolivian Marian shrine. Narratives for example, are useful as religious meaning is constructed in personal stories. A storyteller actively reconstructs her or his role in, and the meaning of, recounted experiences (Jackson, 2002: 15; Orsi, 1996; 136). I agree with Yamane (2000: 173) who argues that when we study religious experience we cannot study religious experience in real time with its physical, mental and emotional constituents, and therefore we must study linguistic representations of religious experience. In fact, we study how an experience is made meaningful through language. In addition, life histories are useful to understand how people construct their pasts into a meaningful whole, and this also enables us to understand in what context the religious experiences acquire their meanings.

Objects also have to be interpreted through reading the stories that accompany them. Objects abound at sacred sites. There is not only the sacred statue of Mary, but also replicas of her and other devotional objects sold to pilgrims, as well as the candles, ex votos, stones and miniatures offered to her. In order to understand the meaning of objects, the personal stories, conflicts, and biographies of people have to be studied, as things derive their meaning from the interaction between persons and these things. The trajectory of the objects used at the site is studied. 'Following the objects', as proposed by Appadurai (1986), Kopytoff (1986) and Hermkens (2005) leads to other places, as the objects move with the pilgrims between the site and their homes. In this aspect, my study follows Coleman & Eade (2004) who proposed studying 'movement' in relation to pilgrimage. The movement of objects reveals the movement of pilgrims, from the pilgrimage site and back to their homes.

The dynamics of performances can be viewed as another form of movement that adds meaning to the religious experience. Studying the performances such as the blessing ritual, the dance processions in honor of the Virgin, or the heavy labor of cutting stones as offerings, can reveal a great deal about the way people experience their religion. Thus, studying the narratives, objects, and performances leads to an understanding of the meanings Bolivian pilgrims give to Mary, and their religious practices at the pilgrimage site, and how they relate these to the problems of everyday life.

Social inequalities in Bolivia

Bolivia borders on Peru in the northwest, on Chile in the west, on Argentina and Paraguay in the south, and Brazil in the east and north, as can be seen on map 1. It has a surface of 1,098,581 square kilometers, but with only 9.1 millions of inhabitants it is not densely populated. It has a varied climate: a large part of Bolivia consists of the Amazon forest and warm and humid lowlands, and another part consists of the *Altiplano,* a flat plateau at 4000 meter altitude, and the mountain range of the Andes. The town of Quillacollo and the city of Cochabamba, where I carried out this research, are situated in a fertile valley of the *Altiplano*, at about 2,500 meters altitude. There is a wet and dry season each year, but during my one-year fieldwork period in 2005, I experienced it as the valley of eternal spring.

Catholicism is Bolivia's national religion. According to the CIA World Factbook (2008) about 95 percent of the population is Catholic, the other 5 percent is Protestant. Bolivia is South America's poorest country with around 60 percent of the inhabitants living under the national poverty line (CIA, World Fact Book, 2008).

The poverty line is the level of income below which one cannot afford to purchase all the resources one requires to live. People who, by definition, have an income below the poverty line have no discretionary, disposable income. According to the statistics of the National Institute of Statistics (INE, 2007) in 2005, 36.7 percent of the inhabitants even lived in extreme poverty, meaning that they have less than one dollar a day per capita. An article in the national newspaper *Los Tiempos* (2007) shows that in the Cochabamba department, 40.4 percent of the people lives in extreme poverty. Despite these high numbers of the poor, it ranks itself as the fourth richest out of nine provinces, after the lowland provinces Santa Cruz with 25 percent of the people living in extreme poverty, Tarija, 32.8 percent and Pando 34.7 percent. After Cochabamba comes Beni, the last of the lowland provinces, with a minor difference of one percent. The other departments, La Paz (42.4), Oruro (46.3), Chuquisaca (61.5) and Potosí (66.7) are all provinces in the highlands of Bolivia, and poorer than Cochabamba. Poverty intersects with ethnicity, as the largest number of indigenous

Map 1: Bolivia and surrounding countries
Source: United Nations, Map no. 3875, August 2004

people live in the poorer highlands.[1] Furthermore, there are considerable differences between the districts in one and the same province. Cochabamba has some of the - mostly Quechua - villages in the entire country where families live on approximately 19 dollars a month.

The minimum monthly salary has been declared to be 525 BOB (€ 56) in 2007 (Ministerio del Trabajo, 2007), and 647 BOB (€ 69) in 2009 (Ministerio del Trabajo, 2009). However, this salary is based on a full-time workweek on the payroll of an employer. In 2007 the official unemployment rate was 7.9 percent, but it must be noted that Bolivia has high levels of involuntary underemployment, as many people have to work in jobs below their educational level, often on a part time basis, or have to work on short term contracts. Furthermore, the majority of the workforce is informally employed, and has to generate its own income with petty trade or services. Most of the people working in the informal economy earn less than the minimum salary. In recent decades, the national government has supported the neoliberal model, a free-market economy that reduces state intervention to an absolute minimum and functions according to the laws of supply and demand. However, many Bolivians and social scientists hold the neoliberal policy responsible for the increased economic inequality in the country (Farmer, 2004, 2005; Goldstein, 2005; Kohl & Farthing, 2007).

The neoliberal model, as installed in 1985, does not bridge the gap between rich and poor, but increases it (Albo, 2002: 64). The salary differences between rich and poor are very considerable, as a rich person can have an income ten to twenty times greater than that of someone with a minimum income. For example, a house cleaner may earn around 300 BOB a month, which is about 30 euros, whereas a lawyer sometimes earns upwards of 600 euros. Although most figures show that the degree of inequality has increased between 1988 and 1997, the total share of the extremely poor has become less in the last quarter of the 20th century. According to the national census of 1976, 85.5 percent lived with their basic necessities unsatisfied, in 2001 their share was diminished, but 58.6 percent of the Bolivians were still unable to afford their basic necessities (INE, 2007: 381).

A second form of social inequality that is deeply rooted in Bolivian society is that of gender. Gender is seen as a cultural construct and refers to the social traits, behavior and characteristics that are associated with each sex (Golombok & Fivush, 1994). Societal norms play a role in the gender differences, and have far reaching implications in the daily lives of the Bolivian women. Women, in general, are less valued than men in Bolivia. A few decades ago gender inequality appeared on the political agenda. For example in 1979 the *Convención sobre los Derechos Políticos de la Mujer*, the Convention on Women's Political Rights, D.S.

1 Indigenous people in Latin America employ the term *indígena* as a self-description, while *índio* is a deprecating term (Field, 1994: 237). Therefore I will use the terms indigenous people or *indígenas* as a neutral term throughout the text, and I will avoid the terms *índios* or Indians.

no. 9385 was ratified; in 1993 a special government institute for gender issues was established, and in 1995 a special law against domestic violence was installed, *Ley* no. 1674. After that, several other laws and conventions to improve women's legal and social positions have been promulgated (INE, 2003).

Despite the progress in women's rights at a national level, there are still large gender inequalities. For instance, according to the national census that was held in 2001, 80.65 percent of the Bolivian women over 15 years old were able to read and write, whereas 93.06 percent of the men over 15 were literate. There are considerable differences between the rural and urban areas, as in the rural areas only 62.09 percent of the women were able to read and write (against 85.58 percent of the men). Literacy has increased in the past decades, as the census of 1976 shows that only 51.38 percent of the women and 75.84 percent of the men were able to read and write (INE, 2003: 101). There are even greater differences in the highest educational level attained. According to the census of 2001 19.87 percent of the female population over 19 years old had not completed education at any level, compared to 7.75 percent of the men over 19 years old. In the rural areas 39.06 percent of the women, against 15.55 percent of the men, did not complete any educational level. In addition, in Bolivia in general, for 42.21 percent of the women and 43.11 per cent of the men primary school was their highest educational attainment; 21.41 percent of the women compared to 29.64 per cent of the men finished secondary school, and 13.10 percent of the women and 16.73 percent of men had completed some form of further education. Finally, 3.41 percent of the women and 2.77 percent of the men followed another, unspecified, form of education (INE, 2003: 111-112). In employment there are also inequalities, as men and women work in areas that are valued differently. For instance, women more often work as street vendors and market traders in the informal economy, whereas more men work in construction or transport. If men and women work in the same branch, a man usually earns a higher salary. Gender norms also prescribe that women have to take care of the children and the household. The responsibility for childcare, means that it is often difficult for them to work outside the home and they are often economically dependent on their husbands. Sometimes the only way to gain an extra income to maintain their families is in the informal economy.

In almost every conversation with women about the differences in prescribed and actual behavior between men and women the word *machismo* comes up. By this the women mean the stereotype man who behaves in a domineering way towards women. The ideal is a strong, masculine man, in competition with other men while acting in a superior manner to women (e.g. Morales-Gorecki, 1998). The high incidence of domestic violence is often explained by this male gender role. Domestic violence is a common problem in Bolivia, and, according to the Bolivian Health Ministry, encountered in 55 percent of the economically active population (Ministerio de Salud, 2004).

As Bolivia is one of the countries with the largest indigenous population of Latin America, ethnicity is another form of social inequality that demands attention. According to the CIA World Fact Book, 30 percent of the Bolivian population is Quechua, 25 percent is Aymara, 30 percent is *mestizo*, or mixed white and indigenous blood, and 15 percent is white. This classification does not take into consideration the fact that there are more indigenous groups in Bolivia. According to Ruiz Martinez (2007) the actual number of ethnic groups fluctuates between 30 an 40. The Quechuas and Aymaras are the largest Bolivian ethnic groups, and they live in the highlands. According to INE in 2004 there were 5,064,992 Bolivians over the age of 15, and of these people 1,555,641 identified themselves as Quechua and 1,277,881 identified themselves as Aymara. Thus, in total, 56 percent of the Bolivians over 15 years old classified themselves as Quechuas or Aymaras (INE, 2004). Furthermore, around 2000 Urus and more than 30,000 Afrobolivianos also live in the highlands. Ruiz Martinez (2007) specifies 30 ethnic groups in the lowlands, ranging from 86,000 Guaranis, 71,128 Chiquitanos to only 19 Pacahuaras.[2]

Ethnicity is also related to inequality: for example, the national census of 2001 shows that Quechua speaking villages in Bolivia are among the most impoverished in the country and, as a consequence, have the highest rate of infant mortality. A hundred out of every thousand babies born of Quechua speaking mothers die in the first year. Guarani speaking mothers followed with an infant mortality rate of 84 out of 1000 babies; Aymaras had an infant mortality rate of 75, that of Spanish speaking mothers was 53, and of Spanish speaking mothers who also speak a foreign language only 40 out of 1000 babies died in the first year (INE, 2003: 70). Also fertility rates coincide with the spoken languages of the mothers. On average Guarani speaking mothers have a fertility rate of 8.5, followed by Quechuas with a fertility rate of 7.5. Next, women speaking other indigenous languages in Bolivia have an average fertility rate of 7.4. Aymara speaking mothers deliver on average 5.8 babies, and bilingual women who speak Spanish as well as their indigenous language, in general, have 4.5 babies, while bilingual women who speak Spanish and a foreign language have only 2.2 babies. Bolivian women who speak only Spanish had a fertility rate of 3.7 in 2001 (INE, 2003: 60). This too shows the intersection of gender and ethnicity that reinforces inequality.

Ethnicity is a complex term, as it can be seen as a classification of a variety of shared elements, such as race, language and customs. In Bolivia - and Peru and Ecuador - people identify themselves as Quechuas and Aymaras if they speak these languages, the two most widely spoken indigenous languages in Latin

2 INE shows different numbers and classifies the Chiquitanos as the largest group *indígenas* in the lowlands, counting 112,216 people, whereas the Guarani consists of 78,359 people, followed by the Mojeño with 43,303. Another 75,237 belonged in 2003 to another - not specified - ethnic group.

America (Hornberger & Coronel-Molina, 2004). Albo (2004) notes that Quechua or Aymara speakers are also likely to identify according to their geographical region and local cultural traditions, such as *Cochabambino/a*, *Tarabuceño/a* or *Paceño/a*. Dress is an important marker to show in which geographical area someone has been born. For example, the Aymaras from the city of La Paz wear long layered skirts and embroidered coats with bowler hats placed on their heads at a slant. The Quechuas from the Cochabamba valley wear shorter velvet skirts without layers, white blouses and white sun hats. When migrating to another area, people seldom change their clothes, as these show their regional and ethnic identity.

The fertile and commercially active valley of Cochabamba has been an attractive area for migrants from the highlands, especially from mining areas in La Paz and Potosí. However, migrants often suffer from double inequality. They already suffer discrimination as *indígenas*, but this is increased because they are *indígenas* from elsewhere. Although ethnic groups have been marginalized in history, in the past decades there has been a revaluation of ethnic identity in Bolivia. The indigenous people in Bolivia dare more and more to stand up for their past, language, religiosity, ethnicity and identity (e.g. Janssens, 2001). In addition, they are revalued by many of the non-indigenous people. Evo Morales, the first indigenous president of Bolivia, elected in 2005, is a good example of one of the consequences of, as well as boost to, this process. At the same time, there seems to be a process of polarization going on, as discrimination and racism increases among certain segments of the population: especially in the lowlands acts of ethnic violence are on the increase.

Research questions

My project focuses on Bolivia, Latin America's poorest and most indigenous country. At the shrine, in particular class, gender and ethnic inequality came to the fore. The main question of the research is: **How do Bolivian devotees deal with class, gender and ethnic inequality at the pilgrimage shrine to the Virgin of Urkupiña?**

The main research question leads to the following sub-questions:

- What meanings do pilgrims give to the Virgin of Urkupiña and what problems do they take to her?
- How do Bolivian devotees deal with class inequality on a macro and micro level?
- What form of gender inequality is expressed, and how do women deal with it in this pilgrimage?
- How do pilgrims deal with ethnic inequality at the shrine?
- In what way do pilgrims feel empowered, and in what way do they feel disempowered?

Research methods

To answer my questions I used an ethnographic approach. This means that people are studied in their everyday context, while making use of a range of different research techniques. An ethnographic study usually focuses on a single setting or group of relatively small scale to show the depth and complexity of the material. The analysis usually involves the interpretation of the meanings of human actions (e.g. Hammersley, 1990: 1-2). My study focuses on the meanings that devotees give to their pilgrimage to the Virgin of Urkupiña in the context of their daily lives.

In terms of Emerson, Fretz and Shaw (1995: 2) the ethnographer seeks a deeper 'immersion' in other people's worlds, by which they mean looking from the inside at how people lead their lives, what is important to them, and how they give meaning to it, in order to grasp what they experience as meaningful and important. This insider perspective has also been termed 'emic', whereas the scholarly perspective is referred to as 'etic' (Young, 2005: 152). This distinction has been made because of the existing duality between human behavior that is observable from the outside, but does not necessarily correspond to the actual human thoughts and feelings that people have while so behaving (Harris, 1976: 329). Of course, the emic and etic approaches cannot be separated entirely. As Harris (1976: 340) remarks, the neologisms invoke a separation of observers and actors and their behavior, that cannot be separated as such in practice. For example, I use both the observations of what I see happening, and the narratives of informants about their interpretation of these events, about what they think and feel. In addition, the informants may also provide either etic or emic descriptions of the events they have observed and experienced. Furthermore, writing up the analyses is an etic process, as it is done by me, a scholar. However, I will elaborate the emic perspective of the informants by using citations, and link my interpretations closely to the interpretations of the people I studied.

In my project an ethnographic research cycle is used, in line with Spradley (1981). In this cycle, participant observation and recording field notes are always followed by data analysis, which leads to finding new ethnographic questions, more data collection, more field notes and more analysis. So the cycle continues until the project nears completion. The research process is one of constant interaction between problem formulation, data collection and data analysis (Walsh, 2000). The principle of saturation (Wester & Peters, 2004: 202; Cutcliffe, 1999) is used to decide when enough data has been collected about a certain topic. When no new issues or stories arose when asking questions of different individuals about a certain topic, I did not repeat the topic in later conversations. The focus in my book is on the meanings that Bolivians attribute to their experiences, pilgrimage, and to Mary. It relates to the symbolic anthropological approach that studies symbols by speaking with, looking at, and listening to people 'in the field' to gain insights in their thoughts, feelings, and interpretations (Driessen & De Jonge, 1994).

This study is based on a first period of eleven months of fieldwork in Quillacollo and Cochabamba in 2005 and a second fieldwork period of three months in 2007. A combination of several research techniques has been used to collect data. The use of multiple methods, or triangulation, is, as formulated by Denzin & Lincoln (2005: 5) 'a strategy that adds rigor, breadth, complexity, richness, and depth to an inquiry'. This thesis largely draws on qualitative research methods, given its focus on the lived religion of the Bolivians, the meanings they give to Mary and to pilgrimage, and the inequalities they experience. Techniques that are used in this study are participant observation at different places and occasions, in combination with informal conversations, interviewing, both ethnographic interviews, life histories and semi-structured interviews, photo-elicitation methods, surveys, an index-list, collection of statistical data, and literature study. These techniques have been used by all researchers in the project 'The Power of Marian Pilgrimage' to enable cross-cultural comparison.

Participant observation and informal conversations

'Participant observation and informal conversations' were important methods during fieldwork, this is used to cover a mixture of observation and informal conversation (Delamont, 2007: 206). First of all, I observed at the central places of worship at the pilgrimage site, such as the church in Quillacollo, as well as at the Calvary Hill, situated out of town. It is important to observe individuals in different environments, as people do not always behave consistently in every context in which they participate. Speaking with the same person in different contexts gave me the opportunity to understand how individuals are constantly adapting their meanings to their contexts (Walsh, 2000). Therefore I tried to expand the domain of observation to outside the pilgrimage site. Especially the key informants, described later in this section under the heading 'life histories', invited me to participate in their daily lives and gave me the opportunity to study the way they 'live' their religion, not only at the pilgrimage site, but also in their homes and the activities they undertake.[3] I went with them to such places as their houses, their families, the market, the church, the cemetery, to religious

3 It took a while before I was invited to the houses of my participants. When I had an appointment to visit them, they tried to change or cancel it because they were embarrassed to show me their bad living conditions. Once I came to the Calvary Hill and heard that Margarita was sick. I was worried and went with a picture to her village to find her. Directed by other Aymara women, I found her in her tiny house, a shared room in which the two beds for her, her son and her foster daughter barely fitted. From that day things changed, and she invited me to accompany her to the mountain where she used to pray and to have lunch in her house several times. In the same way, I entered the personal sphere of Virginia's life. Showing a picture of her I was directed to her house by some children. I noticed that after the first visit I was welcomed again and again.

celebrations, to meetings of the petty-trader associations, to court and to the doctor. The different contexts in which I spoke with the same persons triggered different stories and details, and thereby gave more varied information about the ways religion is experienced in everyday life.

In addition, I participated in several activities related to the pilgrimage of the Virgin of Urkupiña. Before the *fiesta* of Urkupiña I became a member of the dance fraternity *Tinkus* San Simon in Cochabamba, a dance group at University San Simon. The group has more than 300 members, mostly students, and every year performs its dances at several religious and non-religious occasions in the region, and at the major national dance processions, including the religious dance procession for the Virgin of Urkupiña. In 2005 and 2007 I participated in rehearsal sessions and meetings, I went with a number of girls to the market to buy all the elements necessary to decorate the suit, hat and shoes, and I joined in a few local patron saints' feasts in the villages in the region and, of course, I participated in the two days of dance processions for Urkupiña. This way, I could learn about the dancers' motives for dancing, the multiplicity of meanings that dancing had for them, the representations of the dances, the way the dance processions are organized and the emotions and sensations of dancing and sacrifice. In addition, I was able to compare the religious dance in Quillacollo to the original ritual *tinku* that it represents, which I observed closely in both 2005 and 2007 at the *fiesta* for the saint '*Tata* Santiago' in the village Torotoro, in the north of the Potosí department.

In both 2005 and in 2007 I was present at the *fiesta* of Urkupiña and I participated in all events that are part of this annual festival. I joined in the fifteen days of masses and processions, or *Quincena*, prior to the actual *fiesta*; I observed the religious dance processions on the first three days of the feast; I accompanied several pilgrims to the Calvary Hill to make their requests; I observed and participated in pilgrims' rituals and practices, and observed the farewell processions. To compare the different devotional practices and performances of pilgrims in the context of Andean religiosity, several other religious feasts were visited. For instance, the Carnival in Oruro, with its large and famous dance procession in honor of the Virgin of Socavón, as well as the *Fiesta* of Gran Poder in La Paz and a few local celebrations for patron saints were visited for comparative reasons, and to study the general context of dance processions. Furthermore, I visited the *Fiesta* of Santa Vera Cruz, a rural *fiesta* for fertility, and the *Fiesta* of San Isidro, the saint of agriculture, in which the image of the saint is accompanied by the Virgin of Urkupiña and taken to the fields in front of the Calvary Hill to perform land fertility rites. In addition, Easter and *Todos Santos* - All Saints - were celebrated with the family of Virginia, one of the main informants.

Participant observation at previously described events was complemented with digital video recording. These records capture a moment more intensely and completely than just words. As this study is about 'lived religion', it gives an extra dimension to the study of daily life, as it gives concrete visible details in the direct context of where a certain object, performance or narrative gains its significance (Morphy & Banks, 1997: 9). Another major advantage of the visual recording method is that it enabled me to record for later consideration and re-analysis.

Photography was also used as an entrance to occasions for participant observation. On several occasions my informants invited me with my cameras to take a few shots, such as birthdays, at processions, marriages and religious feasts. Making pictures provided a good opportunity to participate in the daily lives of the informants. It showed me what kind of events were experienced as of value to them. In addition, it gave me the possibility to give the informants something valuable in the form of pictures in return for the information they gave me during numerous conversations. Moreover, reflecting on the pictures with them later, enabled me to elicit further information about the event, while also reflecting on the occasion of the picture (e.g. Bunster & Chaney, 1985).

Informal conversations about all kinds of subjects provided a wealth of information and insights into a broad range of themes and issues. In taxis I often had conversations with the drivers about politics, their religious conviction or social inequality in Bolivia. Buying nuts in the street I could have a conversation about societal norms for men and women that expanded into a conversation on domestic violence. In the university library I could come across a lecturer and ask a few questions. I had informal conversations with all types of people of different classes, ethnicities and ages, policemen, taxi drivers, bus passengers, pilgrims at the shrine, believers in the church, students and lecturers at the university, children, lawyers, priests, market women, nuns, school teachers and carpenters. In total, the informal conversations were held, with varying frequency, with around 200 Bolivians.

Interviewing

A first form of interviewing that I used during my fieldwork was semi-structured. In total 22 semi-structured interviews were carried out, in order to gather information and opinions on a wide range of different topics from the perspective of specialists. Nine Bolivian anthropologists were interviewed, two historians and eight specialists of religion, such as priests and theologians. These interviews focused on several topics, such as religious feasts, historical details about the *fiesta*, class, gender and ethnicity in Bolivia, the role and opinion of the church, for instance about domestic violence or the rituals practiced at the shrine. Furthermore, the president of the dance group *Tinkus San Simon*, and two presidents of the organization of the religious dance processions were interviewed. These three interviews especially focused on different aspects of the dance processions, such as the history, representations, meanings, and organization.

The interviews lasted between forty minutes and three hours, and were mostly held in the first six months of fieldwork to learn to understand Bolivian society, the existing class and gender hierarchies, cultural performances, and church politics.

A second set of interviews were the in-depth ethnographic interviews held with 25 Bolivians. The majority of these were with women, six with men, a Bolivian bar owner from Cochabamba, a researcher at university, the sacristan of the church in Quillacollo, one of the pastors in the parish in Quillacollo, a gardener at the Calvary Hill and the only male petty trader at the Calvary Hill. Ten of the19 women interviewed in this group were female petty traders at the Calvary Hill, most of them belonging to the lower class or lower middle class. Many of these petty traders were Quechua or Aymara, and had migrated from elsewhere to make a living in Quillacollo. They were all religious and present every day at the Calvary Hill. As they dominated the sacred space, I met them on a daily basis, and was told their daily frustrations, joys and sorrows. With the daughter of one of them and a niece of another vendor, I also established regular contacts. Two women, a vendor of candles in the town of Quillacollo and the female owner of a *comedor*, or eatery, close to the church, became key informants. Furthermore, in the city of Cochabamba I became friends with a medical student who was also a member of the dance group, a psychology student and a waitress at a bar. All three girls were of the lower middle class. I also met regularly with a devout older woman from Quillacollo from the middle class and an upper class female lawyer from Cochabamba. During the period of my fieldwork, I met these people several times, some even daily.

All these diverse contacts have been selected because they liked to talk to me about a broad range of themes and issues. They were open and willing to answer my ceaseless stream of questions, and there was a natural bonding. In these intersubjective relationships it felt as if they chose me as much as I chose them (see also Aull Davies, 2008: 89). Although more women from the lower class were represented, women from other classes and men were also explicitly selected as informants. Different ethnicities, Quechua, Aymara and *mestizos*, were also represented.

Life histories of six out of these 25 persons were collected. By narrating their life history, the informants were able to interweave different aspects of their lives in a meaningful way (Nijhof, 2000: 8). The histories gave a profound understanding about important life events, personal suffering and the way religion played a role in people's lives. Life histories of the key informants with whom I established profound friendships were collected. Virginia and Victoria are two poor sisters who both work as *sahumeras*, or sellers of blessings, at the Calvary Hill. They are 59 and 69, from Quechua descent, and twenty years ago migrated with their families from a mining town in the Potosí department to Quillacollo. Virginia's humor, openness and self-willed character made me bond immediately the first time I saw her. Because I knew Virginia, I got to know Victoria, her older sister, who is calmer, more tender, and who talks inexhaustibly - if she is able to hear the question. As she is getting deaf, communication was only possible by shouting in her ear. She does not see well anymore either, and walks bent over. I was invited regularly to visit them in their houses that were constructed diagonally opposite each other in the same district. I got to know all the children, their families and grandchildren, and was invited for birthdays, graduations, and religious feasts.

Margarita is another poor petty trader at the Calvary Hill whose entire life story I collected in numerous hours of ethnographic interviewing during the fieldwork period. She is a 44 years old Aymara vendor of offer ingredients, who migrated almost thirty years ago from the La Paz region. During my fieldwork, she took on the role of being my mother. She warned me for all the potential dangers, cared for me when I had problems, and protected me when men were too obtrusive. When my father came to visit me in April 2005, he asked Margarita to look after me, and from that time she often presented me to pilgrims as '*mi hija Susanna*' –my daughter Susanna. Another key informant with whom I established a close friendship was Angela, who sold candles from her stand next to the church in Quillacollo. Angela was a 67 years old friendly *mestizo* woman, who from her twenties until her mid-forties lived as a nun in Brazil, and for the past twenty years with a disabled woman in a room in the house of her nephew. Religion has always been an important aspect of her life and she showed me how her life was interwoven with her devotion to the Virgin of Urkupiña. The other two women whose life stories I collected were two young women from the city of Cochabamba and regular pilgrims to Urkupiña. Yomar is a middle-class Brazilian woman who has lived in Bolivia for seven years. Five years ago she began her medical studies at the San Simon University. We became friends when I joined the *Tinku* dance group, and together we participated in the dance procession for the Virgin of Urkupiña in 2005 and 2007. I met Escarlent as an employee in the bar owned by a friend I knew from fieldwork during my MA in 2001. She is a 25 years old religious *mestizo* middle-class woman, born and raised in Cochabamba, who became a friend with whom I could both laugh and cry.

Elicitation methods

Elicitation methods have been used as a tool to reveal the meanings of appeals addressed to the Virgin Mary. First of all, an 'iconographic elicitation method' was used in which different visual representations of Mary were presented to the informants. For the project 'The Power of Marian Pilgrimage' Notermans designed a box with 21 image cards that all researchers took to their particular research setting to show to people in different contexts, such as Indonesia, Papua New Guinea, Jordan, France and the Netherlands (Notermans, 2008).

In general, in elicitation methods the lively visual material aims to act as a trigger, causing people to tell their own experiences and narratives. The associations that people have with the pictures stimulate people to tell their stories (Samuels, 2004). The pictures act as a 'medium of communication between researcher and participant' (Clark-Ibañez, 2004: 1512). The images in the box we used represent Mary in different aspects (as an independent woman, a mother, a queen), in different kin relationships (with her child Jesus, her mother Anne; her husband Joseph), and expressing different emotions (happiness, sadness, grief, self-confidence), and characteristics (humble, superior, reigning, protective, rich, simple, worried, contemplative). The iconographies represent, among others, Our Lady of Lourdes, the Pietá, Mater Dolorosa, the Holy Family, and Our Lady of Perpetual Help. I added a few famous local images to the box. These images were presented to the respondents in sets of five, and it was asked which particular image appealed to them, which did not, and why (Notermans, 2008). As Notermans (2008: 474) points out:

> This method helped me in two different ways: first, to discover how pilgrims select from various icons and what reasons they have for loving particular ones 'very much' and others 'not at all'; and second, to overcome the problem of reticence encountered when asking about personal relationships with Mary.

Often, pilgrims cannot articulate their feelings for Mary easily. Notermans (2008: 474) notes:

> People's communication with Mary often lacks the words. It is mainly a language of thought, and herewith an inner and silent communication. Another reason is that when people speak aloud with Mary, they often articulate standard prayer texts such as Hail Mary, and do not look for their own words to express their relationship with her. A final and most relevant reason is that Marian devotion is an intensely emotional practice. Mary evokes thoughts that are tightly connected with emotions or troubles that are mostly silently kept as family secrets rather than publicly expressed in everyday life.

A second elicitation method was used by showing people the pictures I made of the local statue, dance processions and religious practices. The visual material gave people an opportunity to reflect on their personal experiences and enabled me to elicit their personal stories and associations. Moreover, it was useful to ask further questions and obtain detailed information on certain occasions (Bunster & Chaney, 1985).

Surveys

Three different types of surveys were carried out to gather background information about pilgrims and their performances. Firstly, 43 household surveys were held in three different districts of Quillacollo. These surveys aimed to gain insight on the socio-economic background of pilgrims by exploring the family composition and living situations, their economic resources and level of luxury.

Next, 86 pilgrim-surveys were carried out at the Calvary Hill to obtain information about the pilgrims' background, their motives for pilgrimage, the rituals they perform, and their devotional practices at home. I usually approached the pilgrims in front of the pilgrimage site, when they came back after making their requests and sat down in the little stands of the *sahumeras* to pray and make offerings. It was a good time to start a conversation, as they already had done what they had to do at the Calvary Hill, and were sitting and chatting with their family or the *sahumeras*, and the objects they used to give material form to their petitions were revealed for blessing, and this gave me a obvious entry to talk about their requests and the meanings they give to the pilgrimage. Often the conversations covered more than the survey questions and led to personal stories and interpretations of pilgrims.

A final type of survey was held with 62 members of the dance-fraternity *Tinkus* San Simon. In contrast to the former surveys, this took the form of a questionnaire that had to be filled in by the dancers, who were mainly students. Half of the questionnaires were distributed, filled in, and returned at the beginning of the *Entrada*, when the majority of the dancers was fully costumed and waiting to start the dance procession. The other half was distributed and filled in during several rehearsal sessions at the university San Simon in the city of Cochabamba. The questionnaire was constructed to gather information about the dancers' experiences, their motives for dancing, their emotions while dancing, and the meanings the dancing has for them.

Index-list, statistical data and literature study

Another way to gather contextual data on the pilgrimage of Urkupiña and Bolivian society was derived from an index-list composed for the comparative research program and by literature study. The index-list consisted of several topics on which information was gathered at each site. The list is divided into the sections core information, topography, cult object, devotion, pilgrimage, pilgrims, other actors, performances, gestures, words, things, statistics and socio-political context. In addition, statistical data has been gathered at the Bolivian National Institute for Statistics (INE) on demography, gender, and economy. Further, literature was collected to study historical and contextual data on the Andean *cosmovisión*, the devotion to Urkupiña, the rituals and performances, class, gender and ethnicity in Bolivia, and the societal and political context and history of Bolivia. The majority of books and articles has been collected at the *Biblioteca Etnológica* of the *Universidad Católica Boliviana* in Cochabamba, the library of the *Instituto Jurídica de la Mujer* in Cochabamba, the library of CIPCA in La Paz, the library of CEDLA in Amsterdam[4] and the bookshop *Amigos del Libro* in Cochabamba. Finally, in order to understand the development of the *fiesta* to the Virgin of Urkupiña, I have collected newspaper articles from 1967 to 2005 from an archive at the public library of Cochabamba.

Reflexivity: Petty-traders, pilgrims and me as a researcher

I acknowledge that the information and findings that are presented in this book are only 'partial', as it is socially constructed through language (e.g. Clifford, 1986: 7; Goodall, 2000: 12). Goodall (2000: 55) explains the partiality of the stories presented in an ethnography in that they represent only the point of view of the raconteur, and thus only reveal that which the teller of the tale wishes to focus on. Therefore, many authors speak of a 'crisis of representation' (e.g. Elliot, 2005: 154; Goodall, 2000: 13; Madison, 2005). Goodall (2000: 12) explains this crisis clearly:

> Representation is about re-presenting a reality, which assumes a correspondence between language used to create the representation and the reality that gets represented. ... What counts as the truth depends on where you are standing when you observe or participate in it, what you believe about it in the first place, and what you want to do with it.

In fact, reality cannot be captured accurately in words. Firstly because reality does not exist: it is a constructed representation, and secondly because words cannot encompass the complexity of reality (Goodall, 2000: 55). However, words are the only means available to write a dissertation.

One way to deal with the 'crisis of representation' is by being reflexive about who you are as a researcher, be explicit about the choices you make, and the relations you build up with the informants (Davids & Willemse, 1999; Elliott, 2005: 153). I view fieldwork and qualitative research as an intersubjective affair, in which knowledge is not discovered by me, but created in the encounter between me and the pilgrims and believers (e.g. Hastrup 1995, Notermans, 1999). In this attention for the context in which knowledge is created, I am aware of the situatedness of all knowledge. Knowledge is produced and constructed in relationship with the individuals being researched (Abu-Lughod, 1993).

As this study focuses on the perspective of the actors at a pilgrimage shrine, I wanted to construct intersubjective relations especially with pilgrims, but because most pilgrims made only short visits to the shrine, it was difficult to establish profound contacts with them. Most conversations with pilgrims at the shrine focused on a specific aspect of their religiosity, such as their testimonies of miracles, the meanings of Mary, the rituals practiced or the petitions they

4 CIPCA is the abbreviation for *Centro de Investigación y Promoción del Campesinado* or Centre for Research and Promotion of Indigenous Peasant People. CEDLA is the abbreviation for Centro de Estudios y Documentación Latinoamericanos or Centre for Latin American Research and Documentation.

made to Mary. As their petitions are derived from the conflicts they experience in daily life, it was a good start for continuing on aspects of their daily lives, for example about economic struggles, unemployment, marriage problems or migration. However, in such a short period of time, and without the trust that is built up in a profound relationship, it is impossible to understand the whole life-context of pilgrims, and these conversations only gave a fragmented view of certain aspects of their lives.

To understand the daily life of the believers, I established profound contacts with most of the petty-traders at the Calvary Hill, who sold blessings, miniatures, materials for offerings, and drinks outside the gate, because their lives were interwoven with the pilgrimage to the Virgin of Urkupiña. Some of them were there, seven days a week, others came several times a week, and all of them practiced actively their devotion to the Virgin of Urkupiña. Most women were grateful to the Virgin of Urkupiña for providing them with their businesses. Mary's name was mentioned in daily conversations, and when having personal troubles many women entered the church to bring flowers and offer a prayer themselves. Furthermore, during or around the annual *fiesta*, they themselves, with their own families, went as pilgrims. On this day, instead of praying for or selling to others, they bought offering elements for themselves, performed their own rituals and prayed for their personal requests.

As the daily life of the petty traders consists, for a large part, of being present at the pilgrimage site, I was able to understand their daily problems and sufferings and how the Virgin of Urkupiña helps them to deal with these. The inter-subjective relations that were established made it possible to relate different aspects of their lives in a meaningful way. All the women were poor, and in their openness and warmth gave me the possibility to analyze their problems that were related to poverty and class from a bottom-up perspective. From their female perspective they also taught me about gender inequality in everyday contexts. They spoke with me about their suffering, about violent husbands, unwanted divorces, dead children, and unequal income levels of men and women. In addition, many had an indigenous background and taught me about their religious convictions that were influenced by Andean cosmology, and about ethnic related problems such as discrimination. Three of the six informants who told me their life story were petty traders at the pilgrimage site. Their stories were complemented with anecdotes, stories and conversations with the other vendors.

The narratives that evolved during fieldwork are the product of the dialogue between the people and me. It is important to understand how, in many ways, I was an outsider: a white, blonde, European woman, at the time of my year-long fieldwork aged 25. Most petty traders at the pilgrimage place were older women and could have been my mother, or even grandmother. Most of them were mothers themselves, and were amazed that I came alone, without family or boyfriend, to Bolivia. The women sometimes felt responsible for looking after me and warned me for all potential dangers and advised me how to deal with difficult circumstances. In addition, most of them were poor indigenous women, and especially in the beginning they felt flattered that I came all the way from Europe to talk to them, to write a book about their devotion to the Virgin of Urkupiña. An advantage of my obviously different appearance was that I could ask all sorts of questions, and everybody was patient enough to explain everything in the smallest details, as they did not presume that I had an exhaustive cultural knowledge. Also in sensitive subjects I could ask 'stupid' questions to gather a complete view of it in all its complexity. From the first day I sat with my notebook on my lap and wrote down everything that was said. The petty-traders quickly got used to it and did not feel inhibited in telling me personal details about their lives while I wrote down their words. Of course, when somebody told me an intimate story, I focused more on eye contact than on the paper. They learned to know me as a happy, enthusiastic, sensitive and curious woman, who kept on asking questions about all kinds of subjects, and who, just like them, went to the toilet under the bridge.

I would like to comment on the fact that most contacts have been established with women, because first of all, I met more women than men during fieldwork. At the places where I went, more women than men were present. More women walk and sell in the streets, more women visit the church and market, and more women participated in the dance group. Although I spoke with several men, it was hard to build up a personal and close friendship in Bolivian society. I had to keep a distance to protect myself as many men - whether single, married, old or young - wanted more than conversation. Especially when alcohol was involved it was hard to have a fruitful conversation with men. At the pilgrimage site, the majority of the pilgrims drank beer while performing libation offerings and rituals. When speaking to families at the pilgrimage site, it was easier to speak with the women than with the men. Most men were not interested in questions on their religious practices but preferred to offer me a beer.

Outline of the book

This book is built up of eight chapters. The first three chapters contextualize the background of the thesis and, as well as this introduction, consist of a description of the research setting and an outline of the overall theoretical concepts that are used. Next, four ethnographic chapters are presented. All these chapters address a different topic and follow an independent argumentation. This dissertation ends with the conclusions, which reflect on the results of the analytical chapters and answer the research question.

The second chapter outlines the general theoretical framework of this study. First, it discusses the concept of pilgrimage and the anthropological focus of lived religion. Next, it discusses the theoretical concepts of Marian devotion, power and empowerment, and the different forms of inequality, class, gender and ethnicity.

The third chapter: 'The Place of Pilgrimage' introduces the pilgrimage site of the Virgin of Urkupiña. It gives a historical outline of the development of the shrine, it describes the legend - the master narrative as well as the subdominant narratives of pilgrims -, and describes the places that are part of the pilgrimage. Next, attention is addressed to the *fiesta* of Urkupiña that is held in August, and describes all activities that are part of the celebrations that last almost a month in total. This chapter also gives an insight into the cogent and personal relationships that pilgrims establish with Mary and demonstrates how devotees transform her image in a person to whom they can relate.

Chapter four: 'Religious Reproduction of Neoliberal Politics at the Pilgrimage Site', focuses on class inequality on a macro level. It looks at the way the neoliberal structures in society are articulated at the pilgrimage site of the Virgin of Urkupiña. The neoliberal reforms in Bolivia's recent decades are seen as forms of structural violence, as they extended social inequality for the majority of the Bolivians. This chapter looks at the implications of these socio-economic politics for economic suffering on an individual level, and how the neoliberal politics are articulated at the shrine. The pilgrimage to the Virgin of Urkupiña is famous for the material exchanges that take place between pilgrims and Mary. Through the detailed case of Vicky, a Bolivian petty trader, it is shown how the neoliberal model is appropriated and materialized. It is argued that despite severe political and social resistance to this model, it is actually reproduced. In fact, in an attempt to deal with the consequences of the violent neoliberal structures in society by engaging in an exchange relationship with the Virgin, they subject themselves to yet another form of violence.

Chapter five 'Miniatures and Stones in a Spiritual Economy' deals with class inequality on a micro-level. It puts the material objects, predominantly used in this particular pilgrimage to symbolize pilgrims' material requests, centre stage. Building on the view that the spiritual and material conflate in the material expressions of religion, this chapter asks how these objects function in the relation between pilgrims and Mary. The pilgrimage to the Virgin of Urkupiña is aimed mainly at material returns, and pilgrims approach the Virgin particularly with economic and materialistic requests. Kopytoff's cultural biography of things is applied to show how people negotiate with Mary in a spiritual economy. The objects come to symbolize the reciprocal relationship between the supernatural world of Mary and the everyday lives of the pilgrims. The concept of reciprocity shows that the pilgrims work together with Mary in a collaborative relationship. Mary shapes the conditions for change, whereas the pilgrims are empowered to continue their own steps towards their economic aspirations. Thus the pilgrimage to the Virgin of Urkupiña not only consoles on an emotive level, but also activates people to confront their problems themselves.

The sixth chapter, 'Domestic Violence, *Marianismo* and the Anger of Women' emphasizes the way women deal with gender inequality, in particular domestic violence, on this Marian pilgrimage. Scholarly literature on domestic violence in Latin America often explains women's acceptance of domestic violence in the dominant notion of femininity: *marianismo,* in which women are said to embrace the values of the Virgin Mary as a passive and submissive role-model. However, these studies seldom look at whether these women indeed refer to Mary as a symbol to endure gender-related suffering. Chapter six looks at women's experiences of domestic violence and connects this to their interpretations of the Virgin of Urkupiña. Although the stories of Bolivian women are full of suffering, it is shown that they do not merely accept their suffering in marianistic terms. Rage, or *rabia,* came to the fore as a central concept in the experience of domestic violence of Bolivian women, and is a reaction that does not coincide with the notion of *marianismo.* They approach the Virgin of Urkupiña to transfer their rage and to ask for intervention. The Virgin of Urkupiña is not venerated for her qualities of the acceptance of suffering, but is perceived as a powerful, vicious goddess of vengeance. Women's experience of rage is mirrored in this image of Mary.

The last ethnographic chapter, chapter seven: 'Meanings of Movement: Constructing Ethnic Difference in Religious Dance Processions' focuses on dance and the construction of ethnicity. During the *fiesta* of Urkupiña religious dance processions, or *Entradas,* are held in which folkloric urban dance groups make their spectacular performances in the streets of Quillacollo. Since 1999 an *Entrada Autóctona* is held a day before the long established *Entrada Folklórica* with the main aim to include the indigenous people in the *fiesta.* The introduction of this dance procession reinforced the debate on authenticity. The main question in this chapter is how ethnicity is constructed in the two *Entradas.* First of all it is shown that both *Entradas* construct different ethnic identities, as the *Folklórica* refers to an overarching indigenous Bolivian past, whereas the *Autóctona* claims its authenticity in showing the actual ethnic varieties in dance. Next to different ethnic identities, inequality is also expressed as the *Autóctona* is marginalized in comparison with the *Folklórica.* Despite this inequality between the *Entradas,* it is also shown how the dancers in the fraternities when dancing experience a sense of 'communitas', an egalitarian state of spontaneous bonding. In fact, the concept of communitas is appropriated by the groups of the different *Entradas* to create differences between each other. The spectacular show that is performed by the *Folklórica* calls upon feelings of communitas for its members, whereas the shared regional background of the dancers creates feelings of bonding in the *Autóctona.*

The final chapter endeavors to provide a synthesis by uniting the major concepts and findings of this thesis. The conclusions will provide an answer to the research question that asked how Bolivian devotees deal with class, gender, and ethnic inequality at the pilgrimage shrine. I will bring together these forms of inequalities and look at the most important intersections. Furthermore, the conclusions will summarize the main findings of this thesis and go into the theoretical contributions it makes.

Photo 2: Reproductions of the Virgin of Urkupiña are placed by a devotee under the altar in the church of San Ildefonso.

2

STUDYING PILGRIMAGE: CONCEPTS AND THEORIES

This chapter elaborates on the central concepts of this study, and on the specification of the main question and sub-questions. As it focuses on the ways that pilgrimage provides space to deal with different social inequalities, the most important concept is pilgrimage. The first section, therefore, will discuss the main theories and insights concerning pilgrimage and its expression as lived religion. The second section will deal with Marian devotion and discusses examples of how Mary, as a symbol, is appropriated by different groups in dealing with class, gender and ethnic divisions. Power is another key concept that requires specification and this is discussed in the third section, and then this chapter continues by considering the different forms of power inequalities of class, gender, and ethnicity.

Pilgrimage and lived religion

In every era and every society people have set out, crossing the boundaries of their familiar territory, in search of the earthly dwelling of their gods and spirits (Morinis, 1992: 1). Pilgrimage is an activity found in all major religions (Coleman, 2005: 385; Reader & Walter, 2001: 3). In recent decades, pilgrimage centers all over the world have been receiving growing numbers of pilgrims (Reader, 2007), and the phenomenon of pilgrimage has received increasing attention from anthropologists since Victor and Edith Turner (1978) proposed their theory of pilgrimage in the book *Image and Pilgrimage in Christian Culture*.

Inspired by Van Gennep's model of *rites de passage*, Turner and Turner (1978) compared pilgrimage to a rite of passage in its ritual structure, a structure that includes separation of the pilgrim from ordinary life, the liminal period of the pilgrimage journey itself, and the return to ordinary life. In particular they emphasized the importance of the liminal phase. This phase stands as the anti-structural counterpart to the structured organization of society, in which the individual gives up his/her normal status and its resulting constraints and enters a state of freedom and of equality with others. According to the Turners, the individuals in this transitional state experience a spontaneous egalitarian bonding and community that they call 'communitas'. In this sense pilgrimage can be said to be anti-structural, because the normal structures of daily life are broken during pilgrimage.

Arguing against the communitas paradigm of the Turners, Eade & Sallnow (1991) stressed the multiplicity of different meanings that are present in pilgrimage. In the introduction to the book *Contesting the Sacred* that they edited, they postulate that pilgrimage, rather than being a state of egalitarian connection between individuals, should be seen as a realm of 'competing discourses'. According to these authors (1991: 5):

> Pilgrimage is an arena for competing religious and secular discourses, for both the official co-optation and the non-official recovery of religious meanings, for conflicts between orthodoxies, sects and confessional groups, for drives towards consensus and communitas, and for counter-movements towards separateness and division. The essential heterogeneity of the pilgrimage process, which was marginalized or suppressed in the Turnerian paradigm, is pushed centre-stage and rendered problematic.

I recognize that communitas may happen during pilgrimage, being temporarily out of time, place and social structure. Later I will show that I found a clear case of this in the dance processions held during the annual festival; these showed a remarkable social bonding among the various members of the dance fraternities. However, I also follow Eade & Sallnow (1991) by focusing on the multiplicity of different meanings that come together and compete at pilgrimage sites. My study will show that pilgrimage is a highly complex and multifaceted phenomenon. In line with Dubisch (1995) and Morinis (1992) I will consider pilgrimage as both an individual and a social process. I argue that the class, gender and ethnic backgrounds of the pilgrims have to be taken into account. During pilgrimage the individual, but socially informed, differences shape the multiple meanings that pilgrims attribute to Mary, to the pilgrimage, and to their lives. My study will look at the diverse meanings that pilgrimage can have for pilgrims and others at this Marian shrine in Bolivia.

Although Turner & Turner (1978) view pilgrimage as an exceptional experience outside the realm of daily life, in my view, daily life is reflected in pilgrimage. Although the pilgrims travel away from their homes to the shrine of the Virgin, their daily struggles and concerns are not left behind. As will be demonstrated in this dissertation, pilgrims often undertake their visit to Mary to express vows and requests that are embedded in the problems they encounter in daily life.

Given the interconnection between religion and daily life, my study approaches pilgrimage as a form of lived religion. The term is defined by Orsi (2002: 172) as:

> Religion as practiced in the context of daily life, and includes people's symbols, objects, performances and gestures as they describe, understand and use them in the circumstances of their experiences. The key questions concern what people do with religious idioms, how they use them, what they make of themselves and their worlds with them, and how, in turn, men, women, and children are fundamentally shaped by the worlds they are making as they make these worlds. There is no religion apart from this, no religion that people have not taken up in their hands.

In addition, I agree with Margry (2008: 17) who defines religion as:

> all notions and ideas that human beings have regarding their experience of the sacred or the supernatural in order to give meaning to life and to have access to transformative powers that may influence their existential condition.

This anthropological definition of religion, with its focus on people's meanings in regard to the sacred or supernatural, is in line with my focus on lived religion, as in studies of lived religion the personal experiences of pilgrims are central. In line with Sklar (2002) I focus on individuals' experiences at the shrines. Sklar's study (2002) is based on the pilgrims' narratives in the *Fiesta* of Tortugas for the Virgin of Guadalupe in Mexico. She concludes that although pilgrimage is often viewed as a mass event in which individuality is absorbed, it is valued by the pilgrims primarily for the opportunity it offers for personal experience. My study will look at the individual interpretations and meanings of pilgrimage.

An individual's lived religion is not necessarily linked to the teachings and prescriptions of an official religion. People are creative in giving their own interpretations to it and shaping their own ritual practices. Interestingly, there has been little study of the lay person's practices and everyday thinking and actions in religion (Hall, 1997: vii; Christian, 1972). Often religion, as practiced by lay people, is called 'popular religion' as opposed to 'official religion' (Badone, 1990; Rostas & Droogers, 1993; Parker, 1996). As the term 'popular' is defined in opposition to official religion, it often has a pejorative connotation, being seen as inferior to official religion. I choose not to use the term 'popular religion', in order to avoid constructing a dichotomy with official religion. I do not emphasize what and how people believe in relation to church teachings, but, from an anthropological point of view, I am more interested in how they give meaning to their lives through pilgrimage. This is not to say that the church perspective has been ignored in my study, it is just not the main focus. In my view, people's religious beliefs and practices are especially important in understanding how people elicit meaning from their lives. By speaking of 'lived religion' the focus shifts towards the way religion is practiced in the context of daily life.

Special attention will be paid to people's practices during pilgrimage, as these can reveal much about their experiences. Studying practices such as the handling of religious objects, the making of vows by hammering stones, or dance performances for the Virgin during her *fiesta* will give insights into what is at stake in people's daily lives. In line with Dubisch (1995: 219) I view pilgrimage as a 'platform for the recognition of distress.' The objects and performances give room to express and dramatize suffering publicly, and to re-enact and re-signify people's lives. This relates to Janssen (2002: 22) who notes that the body in religious performances expresses emotions.

Coleman & Eade, in their edited book *Reframing Pilgrimage: Cultures in Motion* (2004), argue against the largely shrine-centered approaches to pilgrimage of Turner and Turner (1978) and Eade & Sallnow (1991) and propose to study various forms of movement as constitutive elements of pilgrimage. Although my study is also shrine-centered, I do take into consideration Coleman & Eade's (2004) perspective by considering the movement at the shrine. This links to Hermkens, Jansen and Notermans (forthcoming) who take Coleman and Eade's (2004) ideas on movement further, and argue that Marian pilgrimage is a moving experience in four different ways: pilgrims' physical and emotive movement, Mary's movement, and the pilgrimage's relation to social movement. By considering the performances, first of all my study will look at the physical movements that are involved in the pilgrimage to the Virgin of Urkupiña. These movements are not limited to how pilgrims move towards Mary by bus, car or on foot, but also to the movements that are involved when pilgrims practice their rituals. In this study, these include rituals such as dislodging stones, performing blessings, and dancing in folk costumes. These repetitive, collective, multisensory physical movements will be analyzed to see what they reveal about the relationships that pilgrims establish with Mary, and how pilgrims feel empowered by these movements.

In addition, the physical movements engender movements on an emotive level. Feelings of exaltation are experienced that are often translated into religious and spiritual metaphors (Albers, 2007; Peelen & Jansen, 2007). In addition Frey (2004: 91) and Margry (2008: 24) note that pilgrims are often attracted to the metaphorical pilgrimage as an inner journey, and make the physical journey to help them reach their inner destinations. In my study it will be described how pilgrims feel moved by Mary, and how the physical movements call upon emotions and communitas.

The movement of Mary will then be studied. Mary moves literally through Quillacollo before the yearly *fiesta*: during the fifteen days of prayer, she visits the devotees in several districts. How pilgrims turn the Virgin of Urkupiña into a pilgrim herself, and how they endow her statue with particular human characteristics, and personalize their relationship with her will be discussed.

The final form of movement I address in the context of Marian devotion, is social movement. People unite and join with Mary to fight against social inequality, oppression and violence (e.g. Hermkens et al., forthcoming; Rey, 1999; Tweed, 1997). On a broader level, this form of movement is my study's central focus. After all, the research question asks how Bolivian pilgrims deal with different forms of social inequalities at the pilgrimage to the Virgin of Urkupiña. Whether and how Bolivians use the Virgin to deal with, for example, neoliberal violence, domestic violence, or ethnic inequalities will be examined and analyzed.

Focusing on movement in pilgrimage also implies focusing on the dynamics that are inherent in pilgrimage. Pilgrimage is not something fixed and static, but can be seen as a product and manifestation of its social environment, as many people come together with different aims and desires. Because the social environment is always changing, pilgrims adjust to the changing preoccupation of their social environment, and they are creative agents in adjusting the site to their daily needs (Reader & Walter, 2001: 226). Pilgrims continuously create practices and meanings that are not necessarily those prescribed.

The dynamic nature of pilgrimage is also present in the transformation of old rituals to suit new contexts. In Bolivia, this pilgrimage has its origin in the introduction of Catholicism by the Spaniards in the sixteenth century. Over time, pre-colonial Andean religiosity was united with and/or transformed into Catholic religious practices. This study considers ritual as a transforming and transformative practice in which pilgrims actively participate.

Marian devotion

'At the beginning of the twenty-first century, disregarding trends of secularization, Mary, the mother of Jesus, has become a megastar.' With these words opens the book of Hemkens, Jansen & Notermans (forthcoming). All over the world people go on pilgrimage to the Virgin Mary, pilgrimage centers receive increasing numbers of pilgrims, and many new sanctuaries are also being established. It is therefore surprising that only relatively little academic attention has been paid to Marian pilgrimages. My study aims to contribute to the knowledge of Marian devotion in Bolivia, presenting and analyzing the case of the pilgrimage to the Virgin of Urkupiña. Given that over recent decades this pilgrimage site has developed from a local shrine to a place that attracts visitors from all over the country, my study attempts to understand what brings all these people to Mary.

Despite the minimal attention that is paid to Mary in the Bible, throughout the world, the Virgin Mary is worshipped under countless titles and in numerous different images (Boyer, 2000; Orsini, 2000; Taward, 1996; Warner, 1976). Despite the plurality of representations, the Virgin Mary is universally recognizable, and it is this that makes her so powerful: all over the world she is venerated, but at the same time, she is open to multiple appropriations. The various meanings have been culturally constructed by the four different dogmas that the church proclaimed in the past (De Haardt, 2008). The first of these, defined at the Council of Ephesus in 431, proclaimed Mary to be *theotokos*, the Greek word for Mother of God (Gebara & Bingener, 1989). In 533 the second Council of Constantinople declared that Mary was a virgin when giving birth to Jesus. Rooted in the dogma of her virginity, the dogma of Mary's Immaculate Conception was proclaimed in 1854. By being impregnated by the Holy Spirit, for the believers it followed that Mary therefore is spared from all stain of original sin (Warner, 1976). The most recent of the Marian dogmas is her Assumption to heaven that was proclaimed by Pius XII in 1950. Based on these dogmas, the Virgin Mary is venerated for being a caring and protective mother, a submissive and obedient virgin, a pure and good woman, and a mediator between God and mankind (Gebara & Bingener, 1989; Warner, 1976; Woodhead, 1996). In my study it will be asked what interpretations Bolivians have of the Virgin of Urkupiña. Do the people fully share these ideas, or do they (also) have alternative perceptions?

Mary is especially appealing to the oppressed and poor. She generally appears to the less powerful in the religious or social hierarchy, women and children, sick and old, or ethnically and religiously marginalized people (Rodriguez, 1994; Boyer, 2000; Hermkens et al., forthcoming). In the legend of the Virgin of Urkupiña too, Mary appeared to an indigenous shepherd girl. Furthermore, Mary's concern with the oppressed is revealed in the Magnificat, a canticle that appears in the Gospel of Luke (1: 46-55), in which she declares 'the mighty will be put down from their seats, and those of low degree will be exalted.' Her sympathy with the oppressed and poor is often visualized in an image of the Virgin who shelters them under her cloak, the 'Schutzmantel Madonna'. As a symbolic mother figure, Mary stands for warmth, affection, understanding, and consolation. To answer my first two sub-questions it will be asked whether the Virgin of Urkupiña is especially attractive for the poor and marginalized, and whether the poor and the rich have different perceptions of Mary and if so, why. Do they make different requests? Do they perform different rituals?

From the 1970s onwards, liberation and feminist theology have been going against mainstream theology by addressing the historical manipulation of the symbol of a passive Mary, and focusing their attention on Mary as the strong, determined woman who takes action in situations of injustice. These approaches influenced new interpretations of Mary, and emphasized Mary as a role model for liberation and emancipation (Gebara & Bingemer, 1989; Hamington, 1995; Mackelberghe, 1991; Rodriguez, 1994; Schillebeeckx & Halkes, 1993). To answer the sub-question on gender therefore, we need to know whether the Bolivian pilgrims perceive the Virgin of Urkupiña as an active and liberal symbol, or whether they perceive Mary as a symbol for submission and subordination.

In connection with the different interpretations that people give to the symbol of Mary, she is appropriated for the most diverse situations. For example, Tweed (1997) notes how the Marian shrine in Miami serves in the Cuban diaspora to construct a collective identity via a shared national symbol. Orsi (2002) shows how the Madonna of the 115th street in Miami serves Italian migrants in mediating in family disputes, whereas Hermkens (2008) demonstrates how Mary in Papua New Guinea consoles those suffering domestic violence. This demonstrates how Mary can be appropriated and involved in all kinds of situations that occur in daily life. In my study in Bolivia the situations that come to the fore in which Mary is appropriated, and how pilgrims negotiate with Mary to deal with these particular situations will be explored.

Power

When Turner and Turner (1978) launched their theory on pilgrimage, the concept of power was not yet central to the debate. In fact, by stressing that pilgrims experience communitas, power issues were put aside. Arguing against the communitas paradigm of the Turners, Eade & Sallnow (1991) stressed the power dimension of pilgrimage. According to them, social boundaries and distinctions are reinforced throughout a pilgrimage. Moreover, pilgrimage incorporates differences, not only between various groups of pilgrims, but also between the official discourse of the shrine and the private discourses and creative practices of the pilgrims. I follow this line of thought by focusing on power dimensions in pilgrimage.

Pilgrimage can reveal much about the power dynamics of society, as pilgrims often come to a shrine to express the antagonisms in society. Therefore pilgrimage put the power structures in society, as well as efforts to influence them, under the microscope. Studying the events at a pilgrimage shrine provides an excellent opportunity to study how these power structures in society are expressed, contested and mediated.

Power, as a theoretical construct, does tend to take asymmetrical relations and the ways that they are produced, reproduced and transformed as its object (Oldersma & Davis, 1991: 7). In my research I build on Foucaults' (1977: 98) view of power:

> Power must be analysed as something which circulates, or rather as something which only functions in the form of a chain. It is never localized here or there, never in anybody's hands, never appropriated as a commodity or piece of wealth. Power is employed and exercised through a net-like organization. And not only do individuals circulate between these threads; they are always in the position of simultaneously undergoing and exercising this power. They are not only its inert or consenting target; they are always also the elements of its articulation. In other words, individuals are the vehicles of power, not its point of application.

Thus, power is something dynamic that individuals can use. According to Foucault (1982: 788-789) power exists only when it is put into action. Therefore, what defines a power relationship is that it is a mode of action that does not act directly and immediately on others; it acts upon their actions instead. Furthermore, from the perspective of power as only existing in its exercise, power is not unidirectional. It does not take a dichotomous relationship between powerful and powerless subjects, rather, individuals exercise power actively in positioning themselves within competing discourses, rather than merely being 'positioned by' them (Kerfoot & Knights, 1994: 70). In this view, also emphasized by Radtke & Stam (1994) as well as Villarreal (1994), even the dominated are seen as actors who, despite their disadvantage, have some chance of influencing those 'in control.' It implies that the definition of power not only includes coercion and domination, but is expanded to include power as an expression of a capacity to act. Applied to my study, it means that I will view the marginalized as active agents, who disseminate and change the meanings given to the symbol of Mary. I will not regard them as powerless victims, but study their active role in appropriating and transforming Marian devotion and what it represents.

In particular, I will give voice to the pilgrims and other devotees at the site, who in the first instance seem to have less power than priests and other church authorities. However, as Rostas and Droogers (1993: 8) note, power and power relations also depend on the meaning that people attribute to their practices and convictions. In the pilgrimage of Urkupiña it becomes clear that many important aspects, such as the rituals or the interpretations that people have of the Virgin, are largely determined by the subdominant perceptions of pilgrims. For example, the important rituals of hacking stones and symbolizing requests in miniatures, rituals that will be emphasized in chapter four and five, will demonstrate the important role of the subdominant discourse. It will be asked how the pilgrims, especially the marginalized, construct meaning in these rituals. Not only how pilgrims have the power and agency to influence ideas and practices at the shrine, but how Marian devotion also gives them the opportunities to change the problems in their daily lives, is considered. This relates to the main question that asks how Bolivian devotees deal with class, gender and ethnic inequality at the pilgrimage shrine.

Closely related to power is the concept of empowerment. Empowerment is interpreted differently within different contexts, but generally entails the undermining of dominant power relations by strengthening resistance to them (Villarreal, 1994: 227). According to Rowlands (1997: 13) individuals are empowered when they are able to maximize the opportunities available to them without constraints. Empowerment can be experienced and demonstrated on a personal, relational and collective level. On the personal level, individuals are empowered when they develop a sense of self and individual confidence and capacity, and when they undo the effects of internalized oppression. On a relational level, individuals are empowered when they develop the ability to negotiate and influence the nature of a relationship and decisions made within it.[1] On a collective level, individuals can work together to achieve a greater impact than could be achieved individually. In my research I will explore how people feel empowered during pilgrimage. On an individual level, it will be asked how pilgrims are empowered to work towards their goals and on their projects in daily life. On a relational level, it will be asked how they feel empowered by the relationship they build with Mary. Collective empowerment will be studied in relation to dance performance, as this type of pilgrimage performance has more impact because it is experienced collectively.

Several studies have revealed that the Virgin Mary is an empowering symbol for her devotees in diverse contexts (e.g. Hermkens, 2008; Orsi, 2002; Rey, 1999; Rodriguez, 1994; Tweed, 1997). For example Rodriguez (1994: 160) concludes that the Virgin of Guadalupe is 'a role model of strength, enduring presence, and new possibilities' for Mexican American women in the United States. Rodriguez (1994: 134) proposes that Our Lady of Guadalupe is utilized as a 'coping mechanis', and suggests that new research must be done to examine the accuracy of this idea. My research is inspired by this question. Orsi (2002: 60) shows how Mary is an empowering source for Italian immigrants in New York. He shows that Mary exists in relationships, and that she is called on to mediate family disputes, to judge behavior and to listen to the most intimate sorrows and fears. In addition, Orsi's book about praying to Saint Jude (1996: 136) shows that writing letters, recounting narratives and praying - whether to a saint or the Virgin Mary - are empowering activities, as they transform individuals 'from the passive victims into the active narrators of their circumstances.' To answer the final sub-question on how pilgrims feel empowered and disempowered in pilgrimage, it will be asked in which situations Mary is approached by her Bolivian devotees, and whether she offers help on an emotional level, or whether she also activates the believers. Not only the question of how pilgrims feel empowered by the symbol of Mary but also that of how the rituals and performances at the shrine contribute to empowerment will be asked.

Class

Class inequality is a form of power inequality that comes to the fore during pilgrimage. As the Virgin of Urkupiña in Bolivia is especially famous for her help in material issues, she is approached by both rich and poor. Class inequality is one of the most important forms of inequality that is expressed in this pilgrimage.

1 Droogers (2001) defines power as being both the ability to organize one's life, and the capacity to influence other people's behaviour. The first form of power relates to what, in Rowlands' (1997) terms, is called peronal empowerment, the second to relational empowerment.

Social class can be defined as a group of individuals or families who occupy a similar position in the economic system of production, distribution, and consumption of goods and services (Rothmann, 1999: 5). The social classes in a society form a hierarchy of wealth, prestige, and power (Sills, 1979). All complex societies are characterized, to varying degrees, by the unequal distribution of material and symbolic rewards (Crompton, 1998: 1). Societies with large economic stratification generate a structuring of society into social classes, with notably differing degrees of power, with relationships of dominance, and objectively opposing interests (Maduro, 1982: 48). In any system of stratification, individuals belong to strata that are groups in the sense that everybody in them shares some obligatory ways of acting that are typically and intentionally different from those in other strata. In addition, strata are exclusive, so that nobody belongs to more than one at the same time, and they are exhaustive, so that everybody in the society belongs to one, and finally strata are ranked (Sills, 1979).

Crompton (1998: 11) points out the multiplicity of meanings that are attached to the word class. She summarizes, while recognizing the oversimplification of her classification, three different meanings: class as prestige and status, class as structured inequality (related to the possession of economic and power resources), and classes as actual or potential social and political actors. This variety of meanings has contributed to the lack of clarity that characterizes many contemporary debates on stratification. In my research I regard class as primarily a structural form of inequality. At the same time, I acknowledge that it implies that people from different social classes are granted different levels of status and prestige.

In Bolivia great class differences exist. According to USAID (2007: 11) the ratio of income of the wealthiest 20 per cent to that of the 20 per cent poorest of the Bolivian population is 42, which means that the 20 per cent richest have 42 times more than the 20 per cent poorest. It is the largest ratio of income inequality in Latin America and the Caribbean, followed by Haiti with a ratio of 27. In addition, Bolivia is the poorest Latin American country. As we will see in chapter four, many poor Bolivians blame the neoliberal model for their poverty. It will be asked whether the pilgrimage to Urkupiña gives them a space to resist and criticize the neoliberal politics, and if so how.

It has to be taken into account that pilgrims from all social backgrounds come to Quillacollo to visit the Virgin of Urkupiña. As Lagos (1993) points out, the pilgrims adjust their requests to their needs, so everybody is able to receive from the Virgin, according to the class-based background. Rey (1999) points out that with regard to devotional practice, large differences between the Haitian elite and the Haitian popular masses in Marian devotion do not exist, but there are differences in ideological content. For example, especially the lower class devotees in Haiti perceive their relationship with Mary in terms of service; they see themselves as the instrument of her will, whereas the elite focused more on the personally lucrative potential of their piety. In the case of Bolivia also it will be asked whether lower and higher classes perform different rituals and have different interpretations of Mary. Chapter five in particular will focus on the material requests that pilgrims make, symbolized in miniatures. I will consider how people from the higher and lower classes legitimize their material requests and the class differences in them.

Gender

Gender is another form of inequality that is central in this study. A new critical awareness of gender differences, linked to the existing asymmetry in the power relations, representation, knowledge, and scholarship between men and women, challenges the traditional practice and study of religion (King, 1997: 647). It has to be noted that almost all major monotheistic religions are androcentric, meaning that traditionally men have had a dominant role. Men are prominent in religious organization; they lead the performance of the important rituals, formulate dogma and hold the pens that write the 'divinely inspired' texts. They control the powers of female reproduction, and dictate the social and cultural roles of women (Holden, 1983). Paradoxically, women almost everywhere, represent the majority of religious practitioners in day-to-day religion (King, 1997; 647; Weis Ozorak, 1996: 17; Holden, 1983).

On pilgrimage too, gender differences come to the fore. For example, Gemzöe (2000: 29) speaks of the feminization in pilgrimage. With this term, Gemzöe refers firstly to the numerical predominance of women, and secondly to the female process of interpretation of the religious symbols and practices. Women interpret these in terms of their own concerns and experiences. These concerns are 'female' in the sense that they are those of women rather than men, mainly because the domains of male and female activity are kept separate to a great degree. Although in Bolivia men and women come to the shrine in more or less equal numbers, their activities, requests, and interpretations may differ. It will be asked whether there are gender differences in devotional practices, and in what ways gender related problems are articulated at the shrine.

Dubisch (1995) draws attention to, what she calls a 'poetics of womanhood', by which she means the presentation of 'being woman' in public performance during pilgrimage, in the case of Dbuisch a Greek pilgrimage. In dramatic performances, crawling on their knees for example, women present a performance that expresses ideas about femaleness. I agree with Dubisch that religious activities provide a 'space' for women's performances. I will ask if the pilgrimage provides women with a space and discourse to express and negotiate problems that are generated by gender inequality, problems that cannot be solved directly in daily life.

Gender refers to the social traits and cultural characteristics that are associated with each sex (Golombok & Fivush, 1994). According to Moore (1988: 15):

> These associations are not inherent in the biological or social nature of the sexes, but are cultural constructs, which are powerfully reinforced by the social activities which both define and are defined by them. The value of analysing 'man' and 'woman' as symbolic categories or constructs lies in the identification of the expectations and values which individual cultures associate with being male or female.

Gender is a descriptive rather than an explanatory concept. Gender differences do not indicate why relations between women and men seem so regularly to involve domination and subordination. Nor does gender account for the dynamics of these relations; how they come to be produced, reproduced, and transformed in the various contexts of everyday life (Oldersma & Davis, 1991: 5). Gender is related to power inequality as the structuring of society in gender implies that certain groups have access to more power, and this way gender is experienced as hierarchical. Ortner (1996: 21) states:

> The secondary status of woman in society is one of the true universals, a pan-cultural fact. Yet within that universal fact, the specific cultural conceptions and symbolizations of woman are extraordinarily diverse and even mutually contradictory. Further, the actual treatment of women and their relative power and contribution vary enormously from culture to culture, and over different periods in the history of particular cultural traditions.

Moore (1988: 7) also notes that the images, attributes, activities and appropriate behavior associated with women are always culturally and historically specific. What the category 'woman', or for that matter, the category 'man' means in a given context has to be investigated and not assumed (Moore, 1988: 7).

Practices and ideas about masculinity and femininity in Bolivian society will be studied looking through a 'gender-lens'. For instance, notions of Latin American femininity and masculinity are often described in terms of *marianismo* and *machismo*. *Marianismo* refers to the submissive, suffering, and obedient stereotype, derived from the supposed values of the Virgin Mary, of Latin American women. *Machismo* refers to the strong, competitive, masculine, and virile stereotype for Latin American men. In scholarly literature, gender related problems are often explained by these gender notions (Ellsberg et al, 2000; Flake & Forste, 2006; Sagot, 2005). Domestic violence is a dominant form of gender inequality that women articulate at the shrine, and that by these authors is connected to *machismo* and *marianismo*. In my study, in particular in chapter five, it will be asked whether the female behavior is in fact so passive as proposed in literature. In addition, it will be asked what characteristics women attribute to the Virgin Mary to verify the adequacy of the values of *marianismo* that are supposed to be derived from the symbol of the Virgin Mary.

When in the 1970s sexual difference was established as a social or cultural product, the path was opened toward locating relations between the sexes with other socially structured relations of power (Oldersma & Davis, 1991: 4). Moore (1994: 93) even states:

> Difference is a relational concept, and it is always experienced relationally in terms of political discrimination, inequalities of power and forms of domination. There is, therefore, nothing useful to be said about gender outside of the concrete specificity of gender relations.

Gender relations should be specified, and Moore (1994) therefore, suggests asking how the experience, for example, of race and class transform the experience of gender. This idea has been further developed in noting that there is no such category as 'woman', since there is so much diversity among women due to this intersection of gender with class, ethnicity, and other factors of differentiation. Someone's gender identity does not stand on its own, but needs to be considered in relation to other identities such as ethnicity, nationality, class, and age (Davids & Willemse, 1999; Reid & Whitehead, 1992: 3). In this dissertation the intersections between gender and other forms of social inequality will be taken into account.

Gender intersects with class. The study of poverty from the point of view of gender has gained in importance since the 1990s. Poverty affects men, women, boys, and girls, but it is experienced differently by people of different ages, ethnicities, family roles, and sexes. Over the world, more than 60 per cent of the poor are woman. Furthermore, two thirds of the illiterate adults in the world are woman (Social Watch Report, 2005). In Bolivia, 7 per cent of the men and 19 per cent of the women are illiterate (INE, 2003). Gender inequalities within family contexts, which cause differentiated access to resources of the domestic group, worsen women's poverty, particularly in poor households. The division of labor by sex assigns women to domestic work, and limits their access to material and social resources, and their participation in political, economic and social-decision making. Women are at greater risk of poverty because they have relatively limited material assets, and also more limited social assets (access to income, goods and services through social connections) and cultural assets (formal education and cultural knowledge). The consequences of this disparity in diverse forms and in different areas and social structures persist throughout a woman's entire life. The gender approach to the study of poverty unmasks both public and household discrimination by identifying power relationships and unequal distribution of resources in both spheres. The majority of the informants in my research are women, and it has to be taken into account that their gender intersects with other forms of inequality on several issues.

Another way in which gender is relevant in my study is in the feminine symbol of Mary. As Mary has synthesized with the Andean goddess of fertility, Pachamama, feminine characteristics may be attributed to her. In my study it will be asked whether and how Mary's femininity plays a role in the Bolivian men's and women's interpretations of her. It will be argued in chapter four and six that the characteristics attributed to her, in practice, at times invert the doctrinal ones.

Ethnicity

The perception of social classes in Bolivian society is closely linked to notions of ethnicity. When the Spanish colonizers came to Latin America in the sixteenth century, they introduced the term Indian to indicate all conquered peoples in the Americas. They imposed a hierarchic, racially-based social stratification in the American colonies that classified people on the basis of race and racial mixtures. Social stratification was thus based on ethnicity. Whites represented the tiny upper class, and Indians the lower class. The Spanish wanted purity of races, which made *mestizos*, or mixed white and Indian blood, the lowest in the social ranking system. At the end of the nineteenth century, meanings and associations of colonial racial categories were altered. Indians were seen as individuals living in poverty and working the land, whereas *mestizos* were increasingly identified with 'civilization' and urban residence. As the Indians had their own culture and the whites had their European culture, the *mestizos* took elements of both. The reconfigured relations between Indian and *mestizo* took a class form. The *mestizos* did not consider themselves as Indians. The term Indian acquired a pejorative connotation (Wilson, 2000). The Bolivian indigenous people employ the term *indígena* to describe their ethnicity, while *indío* is considered a derogatory term (Field, 1994: 237). For this reason I use the terms 'indigenous people' or *indígenas* throughout my text, and will avoid the terms Indians or *indíos*.

With the Agrarian Reform in 1952, the Bolivian state attempted to forge a national identity without ethnic distinctions. The white oligarchy lost its privileged positions and a more socialistic approach arose, which also had its implications for the ethnic social order. Gill (1993: 75) explains:

> The modernizing ideology of the post-1952 state claimed that all Bolivians were mixed bloods, and therefore equal, in order to create a new national identity. The ideology of *mestizaje* denied class differences and ethnic labels such as white and Indian. The term *indio* was replaced in official pronouncements by the more neutral term *campesino*, or country person, and so-called whites were no longer referred to as such.[2] In this way, the state attempted to negate all forms of ethnicity through which competing groups might assert distinctive identities, lay claim to resources, and distance themselves from one another. Yet despite the

2 I would like to remark that the term campesino in common usage does not translate easily into the concept of 'peasant'; instead it has replaced the term 'indigenous people' (Psacharopoulos & Patrinos, 1994).

> new discourse, the state was unable to form a new, hegemonic cultural order, for class contradictions were intensifying and ethnic loyalties being reasserted.

Nowadays, on certain occasions, ethnicity still intersects with class, as the four richer departments - also rich with oil and gas in the ground - that strive for more autonomy are the lowlands with only a tiny percentage of indigenous people.[3] According to Tapia Vargas' classification (2005: 97) there are three social classes in Bolivia: a higher class, a middle class consisting of three strata: high, middle and low, and a lower class. The most marginalized in society according to Tapia Vargas, are the *campesinos*, whereas the middle class consists mainly of *mestizos*, and the higher class mostly out of white, or predominantly white *mestizos*. However, there are several problems with this generalization. First of all, it is difficult to define the boundaries of the different strata. Not all *indígenas* are poor. For example, in La Paz there is a large community of indigenous women who belong to high society and dress elaborately with expensive *polleras* - layered skirts, earrings, bowler hats, and coats that proudly mark their ethnic identity (e.g. Gills, 1993). In addition, Seligmann (1989) notes that the indigenous market women in Peru have become known as *cholas*, and can be viewed as a distinct social class. Also in Bolivia the concept of *cholos/cholas* is used to differentiate between classes (Lagos, 1997: 172). These indigenous market women belong neither to the *campesinos* nor the *mestizos*, but to a stratum between, at the intersection between rural and urban socio-spatial environment (Seligmann, 1989: 702). As businesswomen and vendors they often belong to the middle strata of society.

Lagos (1997: 173) makes clear that it is not the self-proclaimed links to ethnicity that divide in different classes, but the imagined representations of ethnicity. For example, a man who considers himself as white because of kinship ties with his white ancestors, may be classified by others as *indio* or *campesino*, because he does not speak Spanish or because of dark coloring. Thus, the conceptual dichotomization as urban/rural, *mestizo/indígena*, modernity/tradition cannot be applied so easily (Radcliffe, 1997). The boundaries are constantly changing, and it is not possible to simply classify indigenous people as being at the bottom of the class hierarchy. In Bolivia, class differences are most commonly defined in relation to ethnic differences, but the dynamic, subjective, and historically situated nature of the concept of ethnicity, also makes class a transformative and dynamic category.

Ethnicity is a contested concept, as definitions vary and show several ambiguities. The International Encyclopedia of Social Sciences defines an ethnic

3 In the past few years the question of autonomy erupts regularly. For instance, on 13th of September 2008 at least 16 people (mostly *campesinos*) died in the northern province Pando because of a violent encounter between indigenous Evo Morales followers and opposition groups that aim for autonomy (*Los Tiempos*, 2008).

group as: 'A distinct category of the population in a larger society whose culture is usually different from its own. The members of such a group are, or feel themselves, bound together by common ties of race, nationality and culture' (Sills, 1979: 167). Race, however, is something other than ethnicity. According to Rothman (1999: 7) race is a social construction, typically based on visible physical characteristics such as skin color, stature, and facial features. Ethnic groups, on the other hand, are identified by cultural origins, which may be manifested in language, religion, values, beliefs, or customs and practices. Former descriptions of the term ethnicity show that many different elements are mentioned as markers of ethnicity, making it hard to define the term. Malešević (2004: 4) notes that ethnicity is not a thing or a collective asset of a particular group; it is a social relation in which social actors perceive themselves, and are perceived by others, as being culturally distinct collectivities. Furthermore, ethnicity is a social identity that is collective and individual, externalized in social interaction and internalized in personal self-identification (Jenkins, 1997: 14). The distinctive indigenous societies of Latin America became 'ethnic groups' after they were contrasted and incorporated by the Spanish *conquistadores*. Ethnicity and ethnic group should be understood as processual terms that signify changing identities in relation to colonialism throughout history, rather than as a set of more or less fixed social categories (Field (1994: 240). As will be outlined in chapter seven, I view ethnicity not as an asset of a group, but as a social relation in which groups perceive themselves as being culturally distinct collectivities, and as a distinction that is continuously socially and culturally (re)constructed.

In Bolivia, outward appearance can be one of the main characteristics to classify someone as an *indígena* or not. Physical characteristics such as skin-color and facial features are visible markers, especially in combination with indigenous clothing. Historically, dress made a sharp distinction between *mestizos* and *indígenas*. However, nowadays dress does not form a clear boundary between these groups, as many people abandoned their indigenous clothing in favor of 'western' clothing, especially after migrating to the cities. For example the *cholas*, the market vendors, do not necessarily wear indigenous clothing, or they exchange the self-made hand-woven dresses for skirts and *polleras*, layered skirts that are exclusively worn by *indígenas*, but that can be bought at the market. Women in Latin America retain 'traditional' clothes more frequently than men. Especially with men it is hard to define ethnic groups based only on outward appearance (Radcliffe, 1997). When clothes make no visible difference, skin color and facial characteristics may be the outward ethnic markers. However, during history the races have mixed and it is hard to see whether somebody has pure indigenous blood, or the extent to which she or he is of mixed blood.

From the perspective of the indigenous population language seems to be a key marker of ethnicity. In Peru, Bolivia and Ecuador, Quechua and Aymara are the two most widely spoken indigenous languages. Quechua-speaking people often identify themselves as Quechua-speakers, rather than as 'Quechuas' per se. For many, being Quechua means speaking Quechua. A problem with using language to classify ethnic groups, is that Spanish is seen as the dominant, high-status and official language in the Andes. In a country experiencing increasing globalization, the ability to speak Spanish becomes more and more important. Many people are bilingual, and sometimes the indigenous languages are not passed on to the next generation. In the government statistics, the percentages of indigenous language speaking people do often not correspond with statistics concerning the indigenous population. As with clothing, more women than men are monolingual and speak only Quechua or Aymara (Hornberger & Coronel-Molina, 2004).

Quechua and Aymara speakers are also likely to identify themselves according to their geographical region and local cultural traditions, such as *Cochabambino, Quillacolleño, Paceño*. It is increasingly common for individuals to belong simultaneously to more than one cultural context (Albo, 2004). The beliefs, customs, and religious traditions vary according to the geographical regions as well. There is no coherent 'Quechua-culture' or 'Aymara-culture'. In fact, differences in the cultural practices between two Quechua-communities might be greater than the cultural difference between a Quechua- and an Aymara-community.

Ethnicity is related to pilgrimage. For example, Borland (2003) notes that in a Nicaraguan pilgrimage indigenous and regional identities are asserted. The pilgrims 'folklorize' themselves and perform a 'traditional identity' that is rooted in the indigenous past. In Bolivia, with its many ethnic subgroups, ethnicity is also expressed during pilgrimage, as first of all people from different ethnic backgrounds visit the shrine, and secondly, because the meanings and interpretations that pilgrims give to the symbols and performances of pilgrimage are shaped by these ethnic backgrounds, as I will show in this thesis. To build this argument I will analyze an occasion where ethnic symbols are gloriously carried around and ethnic authenticity is most apparent. Although there are many other indigenous groups in Bolivia, the pilgrimage to Urkupiña has to do with meanings of Andean religiosity of the highlands, of the Quechuas and Aymaras in particular. The shrine of the Virgin of Urkupiña is situated in an area that is mainly inhabited by Quechuas. However, in recent decades many Aymaras have also migrated to the area. During the *fiesta* many Aymara vendors come to the valley to sell their services in pilgrimage. They are important agents in the process of constructing meaning, as they integrate their ideas and practices of the Andean *cosmovisión* with the Catholic ones. As we will see in this dissertation, the meanings that pilgrims give to the Virgin of Urkupiña are derived from the interpretations that people have of the Andean goddess of fertility, Pachamama. In addition, the principle of reciprocity of the Andean *cosmovisión* is also applied to the relationship that pilgrims establish with Mary.

Photo 3: Procession with the Virgin of Urkupiña on the 16th of August at the Calvary Hill (© Alfredo Ramos)

3

THE PLACE OF PILGRIMAGE

’To your feet, to your plants, miraculous Virgencita’

- expression that many sahumeras use in their prayers at he Calvary Hill

Thousands of times I heard the *sahumeras*, the sellers of blessings, uttering their prayers aloud at the Calvary Hill. Over and over I heard: ‘These pilgrims have come to your feet, to your plants, miraculous *Mamita* of Urkupiña.’ Apart from calling on Mary, this also refers to the sacralization of nature that was part of the Andean *cosmovisión*. During colonization many elements of this *cosmovisión* have blended with Catholicism, and even nowadays many convictions and practices, especially those of the indigenous believers, are still derived from it. But where are the Virgin’s feet and plants localized? And who is this miraculous Virgin or *Mamita* of Urkupiña? The shrine of this Bolivian Virgin Mary is located in the indigenous market town Quillacollo, in the Cochabamba department, between the lowlands and the highlands. Being one of Bolivia’s most famous pilgrimage places, devotees come from all over the country to make their requests for her miraculous intervention.

Several inhabitants of Quillacollo told me proudly the same anecdote about the preference of their *Virgencita* for their town:

> One day they transferred the image of the Virgin of Urkupiña from Quillacollo to Santa Cruz. When she arrived it started raining. It was a sign from the Virgin that she did not want to live in Santa Cruz. The Virgin of Urkupiña belongs to the Cochabamba department. After three weeks she was taken back and finally it stopped raining. It was a miracle!

According to her devotees the Virgin of Urkupiña has a tremendous power. Most people believe that Mary can intervene directly in the world of the living. This also has been derived from the Andean *cosmovisión* in which all deities act independently, thus without intervening on behalf of another hierarchically higher deity. People tell each other stories about the miraculous powers of this particular Virgin, and the more people attracted to the shrine, the more power is attributed to the Virgin of Urkupiña. As I have heard many pilgrims remark: 'So many pilgrims come to her shrine, she must be very special.' Devotees from Cochabamba showed that they were proud to live in a province with such a famous and powerful patroness. Pictures of her image can be found in shops and houses all around in the department Cochabamba. Although pilgrims come from all over Bolivia and even abroad, the Virgin of Urkupiña is inextricably linked to Cochabamba.

The Sanctuary of Urkupiña is located in Quillacollo, a town of around 110,000 inhabitants, 13 kilometers to the west of the city of Cochabamba in Bolivia. Cochabamba, with around 800,000 inhabitants, lies between the two main cities, La Paz and Santa Cruz, between the highlands and the lowlands. In addition, since the Virgin was declared the Patroness of Integration in 1992, Quillacollo is also called Blessed Land of Integration, as it is at the pilgrimage site of Urkupiña that pilgrims from all classes and regions of the country unite. Thus, on a local level the Virgin of Urkupiña is important because she is connected to her hometown, Quillacollo, but at the same time she is a national symbol, and famous throughout the country.

In contrast to the city of Cochabamba, Quillacollo has a more indigenous character. Quechua women with white sun-hats, white lace blouses and short velvet *polleras* - skirts for *indígena* women - dominate one's view on the street. Many Aymara and Quechua families from other districts have migrated to the town, in search of better incomes in the fertile area with a big market. The name of the town is composed of the words *Quilla* and *collo*, which mean in Aymara 'hill of ash' and in Quechua 'hill of the moon' (Montaño Aragón, 2006). Because of its fertile grounds and the abundant water supplies, Quillacollo had been inhabited by various pre-Hispanic populations who lived from agriculture. During the Tiahuanacu era, between the ninth and twelfth century, the Aymaras inhabited the region. When the Incas conquered it in the 13th century, they dominated the area, which then became mainly inhabited by Quechuas (Obando Stemberg, 2007, Peredo Antezana, 1990). The Incas used the Cochabamba valley for the production of corn, with which they supplied large parts of the empire. Behind the Calvary Hill, around lake Cotapachi, a few silos, *qollqas*, that date from Inca times can still be found (Erostegui, 2003; Pereira Herrera, 1994).

1. COTA
2. CALVARY HILL
3. CHURCH SAN ILDEFONSO

MAP 2: LOCALIZATION OF COTA, CALVARY HILL AND CHURCH

The pilgrimage site consists of three spaces: Cota, the place where, according to the legend, the Virgin appeared, the Calvary Hill, or the hill where nowadays the rituals are practiced, and the church San Ildefonso in town where people go for Catholic prayer (see map 2). These three spaces are not only geographically separate, but different rituals and actions are performed at the three places. Later I will examine the power politics that are at stake at these places. Before presenting the three main sites of Urkupiña I will address the history and legend of the devotion. After a description of the yearly *fiesta*, I will conclude with a section on the social relations between the pilgrims and Mary in order to demonstrate the personal relations that pilgrims actively construct with Mary.

History of the devotion to the Virgin of Urkupiña

The Andean countries have a tradition of pilgrimage that pre-dates the colonial period. During the Chavin culture, between 850 and 300 BCE, pilgrimages were made to local shrines (Sallnow, 2000). The city of Tiuhuanacu, south of Lake Titicaca, that was the centre of the Tiuhuanacu culture from 300 until 1000 CE, was a cultic center and pilgrimage shrine (Vanlangenacker, 1991). Furthermore, during the Inca-empire from the twelfth until the fourteenth century, existing local shrines were co-opted by the Cuzco conquerors. The Incas conducted rituals in which shrines were united through the medium of sacrificial human blood, transported in living victims. When the Spaniards imposed Catholicism after they conquered the Incas in 1532, the indigenous population offered a great deal of resistance, and continued to celebrate their own deities (Sallnow, 2000).

In order to convert the indigenous population in Bolivia to Catholicism, the Spaniards tried to replace the indigenous feasts by Catholic ones. Most feasts and rituals of the Quechuas and Aymaras were ordered according to the agricultural calendar. The preparation for sowing the earth was celebrated in the month of August and marked an important celebration in the Andean worldview. The *fiesta* of the Assumption at the 15th of August became the Spanish substitute for this indigenous *fiesta*. The indigenous population feigned Christianity and used the Catholic calendar to continue their veneration of agricultural deities (Garcia Merida, 2001: 39). The *fiesta* of Urkupiña also merged with their Andean agricultural feast.

Another tactic to convert the indigenous population was to give a Catholic significance to Andean places. The Spaniards put Catholic symbols, such as crosses and chapels, on top of the *huacas*, the holy places of the Quechuas and the Aymaras. These *huacas* were often mountains, stones or lakes that, in the Andean *cosmovisión*, were perceived to have special energy and powers. It appeared as if the indigenous people came to these 'Catholic places', and the missionaries hoped that by transforming the indigenous *huacas* into Catholic shrines, the symbols would merge over time and they would slowly convert into Catholic places (Salles Reese, 1992: 261). An instance of this is the oldest

Marian shrine in Bolivia; this was already a pre-colonial pilgrimage site and *huaca*,but has been dedicated to Mary since 1583 (Sallnow, 1982).

Not much is known about the history of the devotion to Urkupiña. According to the historian Jose Macedonio Urquidi (In: Peredo Antezana, 2001: 89), the Spanish conquerors entered the valley of Cochabamba in the year 1542. Because of the pleasant climate and the fertile ground, they settled in there, as the Incas did before. According to information found by Adolfo de Morales, another historian, the Catholic clergy of San Ildefonso was established between 1585 and 1600 (Peredo Antezana 2001: 92). The first mention of the devotion to the Virgin of the Assumption dates from 1760. A chronicle that is kept in the *Archiv Metropolitano* in the city of Sucre, reveals that a major expenditure of the clergy of San Ildefonso was 'the feast of the Virgin, as realized by the clergy of San Ildefonso in Quillacollo on the 15th of August' (Peredo Antezana, 2001:96).

The first document in which the celebration was mentioned by the name of Urkupiña, was discovered by Rafael Peredo Antezana, and dates from 1848. In the document it is said that the lighting of the parish was financed by the donations 'that devotees brought to the festivity of Our Lady known by the name of Urkupiña' (Garcia Merida, 2001: 56). Since the beginning of the twentieth century the communication media, newspapers, television, and radio, started to be interested in the *fiesta* of Urkupiña, and information about how the feast was celebrated started in the 1920s (Valdivia, 2001).

In the twenties and thirties, the devotion to the Virgin of Urkupiña was mostly a local affair. The protagonists of the *fiesta* were the *indígenas* who came from the heights around Quillacollo to honor the Virgin with music and dance. These rural *indígenas* venerated the Virgin of Urkupiña to honor Pachamama, the Earth Mother: their main aim was to give thanks, and make petitions to this agricultural deity (Mendoza Flores, 1996; Peredo Antezana, 1990). At that time the feast was not an organized celebration. Little groups from different communities entered the town with their *chicha* - a corn drink containing alcohol - food, and music, and for a few days these groups took over the streets of Quillacollo. During this period, the townspeople reacted to the indigenous people and their celebration in a discriminatory manner (personal communication Mendoza Flores).

A new era began in the nineteen-fifties. The *mestizo* inhabitants of Quillacollo, especially the local entrepreneurs and traders, took over the *fiesta*. According to Mendoza Flores, the *mestizos* also suffered discrimination, as they were always regarded as being a step lower than the white people. By becoming the *pasantes* of the *fiesta* they could show they had money and power. *Pasantes* are responsible for the organization and expenses of the *fiesta* (e.g. Crandon-Malamud, 1993). Mendoza Flores continues:

> As traders they also had contacts in Oruro and the famous Diablada of Oruro, the oldest organized Bolivian dance fraternity from Oruro, that has been funded to dance during the Carnival for the Virgin of Socavon,

was invited to dance for the Virgin of Urkupiña in Quillacollo. This was the start for the organization of other dance fraternities in Quillacollo. The year 1952 marks a milestone that changed the character of the *fiesta*: it saw the foundation of the first dance fraternity from Quillacollo, Centro Cultural Diablada, by employees of the shoe factory Manaco (Valdivia, 2001). Thus, from the fifties onwards, the *indígenas* were replaced by the *mestizos,* and the *fiesta* started to expand into an organized spectacle, in which dance fraternities were funded and processions organized. The upward mobility of the *mestizos* and the competition with other towns gave a boost to the *fiesta*.

Especially in the nineteen-seventies the *fiesta* experienced a boom in the number of visitors (Baptista, 1989). At that time pilgrims coming from Santa Cruz were the main actors. Among them were many migrants returning to their place of origin (Giorgis, 2004). In particular Santa Cruz was doing well economically, and this underlines Wolf's ((1969: 290) argument that people need to have sufficient resources of their own in order to challenge dominant power structures. In the case of the pilgrimage to Urkupiña, these pilgrims from the growing business areas of Santa Cruz had enough money to pay for a bus ticket to Quillacollo and to invest in rituals, and in this way they were able to become important actors who increased the fame of the *fiesta* and the Virgin. Another factor, next to the flourishing economy of the seventies, that contributed to the upswing of the *fiesta*, was the rise of the drugs trade at that time: this created the exceptional conditions in which the miracles of the Virgin could come true. Money was circulating within the country. The results of the material petitions to the Virgin were within anyone's reach (Mendoza Flores, 1996). As a Bolivian anthropologist told me:

> Especially in Santa Cruz coca was planted and cocaine was fabricated there. People saw how people could be poor at night and rich in the morning. As people could not tell openly they were in the drugs trade, it seemed like a miracle. Sometimes they said it was a blessing of the Virgin of Urkupiña and people came to the supernatural with their petitions. Urkupiña became the deity in charge of material things and money. Santa Cruz is a very capitalistic city, and therefore they made more material requests.

His words are in line with Lagos (2001) who notes that especially the Santa Cruzeños have given the Virgin of Urkupiña an even more economic and material connotation. Another Bolivian anthropologist did not want to talk openly about the relation between drugs and Urkupiña. As if he was revealing a secret, he explained that the Virgin of Urkupiña was a special protectress for drugs traffickers and others working in the drugs trade. He whispered:

> The risks and dangers of their profession meant that they needed special protection, which they could find in supernatural spheres, with the Virgin of Urkupiña. She was chosen as she was perceived as *La Virgen de la Plata* - the Virgin of Money.

Another subdominant story about the sudden expansion of the *fiesta* was told by a middle class man from Cochabamba. He explained:

> At the 15th of August in the mining areas of Potosí a *fiesta* was celebrated for the Assumption of the Virgin Mary to Heaven. During the period of dictator Banzer the *fiesta* was so popular, that Banzer was afraid that these gatherings of miners during the *fiesta* would be harmful for his power as it gave them the possibility to become organized. That's why Banzer started to promote successfully the *fiesta* of Urkupiña that was also held at this date. This way attention was distracted from the leftist *fiesta* in Potosí.

Nowadays pilgrims come from all over Bolivia. Many still come from Santa Cruz, but they are no longer the main actors. The Virgin of Urkupiña attracts people from all over the country, and also from abroad: migrant communities in Argentina and the United States started to emulate the celebration of Urkupiña, and many pilgrims come to visit the 'real' Urkupiña in Quillacollo (Giorgis, 2001, 2004; Ontiveros, 2001). The surveys that I held at the Calvary Hill showed that from 86 pilgrims (alone, couples, families or in groups), six people came from Argentina, two from Peru, one from Brazil, and one Chilean couple had come with acquaintances from Cochabamba. A Bolivian man who had migrated to the United States many years ago was also included. The other 75 people came from Bolivia. The surveys also showed that the shrine still attracts new pilgrims each year. Twelve out of 86 people surveyed were at the Calvary Hill for the first time, while another six had come for the first time, but accompanied by people who had visited the Calvary Hill before.

Legends of Urkupiña: The master narrative and subdominant narratives

The reason a certain place has become a place of pilgrimage is usually explained to the pilgrims in a master legend attached to that place. These stories about the origin of shrines can be clustered around several topics. Cults can develop after an object is brought from another place, arise after a certain object is discovered, or after a spontaneously reported miracle; they can also originate with the depositing of ex votos, through which believers give thanks for the salvation from catastrophe; shrines can be developed from devotion to a certain religious figure, relate to events in a saint's life, or the historical development of Christianity. Only few sites have their origin in the legend of a reported apparition or vision (Nolan, 1991).

The legend of Urkupiña traces the shrine's origin back to the appearance of the Virgin Mary to a local shepherd girl, sometime in the eighteenth century. There is no exact date for the origin of the legend, but a painting of the Virgin of Urkupiña that dates from 1761 and a chronicle from 1760 that mentions the celebration of the Virgin of Assumption, demonstrate the antiquity of the veneration (Peredo Antezana, 1990: 27; Peredo Antezana, 2006: 55). Thus the devotion originated long before the Lourdes legend of Mary, or other 19th century apparitions in France.

According to the master legend of Urkupiña, as told by the church representatives, a beautiful lady with a child in her arms appeared several times to a local shepherd girl who was grazing her sheep at the foot of a hill outside Quillacollo. Nowadays this hill is known as Cota. During these visits, the little girl played with the child of the beautiful lady. When she told her parents about it, they wanted to find out the identity of this mysterious lady with her son. Therefore they asked their daughter to inform them next time the lady appeared. One day the lady appeared and the shepherd girl ran to her parents. Together with her parents, neighbors, and the villagers she returned to Cota. There they saw the Virgin walking up the hill. The shepherd girl shouted in Quechua: '*Orqh'opina, Orqh'opina*', which means: 'there she is, on the hill.'[1] When the crowd of townspeople went up the hill to search for the lady, they found on top a stone image of the Virgin (Taboada Teran, 1999; Cano Galvarro, 2001). As well as this legend propagated by the church, legends also exist in which not the apparition of the Virgin is emphasized, but her miraculous power.

The master legend is relatively simple, compared to other apparition legends of the Virgin Mary elsewhere in the world. No political messages such as in the apparition of Fatima, where Mary warned against communism, no instructions to build a chapel, such as in the legend of Lourdes, and no apocalyptic predictions such as in Kibeho, Rwanda (e.g. Matter, 2001; www.apparitions.org) occur in the story of Urkupiña. The stone image found on the mountain is mentioned in the official legend, but no importance was given to it thereafter, even though it could have been considered material proof of Mary's appearance. During my fieldwork, nobody could tell me where the stone image had gone. When I spoke to one of the priests of the parish of San Ildefonso, he made no mention of the stone image. His story stopped with the girl shouting '*Orqh'opina*'. Surprisingly, the stone image was not emphasized by the church representative, whereas, as we shall see, stones are the central elements in the legends of pilgrims.

1 There exists confusion about the correct orthography of the word Urkupiña. Sometimes it is written as UrKupiña, sometimes as UrQupiña and few times as UrCupiña. According to Quiroga Flores (2006) the right spelling is with a 'q', as the Quechua word for hill is *Orqho*. In contrast, Garcia Mérida (2001) advocates UrKupiña, as the word is derived from Quechua but has been Hispanicized in history and the use of the consonant 'k' indicates its Quechua-origin. In addition, according to Garcia Merida, writing it with a 'q' is only an invention of Bolivian academics. The majority of the Bolivians spontaneously write UrKupiña with a 'k'. Furthermore, he points out an orthographical contradiction, as in Spanish the 'q' is accompanied by an 'u' to give sound to the following vocals 'e' or 'i'. The other vocals 'a', 'o', 'u' are always preceded by the consonants 'c' or 'k'. I agree with Garcia Merida and choose to write Urkupiña with a 'k' throughout my dissertation.

The master legend does not emphasize any miraculous power of the Virgin, but draws attention to the unusual name of Urkupiña. Urkupiña is not a Spanish word, and has its origin in the Quechua language. The master legend of the church is mainly a message for the purpose of converting the indigenous people to the Catholic religion. As the name Urkupiña is derived from the indigenous Quechua language, the master legend outlines the appearance of Mary to an indigenous shepherd girl. Mary, as an embodiment of Spanish Catholicism, is shown to be receptive to the indigenous population. In this way the master legend resembles the legend of the appearance of Our Lady of Guadalupe to Juan Diego in Mexico, who with her appearance to an indigenous man, just after the colonization in 1531, stood as the mother of the poor (Sklar, 2001).

Although the official legend emphasizes the apparition, the believers also emphasize the power of the Virgin to realize miracles in their personal version of the story of the origin. In contrast to the official legend, the pilgrims do not highlight Urkupiña's name in their versions of the legend. Almost all people know that the name Urkupiña is derived from the words '*Orqh'opina*', as shouted by the shepherd girl when the woman climbed up the hill. Most pilgrims then added that this Virgin is '*es muy poderosa, muy milagrosa*' – very powerful, very miraculous. Her power is especially connected to the stones and their miraculous ability to transform. According to Vicky, an older Catholic vendor selling blessings on the Calvary Hill, a shepherd girl was crying close to the Calvary Hill because she had lost all her sheep. Then the Virgin came and told the girl to pick up little stones and take them home in her *awayo* (indigenous cloth to carry things on the back). Back home, the girl discovered that the stones had been transformed into gold. A similar story was told by another pilgrim. She tells again about a girl who lost her sheep:

> A lady appeared and told the shepherd girl to take home little stones and put them in the sheep pen. She did as she was told. Her parents became angry because of the lost sheep. However, the next morning the pen was full of sheep. The stones had been transformed into more, and more beautiful, sheep than they had ever had before.

The central focus of these subdominant stories is on miracles and stones. The stones change into either gold, or sheep, or whatever people are desiring at that time. People draw attention to the multiplicity of abundance. This has also to do with the importance of fertility on which the Andean *cosmovisión* is based. The key value of fertility is experienced as reproduction, prosperity, and multiplication (Harris, 2000; Lagos, 1993).

Another important difference between the master narrative of the church and the narratives of the pilgrims, has to do with the interpretation of Mary's image and feast day. Some pilgrims link the cry '*Orqh'opina*' to the feast day of 15th of August, the day of Mary's Assumption to heaven. According to the pilgrims, the part in which the Virgin walks up the hill, symbolizes her Assumption to heaven. However, the image of Urkupiña, which represents the legend of her apparition, does not correspond with the images representing Mary's Assumption. According to Javier Baptista, a Bolivian priest, the Assumption should be pictured as a woman alone, with her hands open to ascend to heaven. The image of the Virgin of Urkupiña is that of a woman, carrying her son Jesus. Images that present Mary together with Jesus correspond liturgically to the *Fiesta* of the presentation of Jesus to the temple on February the second. The famous image of Urkupiña, thus, is used liturgically incorrectly, as it does not correspond to the doctrinal order. In the Catholic calendar, Mary cannot ascend to heaven with her son Jesus, because Mary died after Jesus. The pilgrims, however, do not seem concerned with the inconsistent logic about Urkupiña's image. Baptista explains: 'People don't care. They know Mary ascended to Heaven, and they know she had a son. They don't mind whether or not the image is in accordance with the biblical dates.' He told me that the church wanted to change Urkupiña's image of a mother carrying her son to an image in which she appears without her son, but the people protested: 'This way, they did not recognize their *Mamita*, and the church had to accept that she could not be changed.' As a pilgrim said: 'The Virgin of Urkupiña is always depicted with her child. If the little kid is not there, it is not Urkupiña.' This demonstrates the power of the subdominant discourse of the believers: although the church wanted to transform her image, the townspeople did not allow it, because for them the Virgin of Urkupiña appeared together with her son to a little Quechua shepherd girl.

Cota: The place of legend

According to the legend of Urkupiña, the Virgin appeared at the hill of Cota. This hill is about one kilometer away from the Calvary Hill, a part of the same chain of hills to the south of Quillacollo. Surprisingly, pilgrims do not attach much importance to this location, whereas at many pilgrimage sites the place of apparition is the most central and powerful place, for example in Lourdes in France or Guadalupe in Mexico City. Many people I spoke to did not even know that Cota is the location of Mary's appearance. Many pilgrims just think Urkupiña appeared on the Calvary Hill, as, for them, this is the most important site.

One day I walked from the Calvary Hill to Cota along an unpaved road following the Sapenko river. The road first bends around the migrant district *Villa Urkupiña*, and then the Calvary Hill. Depending on the season, the river can be high or very low. In the dry period the river has dried up, and it looks more like a garbage dump. Little bushes grow on the banks. When I walked there I saw small, barefoot children with dirty clothes playing with home-made little catapults, trying to hit an empty Coca-Cola bottle floating in the river. On the barren surfaces of the hill, I saw an indigenous man grazing four thin cows. Further away, a woman with a colorful *awayo* - woven cloth - with a baby in it, was guarding a few sheep. Another woman with two little children walked to the river. I saw them disappear in the bushes. When I passed, I saw the three of them were squatting on the river bank to urinate.

The lack of signs giving the direction of Cota shows how little importance the locals attach to the site. Both the river and the road curve; the path stops at a small, empty, flat, rocky space. A little path, made by people walking, leads to a little chapel made of rocks at the foot of the hill. Further to the right stands a little unfinished brick building. A bit further on are some bushes, and through these the river can be reached. At the other side of the river, another unpaved road has been constructed leading from the river to the inhabited areas of Quillacollo. However, there is no bridge to connect Cota with this road. It gives the impression of a desolated and neglected area.

Before the boom of the *fiesta* in the 1970s, the annual celebration for Mary was on Cota. The chapel at the foot of the hill is an open building with a corrugated iron roof. A few stairs lead to big silver-painted rocks and to a little glass case in the middle of these rocks. The glass case is fastened with a big padlock, but there is nothing in there - not even an image or picture of the Virgin. To the right there is a little door in the rocks. It is open, but once again, there is nothing there. It appears abandoned, no vendors or other people are present. But there are signs of human activity - a few flowers stand in vases in the chapel, and the lower part of the rocks is completely blackened by smoke and candles.

According to some vendors on the Calvary Hill, *yatiris*, Andean medicine men, sometimes go to Cota to perform their rituals for pilgrims. An historian told me that Cota was once a *huaca*. Remainders of offerings to Pachamama can be found in several places. The ash of the burnt offerings is still there, together with coca leaves, as well as empty beer bottles and little empty plastic bottles that once contained pure alcohol as an offering. Every first Friday of the month, Pachamama is venerated in Bolivia and people perform a *k'oa*, an offering of burnt sweets, herbs and incense to their homes, shops or fields. Some people, especially the *yatiris*, still visit the old pre-colonial *huacas* to render their offerings, as the energy is especially strong in these places (Janssens, 2001).

Starting at the little chapel, a path made of stones leads up the hill. This is also remarkable, since nobody lives around Cota. I followed the path that curved, forming a loop from the chapel, over the hill back to the chapel again. Halfway along the road, on the outer edge, stood a rock on which was painted: 'Virgen de Urkupiña.' One of the vendors of *alasitas* on the Calvary Hill, told me that this rock represents the exact place where the Virgin of Urkupiña appeared.

Closer to the river stands a partially constructed chapel. The construction of this newer chapel was started in 1992, but it was never completed. According to a notice the chapel is evidence of the gratitude of a family from Santa Cruz. Close to this chapel is a well dug by pilgrims. An old woman in town told me that when she was young, people used to take water from this well for healing purposes, but this practice has fallen into disuse, as the water is polluted. The sacristan of the church told me that the parish never agreed with this custom, due to the harmful bacteria in the water.

Only on one day, the 17th of August, the day after the three day *fiesta*, a group of fifty to a hundred devotees from Santa Cruz take the Virgin of Urkupiña from the church in procession to Cota. It is their yearly farewell celebration to the Virgin. This day an open air mass is celebrated. The statue of the Virgin is placed in the partly constructed chapel, while plastic coverings are attached to form a church roof for the little mass. Pilgrims from Santa Cruz are in charge of this procession, and join together at Cota to celebrate their own *fiesta*. After mass they share food, drink, and music, and in the evening the image is taken back in procession to the church in Quillacollo. Remarkably, almost no Cochabambinos are present at this farewell procession. Most Santa Cruzeños told me with pride that, since the Virgin had appeared here, that was their reason to come to this place, and not to the Calvary Hill. Most people from Quillacollo perceive it as a place taken over by the Santa Cruzeños and they want to have little to do with it. In Bolivian society there is a tension between the people from the lowlands, also called Cambas, and the people from the highlands, called Kollas, who have different ethnicities (e.g. Friedman-Rudovsky, 2008; Margolis, 2008). People from Santa Cruz, in general, are whiter and richer than the people from the highlands. At the pilgrimage site, this is another manifestation of power politics than that of the church and its devotees, that comes to the fore.

Calvary Hill: The place of petitions and rituals

About 20 years ago, the central pilgrimage space was transferred from Cota to a hill at one kilometer away, which then became known as the Calvary Hill, and where there was yet another chapel to the Virgin. Most people give as the reason for this replacement the easier and more direct access to the Calvary Hill from the church in town. This site, occupying around four hectare, is also a larger place to host the thousands of pilgrims that arrive during the *fiesta* to perform their rituals. According to the gardener of the Calvary Hill, this terrain was already church property, while Cota is not a church domain but belongs to a rich family, who does not want to sell their lands to the church. According to an ex-priest of Quillacollo, the Calvary Hill is bigger and therefore able to host the large number of pilgrims that visit the shrine in August each year. Map 3 (p. 54) shows the Calvary Hill and map 4 (p. 55) gives a close-up of the start of the Calvary Hill. The trip from Quillacollo to *el Calvario* follows the almost two kilometer long straight paved road '6 de Agosto', that ends at the entrance of the Calvary Hill, just after crossing the bridge over the narrow Sapenko river. From far away, the large white curved gate that functions as the welcoming portal of the sanctuary is visible. According to Natalia, one of the sellers of blessings, its construction, around twenty years ago, was a donation by Max Fernandez, who was one of Bolivias most famous beer brewers from Quillacollo.

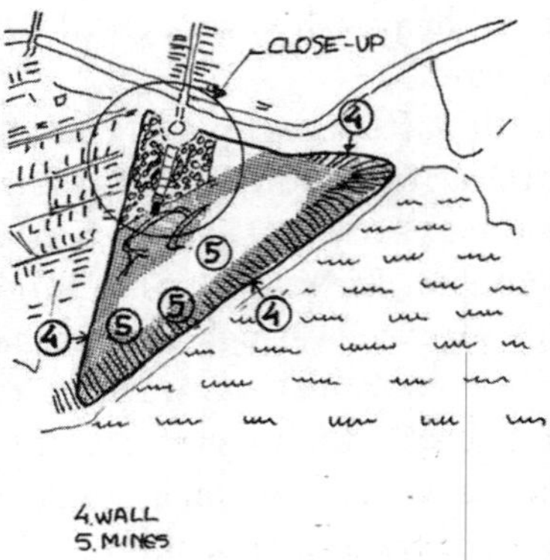

MAP 3: THE CALVARY HILL

⑤ THE MINES

Most pilgrims arrive at the sanctuary by bus or car. When getting out of their vehicles, they are harassed by swarm of vendors who all want to sell their goods. Little stalls stand on both sides of the road. As the obtrusive vendors can be an annoyance to pilgrims, the parish has prohibited them entering the Calvary Hill, to keep the site 'pure and spiritual' as Federico Torico, an ex-parishioner said. In 2005 the construction of a two meters high wall was finished, marking the boundary of the Calvary Hill and enclosing the four hectares. According to one of Quillacollo's priests, the walls are a clear demarcation between the 'sacred' pilgrimage site and the 'profane' outer world. Interestingly, the church tries to transform the Calvary Hill into a clearly defined holy place, but at the same time the pilgrims and vendors appropriate it, and adjust the site and its performances to their wishes. Again, the power politics between church and devotees is at work here.

In front of the gate, the paved road ends and a sand road continues to the left and right around the Calvary wall. The road on the left leads through the fields to some small communities outside Quillacollo, that on the right leads to the district *Villa Urkupiña*, a poor suburb of Quillacollo. The district has been established only recently, and is inhabited predominantly by migrants from several highlands towns in Bolivia. There are few resources, no paved roads and not everyone has access to water or electricity. Many of the vendors working in front of the Calvary Hill live in this area.

Beyond the bridge at the end of the Avenida 6 de Agosto a square has been constructed. At the end of the square, a white cobblestone path leads through the curved white gate for about two hundred meters, gradually rising to the chapel of the Virgin of Urkupiña. To the left and right of the path a park has been laid out with grass, flowers, and trees. Every weekday a gardener and a few helpers are present to keep the garden in top condition. The park is a quiet and clean place to relax, and especially on Sundays, families and friends come to this spot for a picnic.

When entering the gate, the visitors are presented with numerous large signs with texts such as: 'For God everything is possible' and 'Mary, bring us closer to the heart of your son'. On the left, before the chapel, a tiny health post is located: this is a gift of thanksgiving to the Virgin of Urkupiña from a group of Bolivian immigrants in the United States. The place is run by volunteers, and the medicaments they distribute are donated by the bishop's convention in Cochabamba. People from nine poor communities in the area round lake Cotapachi receive help at the post. Behind the health post there are three other buildings. In one of these, four nuns live. Another tiny house has been built for Doña Gregoria, who is in charge as the guardian of the Calvary Hill. She lives here together with her husband and five of their children. She also keeps eight dogs that walk freely around the site. They are taught to protect the site from potential burglars at night. Behind the house of the guards there is a canteen for about forty poor children from the area who, during the week, come to eat at the expense of the parish in Quillacollo.

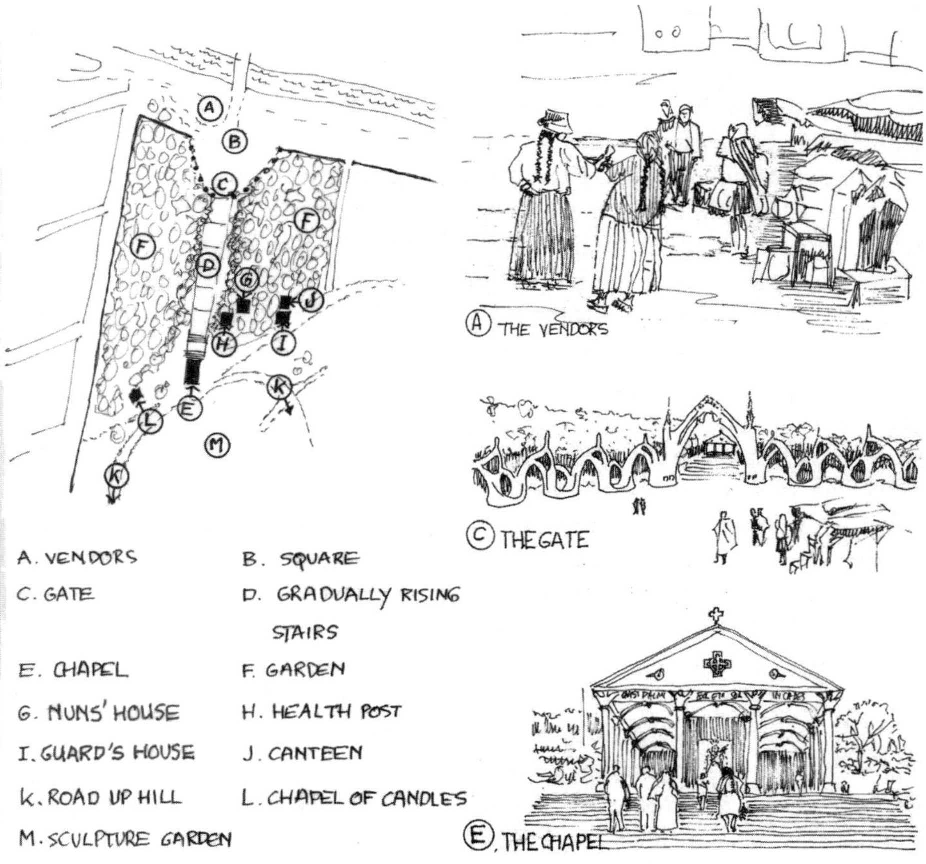

MAP 4: CLOSE-UP OF THE ENTRANCE TO THE CALVARY HILL.

The chapel on the hill was built on the orders of father Monseñor Francisco Cano Galvarro, who was the priest of Quillacollo in the nineteen forties and fifties. In 1947 the land was bought by the church, and in 1951 the actual chapel was built (Obando Stemberg, 2007). It is a simple building, mostly concrete, open and pillared, with a corrugated iron roof. It contains about 20 pews, all gifts of pilgrims. Every Sunday a mass is held in the morning in the open chapel. At the back of the building, behind a stone altar, stairs lead to a platform on which pilgrims can pray and stand in front of a replica of the Virgin of Urkupiña. From the platform pilgrims are able to touch the image, as it is not protected by glass. The replica is smaller than the statues kept in the church.

Behind this chapel a white statue of the Virgin, together with white statues of sheep and an indigenous shepherd girl, represent the legend of Urkupiña. Curved around both sides of these statues, a sand path leads further up the hill. On top of the hill is a large flat area. This gives a view over a valley with fields, where during the wet period a lake - Lago Cotapachi - emerges. Walking over the flat area in the direction of the lake, the hill takes on a different look. At first sight, from the end of the flat area and where the hill slopes down, it gives the impression of a war zone, a large field with so many holes that it looks as if lots of little bombs have been dropped there. However, the most famous ritual of the pilgrimage of Urkupiña is the cause of these holes. Pilgrims come here to hack stones out of the rocks. With big, heavy hammers pilgrims make their offering by slamming on the rocks. The stones they chisel loose are blessed in name of the Virgin, then taken home, and brought back to the Calvary Hill after a year. The holes are called mines, as the hacking resembles the work in the mines, and also because in mines wealth can be found, and wealth is an important motivation for pilgrims to approach the Virgin of Urkupiña.

For years the church has had plans to build a Cathedral, and the symbolic first stone was laid in 1994. Since then no second stone has been added. However, the new parish council of 2007 spoke seriously about the plans, saying that the construction would begin shortly and that they were busy with the preparations. According to one of the priests:

> We want to construct a great basilica that covers a large part of the Hill. We want to make it so big that it can compete with the sanctuary Our Lady Aparecida in São Paulo or Guadalupe in Mexico City. We want to transform the site into a calm and spiritual place.

The plans for transforming the Calvary Hill into a church-controlled pilgrimage place again demonstrates the power politics at work between church representatives and devotees. The plan to build a basilica is meant to attack the 'pagan custom' of hacking stones, as the priest said. In the *fiesta* of 2007, the priests already started the purification of the mining field by closing more than half of the mines with sand. However, this was a vain effort, because during the days of the *fiesta* of Urkupiña, the mines have particular owners; several inhabitants of Quillacollo pay a permit fee to the local *alcaldía* - city hall - and in return they can make money during *fiesta* days by renting out hammers and selling beer to pilgrims at 'their' mine. A few days before the actual *fiesta* most of them came and with their own hands cleared away the sand from their mines. Others found other solutions. A mine owner whose mine was filled with sand said:

> When I came here my mine was gone! There were no holes anymore, everything was full of sand. It was just a flat area. I saw people with a tractor and I paid them to tow away a big rock from another mine. It is hard to speak of a mine this way, as there is no hole in the ground, but at least our regular customers can come to our spot and dislodge stones!

The majority of the mine owners and the pilgrims were angry about the unannounced closure of the mines in 2007 and refused to accept it. For most of them, the ritual of hacking stones is an integral part of the pilgrimage to the Virgin of Urkupiña. For them it is out of question that the custom will be eradicated in the coming decades. It shows the strength of the vendors and pilgrims to undermine the power of the priests.

Other than during the *fiesta* time, there are few pilgrims present at the Calvary Hill, but it is not a desolate area either. Walking around the mines and the surrounding area, you always hear people laughing, singing, proposing toasts or praying. Often people come with their families to the site, so children can play in the rocks, while everyone dislodges a few stones. This gathering of groups looks like open air *fiestas*, because of the sharing of bottles of beer. The ground in and around the mines is strewn with beer caps, because of the beer that is used in libation rituals at these spots.

After the dislodging of stones, pilgrims can burn candles in the new chapel of candles built in 2007, replacing an old open building with a corrugated iron roof. This chapel of candles is built about 30 meters to the right of the chapel with the tiny replica of the Virgin of Urkupiña. The new building is a spacious round construction, with a high ceiling and many stained glass windows.

Church of San Ildefonso: The place of the dominant discourse

The original statue of the Virgin of Urkupiña, together with several replicas, is kept in the church San lldefonso throughout the year. The church is in the central part of Quillacollo and easily accessible. It is only three blocks away from the main square of Quillacollo, that is attached to the wide and busy Avenida Blanco Galindo that connects Quillacollo to Cochabamba. It is the town's most important church. The building of the church was initiated by father Fructuoso Mencía, and the construction took place between 1908 and 1947. It is built with stones that have been carried from the Calvary Hill (Delgado Morales, 1990: 154). In 1992 the church was declared a National Monument (Orlando Stemberg, 2007).

The church, painted in white and yellow, has a picturesque allure with its two towers overlooking the square that is full of coaches and trees. Every morning several masses are held from six o'clock until twelve o'clock. During these hours a few women are to be found standing in front of the entrance to pin little images of the Virgin on the clothes of churchgoers, in the hope that pilgrims will buy the little pins when they are stuck in their clothes. The mass is an informal event, as people walk in and out. Not everyone attends mass; some just enter the church to greet the Virgin of Urkupiña when they pass by. In the afternoon the church remains open and people can walk in and out to pray. At night the church is closed. Day and night a few, mostly disabled, beggars install themselves at the entrance to the church and try to obtain a little money to buy some food.

Inside, visitors are treated to an impressive dose of gold and kitsch. The decorations are of neo-classic style (Cáceres, 2001: 150). At the left and right side of the nave, different images of saints and of Mary, full-length, are placed in glass cases. When entering the church, the eye is immediately drawn to the statue of the Virgin of Urkupiña, behind the main altar at the back of the chancel. According to the sacristan the image came originally from Spain and was brought to Bolivia by the Spanish colonizers. Nobody I spoke to knew the exact origin of the statue. It is placed high up in a glass case. Six large angels, three at each side, forming a triangle, focus attention on the seemingly small figure, which the pilgrims are not allowed to approach. Above the image a religious scene is painted, showing Mary ascending to heaven, accompanied by God and angels. The little shepherd girl's encounter with the Virgin of Urkupiña is depicted in the lower part of this painting.

Another image is placed in a transept of the church, which is dedicated fully to the devotion to the Virgin of Urkupiña, where there are always pilgrims who place flowers, light candles, and pray. On a little scaffold in front of the image pilgrims can put flowers, and there are always numerous bouquets standing there. The church officials never have to buy flowers, as so many people come to put their bouquets in front of the Virgin's statue. Although this image has exactly the same size as the main one behind the altar - 1.20m - she appears to be bigger, as she is placed lower, her feet at eye-level. This statue, like the one behind the altar, is also placed in a glass case, but pilgrims do not hesitate to approach her and touch the glass with hands and flowers. Once a year this image leaves the church for a short procession in the square, carried by a group of candle vendors who donated this replica to the church around 15 years ago. For all other processions, a third replica is used that is not exposed directly to the public. This image looks the same as the one in the transept, and is kept in a little room where pilgrims can approach the sacristan or pastor to ask for blessings and blessed water to take away.

Men, women, rich, poor, young, old, urban and rural people, they all come to visit the Virgin. Every day when the schools finish, around twelve o'clock for the morning session and around five o'clock for the afternoon session, little groups of friends stroll around in church; boys in blue pants and white blouses, girls in white school tunics and bare legs. Many people come to light a candle in the side chapel. Women often light more than one candle. They put them in little groups on the iron plates. When I asked if one was not enough, they all told me they lighted a candle for each family member. Sometimes I saw people taking a flower from a vase and brush the glass case with it.

The vendors of religious objects and candles are not allowed to block the entrance to the church with their stalls. These are found to the left and right of the church on the corners of the square. Every Saturday and Sunday cars are blessed in the street behind the church. In the weekends the street is full of vendors of ribbons, bands, flowers, confetti, and other decorations for the car blessings. People can come with their decorated cars, taxi's, buses, and trucks to church where they pay for a blessing by the priest, in name of the Virgin of Urkupiña. The blessing is meant to give protection and durability to the car. The driver gets a key ring with a picture of the Virgin on one side, and on the other side a little prayer. After the church blessings most devotees perform their own libations by sprinkling beer on the cars.

Fiesta of Urkupiña

The month of August is almost entirely dedicated to the festivities of Urkupiña. The *fiesta* itself takes place from the 13th until the 16th of August, but is preceded and followed by several other rituals around the Virgin of Urkupiña. Two weeks before the actual *fiesta*, the *Quincena* is held. The *Quincena* is derived from the Catholic practice of the 'Novena' consisting of prayers on nine successive days. The Bolivian variant is not limited to nine days, but lasts for fifteen days in a row. During each of these fifteen days of prayers a mass is dedicated to the Virgin Mary. Also part of the *Quincena* are processions with Mary's statue to several districts of Quillacollo. On the first day several devotees from one district in Quillacollo await the statue of Mary in the church. A group of neighbors, singing Marian hymns and reciting the rosary aloud, takes the image in procession to a house in their district in Quillacollo, where she will stay one night. There, a mass is held by one of the priests who accompanies the procession. After the mass, the priest returns home while the neighbors share a little food and drink. The next afternoon, Mary is brought in procession to the main plaza in Quillacollo where she is handed over to the next group of devotees from invited parishes from Cochabamba. These groups take the image in a short procession from the main square over the three blocks back to the church where she is received by inhabitants from another district in Quillacollo. Immediately after its return they take the statue to her next venue, while the devotees from Cochabamba stay in church to attend a *Quincena* mass.

The custom of Mary visiting the different districts of Quillacollo started in 1989. Federico Torrico, the priest in charge during the introduction of the Marian visits in Quillacollo, explains:

> It started with the visit of Pope John Paul II to Cochabamba in 1988. To prepare the people, different parishes in Cochabamba were visited, together with the statue of the Virgin of Urkupiña. In 1989 the parishes from Cochabamba had to pay a return visit to the Virgin in Quillacollo. However, the need arose to welcome and receive the pilgrims from Cochabamba. Therefore, we wanted the *Quillacolleños* - inhabitants of Quillacollo - to be involved in the new event. A way to do this was to invite every district to participate in the procession and make them receive the pilgrims. Then the idea started to let Mary visit the districts beforehand. As most inhabitants are busy negotiating during the actual *fiesta*, they were provided with an opportunity to reflect upon Mary and their religiosity before then.

In the past decades Quillacollo has expanded greatly, and not all districts participate in the custom. It is more or less the same districts that participated the first time that still receive Mary during the *Quincena*. For most of the devotees it is a great honor when Mary stays the night in their house. They experience it as a special blessing for their family. A pilgrim who hosted Mary in her house recounts with tears in her eyes:

> I can't describe what it means to me that the Virgin stays with our family tonight. We feel so proud that she wants to sleep in our house! I am convinced she will give us all her protection next year.

The fifteen days of processions through different districts of Quillacollo show that the Virgin of Urkupiña herself becomes a pilgrim by visiting the people in town who are closest to her, before they and others make their yearly pilgrimage to her shrine on the 16th of August.

Mary's peregrinations through town has in particular meaning on a local level. However, three years ago this local movement was connected to a movement of Mary on the national level. In the weekend before the actual *fiesta*, different Marian statues from all over Bolivia come to Quillacollo and join the Virgin of Urkupiña in a collective pilgrimage in which for more than two hours all the statues are carried through town under the eyes of many spectators. In Bolivia it is common practise for syndicates to organize a feast for the Virgin in return for protection. The celebration of the *llegada de las Virgenes* - arrival of the Virgins - is an initiative of the syndicate of the local press. According to one of the organizers the idea started in 2006:

> For the simple reason that there is a lack of unity in Bolivia. With so many issues, like the Assembly Constitution and the Autonomy. There are so many situations in Bolivia, and the power of the Virgin of Urkupiña is that she integrates people from all those backgrounds, with different interests. She is the Patroness of National Integration, so the idea arose to invite other Virgins from different departments.

In 2007 the collective pilgrimage of Urkupiña and 'her friends', as many devotees call the accompanying statues of Mary, started in the neighboring village of Vinto. From there the different depictions of Mary moved together in the direction of Quillacollo. Eight famous representations were present, like the Virgin of Copacabana from the La Paz department, the large painting of the Virgin of Socavon from Oruro, and the tiny image of Cotoca from Santa Cruz. Some images had travelled by truck, bound to a jeep, or arrived in Quillacollo on the night bus along with their representatives. Mostly migrants that live in Quillacollo group together with the image from their original department. Many devotees also brought their images from their house altars to town and put them on the same platform as the travelling statues[2]. With all the Marian representations, a mass was held outside at the square of the church of San Ildefonso, after which another short procession was held round the four corners of the square, and then the images stayed together and 'slept' in the church during the night.

Few authors have paid attention to the literal movement of Mary. Both Morgan (forthcoming) and Hermkens (forthcoming) look at the 'International Pilgrim Virgin Statue of Our Lady of Fatima' who herself travels around the world and visits the devotees in diverse contexts. By letting an image travel around the world, the Virgin of Fatima is able to reach more devotees, her image coming to the people rather than the reverse. This also happens in Bolivia, as Mary visits the people in the different districts of Quillacollo and Marian representations of all regions travel to the town of Quillacollo to make contact with the devotees. The power of pilgrimage lies not only in people travelling to Mary. Turning Mary into a pilgrim is also a message about presence. Hermkens (forthcoming) notes that by communicating Mary's presence the devotees from Papua New Guinea also imbue the statue with the power to reconcile and convert people in order to bring peace in the conflict area of Bougainville. The mobility of the statue aims at bringing about moral and social reform. In Bolivia, the mobile image of the Virgin of Urkupiña, together with her friends, has a cohesive force, as the custom has been instigated in an attempt to unite the different provinces in Marian pilgrimage. At the same time, it divides the devotees because the migrants join their 'own' Mary.

2 Many devotees in Bolivia have personal altars, for example a devotional corner in house with a picture or statue of the Virgin and other saints. In the private surroundings of the family the images and representations derive their meanings and importance. In the private sphere these altars give them the space to connect to Mary (e.g. Margry, 2003).

From the 13th till the 16th of August, the actual *fiesta* of the Virgin of Urkupiña is held. During the first three days of the *fiesta* there are dance processions in which the streets of Quillacollo are the décor for a spectacular display of dances. By dancing, devotees can embody their vow and ask for Mary's support. Most of these dances refer to ethnic and cultural events in the Bolivian past and present. The 13th of August starts with a dance procession for the indigenous people, called the *Entrada Autóctona*, in which dance groups can display the variety of regional differences in dance. In the official discourse this dance procession does not count as the first day of the actual *fiesta*. The more spectacular dance procession, by mostly urban groups from all over the country, that is held on the 14th and 15th of August and is called the *Entrada Folklórica*, is seen as the beginning of the actual *fiesta*. This event also attracts visitors from all over the country, and from early in the morning until late at night the most beautifully dressed and decorated dancers perform over a distance of four kilometers in front of a large crowd that comes to watch.

The official second day of the *fiesta*, the 15th of August, starts at 10 o'clock with a mass celebrated by the Archbishop of Cochabamba. After the mass, the statue of the Virgin is taken in procession round the four corners of the main square in Quillacollo. The dance groups of the spectacular urban dance procession again perform their dances on this day. The third day actually starts at night in the city of Cochabamba where thousands of pilgrims, especially youth groups, gather to start their pilgrimage of 16 kilometers on foot to the Calvary Hill outside Quillacollo. When they have walked 13 kilometers they pass the church of San Ildefonso and they can join a morning mass. At ten o'clock the statue of the Virgin is taken in a procession of pilgrims to the Calvary Hill. This third day is also called 'Calvary Day', because so many pilgrims come together - on foot, by bus or other transportation - at the Calvary Hill to hammer out stones that symbolize their wishes and perform their own calvary. After these intense feast days, farewell processions are held with the image of Urkupiña. In three days, the statue is taken in four directions around Quillacollo. She goes to the north, south, east and west. Every year the same places are visited, where masses are held and people join for a *fiesta*. The procession to Cota, performed by the Santa Cruzeños is one of these farewell processions.

The Urkupiña month ends at the 24th and 25th of August with the Days of *Alasitas* in Quillacollo. On these days the main streets of Quillacollo change into a market of all possible sorts of miniature foodstuffs. People take or buy a basket and collect all kinds of real food in miniature. There are mini-potatoes, mini-roots, mini-cuts of meat, and so on. The first day, the image of the Virgin is placed outside in the round open kiosk in the square in front of the church, the second day she is taken to the covered market of Quillacollo. People line up in front of the Virgin with their baskets with food, to have them blessed in name of the Virgin. Priests are present to bless the food with sacred water. The people have a tremendous faith in this custom, as the goal is: 'that in my house there will be no lack of food in the coming year.' After the blessing they take their baskets home, and prepare a meal from these ingredients, and shared with all family members.

From icon to person

One day I had a conversation with a player of the *zampoña,* an Andean flute, who used to accompany a religious dance group with music during their performances on several patron feasts in the Bolivian country. He told me:

> Some years ago, during the *Entrada* in honor of the Virgin of Urkupiña, I entered the church with the dancers and the other musicians. Inside, everyone started to make their vows and requests. I didn't want to ask the Virgin anything; I only entered to thank her for everything she gave me in that previous year. On my *zampoña*, I played a little melody in her ear. When I looked at her, I saw a tear slip away from her eye... She cried for my song.

Many believers told me similar stories about the Virgin's changing facial and emotional expressions. Her devotees did not see her statue as a static representation of the Virgin Mary, but as carrying her presence inside. Believers approach Mary to experience something of her presence (De Haardt, 2008). Pilgrims are affected by her statue, but it is not the image itself that causes sentiments, but pilgrims' attribution of Mary's presence within the image. Bolivian pilgrims humanize the image by attributing human characteristics to it, and also personalize their relation with Mary in their acts and narratives. Pilgrims humanize Mary in order to relate to her.

The *Mamita* of Urkupiña is always shown with her child Jesus on her left arm and a staff in her right hand. One of her characteristics are her healthy apple-red cheeks. Most pilgrims distinguish 'Urkupiña' from 'Copacabana', another famous Bolivian image of Mary, on the basis of her skin color and hairstyle. Copacabana is a brown skinned Virgin with black hair, whereas Urkupiña is a white skinned statue with dark blond curly hair. It looks as if she is wearing make-up, as she has long, dark, full eyelashes. Her lips are small, but do not necessarily evoke Mary's chastity, as the deep red color give the appearance she is wearing alluring lip-stick. A halo, mostly made of gold metal, frames her face.

Freedberg (1989: 91) notes that religious icons and images are often imbued with presence and sacral power from the perspective of the believer. He writes:

> People do not garland, wash, or crown images just out of habit; they do so because all such acts are symptoms of a relationship between image and respondent that is clearly predicated on the attribution of powers which transcend the purely material aspect of the object. These are acts that bespeak the transition from human product to sacredly endowed object and from impotent manmade piece of material to beneficent - or maleficent - representations.

Believers perceive a sense of presence of the sacred in the material image. Orsi (1997: 50) states that 'encounters with images of the Virgin are encounters with presence.' Believers approach images with human behavior. They kneel, sing, dance and cry for these images (e.g. Freedberg, 1989: 91).

In Bolivia, pilgrims approach the Virgin of Urkupiña as a woman of flesh and blood, just like themselves, rather than as a static, lifeless statue or a mere representation. Sometimes devotees write letters to the Virgin Mary, in which they set down their everyday concerns and ask for Mary's help. These letters are put as close as possible to the statue. Around the replica at the Calvary Hill, where pilgrims come to make their requests, letters can be found directly under the dress of the statue. In the church San Ildefonso, these letters are put in the chinks of the wooden frame that holds the glass case in which the image is placed. Most of the letters are put into envelops that are directed to the Virgin of Urkupiña and even include a personal address, such as 'Church San Ildefonso in Quillacollo', or 'Calvary Hill in Quillacollo'. The writing of letters shows that pilgrims approach Mary as if she is a real person, living at a specific address.

In letters and prayers, pilgrims also demonstrate a personal relationship to Mary. They often address the Virgin of Urkupiña with diminutive terms as, *Virgencita*, or *Mamita de Urkupiña* that express an intimate relation (e.g. Rodriguez, 1994). In their speech and writings, pilgrims tell her about their daily lives, about their worries and struggles. They tell their stories to a person, Mary, who is supposed to listen to them and will intervene. People travel to her statue, because just delivering a request at home is not enough. When pilgrims approach the statue, they want to touch her dress, they want to kiss her hands, they want to feel her face. During the main procession with the image on August 15th a large force of soldiers and policemen is mobilized to protect the statue. Sometimes, tumult arises among the crowd that gathers at the square. In 2005 I noticed how several devotees tried to fight a way through the line of policemen to be able to touch the image. It was almost necessary to use violence to establish order again. This account shows clearly that from the perspective of the believers, the statue is imbued with Mary's presence.

Another way in which devotees treat her as a person, is by giving her presents. Jewellery and clothes are specially popular gifts of pilgrims. In the room next to the altar, there are six large wardrobes full of different dresses and cloaks, all gifts of pilgrims. The Virgin actually has more than 1,500 different dresses in different colors. According to a pilgrim 'she wears all colors, but prefers to wear light colors.' Pilgrims tailor special clothes for Mary, so they can personalize the clothes to their own esthetic preferences. They can choose the color and fabric they like, and decide what decorations they want. Most dresses of Urkupiña are full of fringes, brilliance and embroidery. Pilgrims often have their names be embroidered on the lowest border of the dress. According to a Bolivian priest the way people want to dress her, full of glitter and glamour, makes her 'look like a Hollywood-star on her way to the awards.' A pilgrim described her as 'a big Barbie'. Most Bolivian devotees explained that her outward appearance of richness made her attractive. When I showed them Marian images from all over the world, most respondents were not attracted to the simple and undecorated women such as the Lady of Lourdes. They preferred the more elaborate ones, also because, in that aspect, they resembled the Virgin of Urkupiña, who is the image with which they are most familiar and in which they have the most faith.

According to the priest of Quillacollo, Urkupiña receives between three and ten new dresses each year. Before an important annual celebration, such as Easter and Christmas, her dress is changed. During the *fiesta* of Urkupiña she wears a different dress every day. According to the sacristan: 'The annual *fiesta* is like her birthday, so on these days she will wear her most beautiful new clothes.' The dean is responsible for changing the statue's clothes and does not allow pilgrims to be present when changing her dress. He explains: 'It is inappropriate to see the Virgin naked.' This is rather interesting, as from the replica on the Calvary Hill I know that under her dress she does not have a body but a sculptured under dress.

The Virgin of Urkupiña is also the owner of a tremendous amount of jewellery. Pilgrims give her golden necklaces, rings and earrings. Together with the dresses, her jewellery is changed regularly. Because of these gifts that are related to Urkupiña's appearance, she is interpreted as rich and vain by pilgrims. One woman told me: 'Urkupiña is very ostentatious. She loves gold and jewellery. She even collects it!' This shows that pilgrims express a personal relationship with Mary, both in words and in actions. They talk about Mary as about a human person to whom they relate.

There are several days of the year that Mary is taken out of the church, most of them in the month of the *fiesta*, in August. In May, at the *fiesta* of San Isidro, the saint of labor, the replica of the Virgin of Urkupiña that is used for all processions accompanies the statue of San Isidro to the Calvary Hill, where fertility rites related to the start of the sowing season are carried out. That day her golden crown is changed for a white sun hat. When she arrived by truck at the Calvary Hill, the pilgrim next to me said: 'Look, she is wearing her outdoor clothes.' When I was talking with a candle vendor in Quillacollo about the image being carried around to several districts in Quillacollo during the *Quincena* processions, she told me: 'Urkupiña is a very good hiker!' It reminded me that my view of her as a statue, carried around by her devotees, was not shared by those devotees. According to the interpretation of this woman, the amount of processions showed that the Virgin 'really likes walking, when she goes on holiday'. In their personalized view, Mary's presence is able to move through the streets, enter and sleep at the homes of the devotees. Mary is transformed into a pilgrim herself.

The treatment of the Virgin of Urkupiña as a person can also be seen in the miniatures that are sold in front of the church. For instance, vendors sell identity cards and driver licenses of the Virgin of Urkupiña. These identity cards show a passport photo of her face and sometimes even a fingerprint. Her place of residence is filled in as: 'close to heaven', 'eternal paradise' or just 'Quillacollo'. She is also given a profession, such as 'philanthropist' or 'miracle-maker'.

Mary is endowed with human traits by pilgrims who speak about her as if she is a person: they tell me she is vain, she collects jewellery and her hobby is hiking. I wondered whether pilgrims attributed the same characteristics to the other Bolivian representations of Mary, but I found out that different characteristics were associated with other images. The Virgin of Urkupiña is seen as one of the most powerful images of Mary, together with the Virgin of Copacabana. However, Urkupiña is seen as especially willing to intervene in material matters. The Virgin of Copacabana is perceived as more helpful in occasions of sickness. Several pilgrims also told me that Copacabana has a very jealous personality, whereas Urkupiña acts more out of a sense of justice. It surprised me that pilgrims spoke about different personalities of these images of Mary, as they all represent one and the same Virgin Mary. Often, pilgrims told me that they were all different sisters. 'Look, you have the Virgin Mary, you have the Virgin of Urkupiña, you have the Virgin of Copacabana, Cotoca, Socavon, they are all sisters.' When I commented that according to the church there is only one Virgin Mary, most pilgrims replied that there is only one Mary, but with different stories and appearances, 'therefore, they are all like sisters.'

According to my Bolivian respondents, Urkupiña is seen as a woman with emotions. She can cry and express her preferences. Reference to her changing facial expressions were made not only by the *zampoña*-player and in the story of her trip to Santa Cruz, but also by many others. Julia, a vendor of drinks at the Calvary Hill told me that her cheeks turned into a more profound reddish color when you look her in the eye. During the political economic crisis in 2005, several people told me that Urkupiña looked worried or angry about the situation. All this reveals that Urkupiña expresses different moods and emotions.

Pilgrims with their performances, gestures and interpretations give the image an individual character. They personalize the Virgin of Urkupiña by acting and perceiving her as a real person. It shows pilgrims' power to transform her into a human being to whom they can relate. They write her letters, give her presents and attribute personal characteristics and emotions to her. The Virgin Mary becomes the Virgin of Urkupiña, a special woman for these believers in Bolivia. Next to personalizing her image, thus making a person of her, pilgrims also personalize their relation with her by using diminutives and touching her. In imbuing her image with a personality and personalizing it, pilgrims make the sacred intangible world of Mary come closer to them. The icon has become a person.

Photo 4: Virginia after performing a *sahuma* at the Calvary Hill

4

RELIGIOUS REPRODUCTION OF NEOLIBERAL POLITICS AT THE CALVARY HILL[1]

'Capitalism is humanity's worst enemy'
- Evo Morales, October 2003

In January 2006, the populist indigenous leader Evo Morales Ayma was inaugurated as the new president of Bolivia. This event demonstrated the popular desire for a change in the dominant neoliberal socio-economic ideology that had characterized Bolivian politics since 1985. Neoliberalism is a market ideology characterized by the reduction of state intervention to an absolute minimum. Production and consumption are left to the laws of supply and demand. Morales articulated the growing discontent of the majority of the Bolivians with this neoliberal policy when he said:

> The worst enemy of humanity is capitalism. That is what provokes uprisings like our own, a rebellion against a system, against a neoliberal model, which is the embodiment of a savage capitalism. If the entire world doesn't acknowledge this reality, that the national states are not providing even minimally for health, education and nourishment, then each day the most fundamental human rights are being violated (Evo Morales, October 2003 In: Westmore, 2006).

Morales criticized the neoliberal model and held it responsible for the deteriorating Bolivian economy, a view shared by a majority of Bolivia's poor. Several social scientists also agree with him that neoliberal politics have rarely served the interests of the poor (e.g. Farmer, 2005: 5; Goldstein, 2005). Morales points out that these socio-economic forces have a severe impact on the lives of most Bolivians, as state protection is minimized, companies are privatized, and the

1 Parts of this chapter have been published: Derks, S.W. (forthcoming). Religious materialization of neoliberal politics at the pilgrimage site of the Virgin of Urkupiña in Bolivia. In: *The Power of Marian Pilgrimage*, edited by A.K. Hermkens, C. Notermans and W. Jansen. Aldershot: Ashgate.

economy is left to the mercy of the laws of the free market. For the majority of the Bolivians neoliberal policies imply working on short term contracts for low salaries or, when faced with unemployment, trying to survive by means of the informal economy. The people themselves are responsible for the almost impossible task of generating the necessary money to pay for their most basic expenses, such as food, rent, and doctors' bills. During the previous socialistic period, Bolivians had become used to relying on the state to solve such problems, but during the neoliberal years state protection was removed, so they felt abandoned.

This negative impact exercised by the neoliberal state has been labeled a form of structural violence, as it is institutional, systemic, and blamed for increasing social inequality for the majority of Bolivians (Farmer, 2004, 2005; Goldstein, 2005; Kohl & Farthing, 2007). The consequences for the daily lives of individuals can be termed social suffering (Kleinmann, Das & Lock, 1997). Morales's socialistic challenge to the neoliberal political economy earned him an absolute majority in the election. However, when I was in Bolivia in 2007, I noticed that discontent with Morales's policies was increasing: most people complained that there had not been enough changes. The neoliberal market model still dominated the daily economy of most Bolivians, and the level to which they could rely on the state was less than they had hoped.

In 2006, the Human Development Index (the measure of life expectancy, literacy and standard of living for countries worldwide) for Bolivia was 0.692, which ranks Bolivia 115th out of 177 countries (United Nations, 2006). According to the National Institute of Statistics in Bolivia (INE, 2007) 59.6 percent of Bolivians lived in poverty, while in 2005 36.7 percent lived in extreme poverty, and although the official unemployment rate was 8.15 percent, Bolivia faces high levels of involuntary underemployment

This chapter highlights the role of the pilgrimage to the Virgin of Urkupiña as one of the ways in which people deal with these disempowering circumstances of daily life. Many Bolivians come to the Virgin of Urkupiña in search of protection and mediation. As such, pilgrimages to Mary bring to the fore social inequalities, such as poverty, and may offer a discourse to both express social suffering and to deal with it more adequately in one's personal life.[2] In this chapter I will look at the macro-level of class inequality as I study the socio-economic policies of neoliberal politics and their implications for economic suffering at an individual level. In addition, the question is posed as to how these neoliberal structures are articulated at the pilgrimage site of the Virgin of Urkupiña in Quillacollo.

2 The relation between poverty, social injustice, and religion has also been indicated in Latin American liberation theology, a practical theology from the perspective of the poor and marginalized (Pilar Aquino, 1992; Rowland, 1999; Tombs, 2002). The theological discussions about poverty and pilgrimage are an important field to be explored in further research. It is, however, beyond the scope of this thesis to go further into these discussions.

Making requests of the divine is very common in Bolivia. During the Spanish colonization, several aspects of the Andean *cosmovisión* were incorporated into the Catholic religion. The principle of reciprocity - to be able to receive, one should give something in return (e.g. Mauss, 1990) - structured the relation between the Andean people and Pachamama. Because of the integration of Pachamama with the Virgin Mary, this principle of reciprocity was also applied to Mary, and forms the basis of the exchange relationship pilgrims establish with her. In the next chapter, I will go further into this exchange relationship, and look at the expressions of class inequality on a micro-level, and how this structures inequality between rich and poor. In this chapter it is mentioned in order to understand the ritual acts performed at the place of pilgrimage.

To explore how neoliberal structures in Bolivian society are articulated and mediated at this particular pilgrimage site, I will first look at the concepts of structural violence and social suffering, after which I will elaborate on Bolivia's neoliberal history and its implications through the case study of one particular individual. The impact of this particular mode of government and how it leads to social and individual suffering on a structural level, is best grasped from the experience of the poor, such as the case of Virginia, a fifty-nine-year-old religious Quechua petty trader living in Quillacollo. She is one of the persons whose lives I followed intensively during fieldwork, and her life history speaks of a great deal of social suffering. Virginia's life story is embedded in the context of Bolivian society and will show at an individual level how people are victimized by neoliberal societal structures. In particular, I focus on the economic hardships she endures and the religious ways she deals with them, through her invented job at the pilgrimage site, and by being a pilgrim herself. Pilgrimage cannot be explained only as a reaction to economic deterioration and resistance to the neoliberal policy, and on the basis of this case, I will forward more complex explanations.

Structural violence and social suffering

As the neoliberal policy has severe negative consequences for the daily lives of most Bolivians it has been labeled structural violence. Structural violence occurs when certain segments of society are systematically deprived of the satisfaction of their needs by the economic and political structures. In general, the poor are the most severely affected (Christie, 1997: 305). The term structural violence refers to long-lasting forms of social inequality that embody individual experiences (Farmer, 1997). The term dates back at least to 1969, to Johan Galtung, as well as the Latin American liberation theologians, to describe social structures characterized by poverty and steep grades of social inequality. Structural violence is violence exerted systematically by everyone who belongs to a certain social order (Farmer, 2004:307).

Structural violence is thus institutional and systemic. It is frequently initiated and maintained by existing systems, such as the state and its social institutions, rather than by identifiable individuals. In the context of structural violence, power relations are omnipresent, and are exercised from innumerable points (James et al., 2003: 130-131). The politics of neoliberalism in Bolivian society can be seen as structural violence, as these socio-economic structures affect the poor in numerous aspects of their lives, such as incomes, jobs, living conditions, and access to health provisions.

Related to structural violence is the term social suffering. Social suffering results from what political, economic, and institutional power does to people, and reciprocally, from how these forms of power themselves influence responses to social problems (Kleinman, Das & Lock, 1997: ix). Social suffering refers to the devastating injuries that social force can inflict on human experiences. It indicates the, often close, link between personal problems and societal problems, as individual experience is embedded in the larger social matrix (Farmer, 2005: 30). It also reveals the interpersonal grounds of suffering, that suffering is a social experience, in the sense that it helps to construct the social world (Kleinmann, Das & Lock, 1997: ix). Social suffering is, at the same time, both collective and individual. Neoliberalism has had a severe impact on the daily lives of the Bolivian people, especially the poor. They suffer at an individual level from what has been done to them at the level of the state. I recognize that social suffering is more than neoliberalism, as it refers to the consequences of several forms of social inequalities, such as class, gender, ethnicity, health, and age. In this chapter, however, I will give special emphasis to economic suffering as a result of the neoliberal policies, as a form of social suffering, as this form of suffering came to the fore most explicitly in my fieldwork material, and because neoliberalism in particular represents an economic structure.

Social scientists have often offered legitimizing rationalizations of inequality and injustice that explain the origins of inequality, but seldom address the existential meaning of human suffering in life and society (Morgan & Wilkinson, 2001: 199). Morgan & Wilkinson (2001: 205-206) raise two considerations. First of all, suffering is often 'beyond language', and this makes it difficult to articulate the experience of suffering. Following Scarry (1985), they describe it thus:

> Suffering is always more than physical pain; more than violence; more than material deprivation; more than destruction; more than loss: suffering is a state of being which "unmakes our world". Whilst the nature of suffering evokes a quest for meaning, the experience is intensified by the brute fact of its senseless irrationality.

Secondly, measures to quantify the consequences of affliction in social science tend to trivialize suffering by consistently failing to capture the intensity of personal awareness and its cultural complexity. These considerations are partly responsible for a distortion of recognition and communication of what the experience of suffering actually means (Morgan & Wilkinson, 2001: 205-206).

Virginia's case will demonstrate that it is hard to articulate the experience of suffering, as language alone cannot express the full impact of social suffering in all its complexity. Detailed description and analysis come closest to grasping at least a small part of the experience. Still, there is a crisis of representation, as mentioned in the introduction, as reality is only reconstructed in words, and words cannot encompass the complexity of reality. Moreover, the sense of the pain of the other is difficult to feel and to translate by the author. Although words are not enough, I do not have other means than words to describe Virginia's experience of suffering. Before continuing with Virginia's case, I will describe the neoliberal politics in Bolivian society to explain why it can be seen as a violent structure, and to understand its impact on the poor.

Neoliberal politics in Bolivia

Before the initiation of neoliberal regime, Bolivian politics were socialist inspired, due to the Agrarian Reform of 1952. The MNR, the National Revolutionary Movement - a multiclass coalition of peasants, workers, and members of the urban middle strata - nationalized the tin mines, established an agrarian reform in which land was expropriated from the feudal landlords and given to the indigenous population, and abolished unpaid labor. Because of these measures, the Bolivians became increasingly dependent and oriented on the state.

From 1964 until 1982 the political scene was characterized by military governments, which kept the economic policies introduced by the MNR more or less intact (Albo, 2002). The later years of authoritarian rule were harsh: repression was severe, corruption widespread, and drug trafficking blossomed under the protection of the military. When democracy returned in 1982, expectations were high. However, the first government failed dramatically, with hyperinflation hastening early elections in 1985 (Salman, 2006: 164).

As a response to the existing economic crisis and hyperinflation, former president Victor Paz Estenssoro from the MNR initiated the New Economic Policy, promulgated in Presidential Decree 21060. In accordance with this decree, state-owned enterprises were privatized, direct foreign investment increased, protectionism and import substitution were ended, and state mines were closed (Kohl, 2006: 310). Between 1985 and 1990 privatization led to a loss of more than 35,000 jobs in the former public sector manufacturing industries (Kohl, 2006: 311). Furthermore, in 1985 the price of tin bottomed out, and the government took the opportunity to privatize or close the mines, forcing nearly thirty thousand miners to migrate in search of other jobs (Webber, 2005: 3; Felix Arias, 1993: 14). The neoliberal reforms deprived the miners of much more than a job: their entire way of life in remote highland mining centers was devastated, and they had to create a new future in distant and unfamiliar cities and regions (Gill, 1997: 294). El Alto, a city that started as a suburb located on the heights of La Paz, increased its population sixfold between 1985 and 1993. The city is now inhabited almost exclusively by Aymara migrants (Felix Arias, 1993:14). Quillacollo has also increased greatly in recent decades, and is inhabited almost exclusively by an indigenous population, both Quechuas and Aymaras. Between 1976 and 2008 the population of the town, including Colcapirhua, a district incorporated in Quillacollo, grew from less than 20.000 inhabitants to more than 200.000 inhabitants (INE, 2004, based on progression calculations).

Through the introduction of neoliberal policies by Decree 21060, hyper-inflation was successfully halted and the economy stabilized initially (Van Dijck, 1998: 1), but, in the long run, unemployment rates rose, taxes increased, social security was reduced, and poverty worsened for the majority of Bolivians. Supreme Decree 21060 marks the beginning of the neoliberal era, and it has even been turned into the Bolivian expression '*veintiuno zero sesenta*' that has come to symbolize collective misery due to economic policies (Gill, 1997: 294).

Over the years, criticism of the new economic approach grew (e.g. Albro, 2005; Kohl, 2006; Salman, 2006). In particular parties of the left, trade unions, and popular organizations held the neoliberal model responsible for the extremely high level of poverty in Bolivia, and emphasized the way it sustains existing forms of inequality and social suffering (Manzanera, 1993: 20-22). The predominantly white capital holders especially benefited from the policy, whereas the majority of Bolivians saw themselves impoverished by it. As Paulson & Calla (2000: 124) note:

> Part of the seduction of neoliberalism is precisely the promise of a kind of moral equality to be obtained by applying the rules of the free market equally to all peoples. In a country where inequality has been institutionalized throughout a history of legal, economic and political systems explicitly based on class exploitation and ethnic and gender inequality, such a universal principle is tremendously attractive. In recent years, however, contradictions and tensions are rising with the growing certainty that neoliberal politics are exacerbating the very inequalities that they had promised to overcome.

In recent years, the battle continued and unrest grew, concerning the hydrocarbon law and the establishment of a Constituent Assembly, reaching its climax at the beginning of June 2005, when President Carlos Mesa Gisbert resigned and snap elections were held (Kohl, 2006). In 2005, after two decades of neoliberal rule, Evo Morales Ayma was elected.

The market ideology of neoliberalism has had a severe impact on the lives and values of most Bolivians. In the realm of labor policy, Bolivia has emphasized a program of making labor flexible, a mainstay of Bolivian economic policy since 1985. Being flexible in the Bolivian context means being willing to work on short-term contracts, in home-based industries, and, increasingly, in the informal economy, creating one's own income-generating opportunities when the regular economy fails to provide work. Flexibility also means caring for oneself and one's family by working without a safety net, through self-employment and without benefit of public provision of social security (Goldstein, 2005: 396).

The overwhelming majority of the Bolivian workforce is 'informally' employed, that is, they have no job protection or health insurance, and their livelihood depends on a precarious income. In 1976, before the introduction of neoliberalism around 40 per cent worked in the informal economy, whereas in 1992, 56 per cent was informally employed (Emmerij, 1997: 11). The percentage of people working in the informal economy in 2005 is calculated at 67.2 per cent (Schneider, 2007: 18). The neoliberal policy invokes self-responsibility, as the state does not provide a social security system, and most Bolivians are responsible for creating their own income and protection (Goldstein, 2005: 405-406). Money is needed in a capitalist world, and it is hard to find a well-paid job. In light of this lack of sufficient economic resources, consumption is more and more valued, while competition increases (Morales Basadre, 2000: 15).

Poor Bolivians feel that their poverty has its roots in transnational capitalism, and that the forces of privatization and the open market have had a negative impact on their employment opportunities, standard of living, and access to basic services (Goldstein, 2005: 405-406). Poverty is still prevalent in Bolivia, and in large parts of the country people do not have access to basic services. In Quillacollo around 75 percent of houses has a toilet on the property, but only 34 per cent is connected to a sewage system (INE, 2007: 295). In addition, in Bolivia 32 percent lives without electricity (INE, 2007: 269).

The contradiction between liberalism's promise and its reality in Bolivia is manifest in the lives of people living under its rule. Seen in this light, neoliberalism is a form of structural violence, or as Goldstein (2005: 390) argues, 'neoliberal violence,' which he describes as:

> structural and undeniably physical violence that entails an inequitable distribution of resources within a rigidly hierarchical society, which ultimately must be implemented and maintained by state violence, and which in turn engenders violent responses. This violence is quotidian - it marks the everyday lives of poor, marginalized people, creating a profound sense of insecurity, an anxious and fearful 'structure of feeling.'

Neoliberal violence violates not only the political and civil rights of individuals, but also their social and economic rights. People generally suffer from different sources of inequality, and because of its complexity, detailed case-studies are necessary for an understanding of the meaning of social suffering. Therefore, the case study of Virginia is used to show the complexity of her suffering. Case studies can be useful as they give a profound understanding of the diverse aspects of daily life, and add to an understanding of how meaning is attributed to daily life. They also contextualize statements, relating them to the situation in which they are made. It has to be taken into account that several techniques, such as multi-sited participant observation, recording of rituals and events, and non-structured and semi-structured interviewing have been combined. Furthermore, it must be noted that Virginia is not the only person to whom I have spoken in Bolivia. Her case echoes similar stories I heard from numbers of other people. Virginia is chosen because she is exemplary for the suffering I want to describe and because I have collected the most details on her life.

Virginia's life

Once I asked Virginia what she would change first if she were the new president of Bolivia. She answered:

> I would work for the poor. I would make health care free, education compulsory, and I would establish lots of day care centers. But first of all, I would take back all the money the government has stolen from us. When a new president comes, I will have at least enough to survive.

She continued talking about politics: 'All presidents want this country to go to hell. I just go to all the campaign speeches, so at least I will get something. Last year they gave us pencils and another party gave us sandwiches.'

Virginia, like most Bolivians I spoke to, is profoundly negative about politics and politicians. As one of the many victims of the neoliberal model, her life is just one long struggle to survive. She was born into a poor family in the northern Potosí department, was unable to complete primary school, had three babies before she was sixteen, and worked as a food seller in the mines. When she was seventeen she married the father of her children, for purely economic reasons. She says:

> There was no love between us. He just abused me, and every time I got pregnant again. He was a miner in the village, and I needed his income to take care of my children, as the little money I gained by selling food was not enough. For the sake of my children I married him.

This account shows how her economic suffering intersects with other forms of social inequality, such as gender inequality. As a woman, she was expected to take care of the household and children.

After the introduction of the neoliberal model, for her and her family poverty only worsened. Because of the privatization of the mines in 1985, her husband lost his job as a miner; they also lost the state security that came with his contract. Sick pay, chits to exchange for food, and a steady income were all now ended. The state had offered miners a great deal of protection, and it was hard to lose all those extras in addition to the miner's job. In three years, all mines in Virginia's region were privatized, and thousands of miners lost their jobs as a consequence. Most of them migrated to the cities in search of a new means of earning a living. Virginia's family decided to go to Quillacollo. At that time Virginia was thirty-six years old and had given birth to ten children, of whom four had died:

> People told us the Cochabamba Valley was very fertile, so we thought there would be enough food and fruits. They also told us there were big markets, so we hoped to find something in the commercial field. We sold everything we had in Potosí and took all we could carry by hand on the bus. So we arrived in Quillacollo, with my six little children, my husband, and me.

However, life in Quillacollo was not what they had expected it to be. Virginia says: 'People here threw rocks at us. We were not welcome because we came from another area. We were ex-miners and they thought we were dirty.' Ethnic violence was added to the suffering and indignity of neoliberal and gender violence. Her husband, also of Quechua descent, found it difficult to find a new job: unemployment rates were high, and competition for jobs had increased, while his only work experience was as a miner. He tried several jobs, eventually finding work in a chicken factory, where he has been employed for the past ten years. This means that at least he has a fixed salary. However, one-third of his daily pay has to be spent on transport to the factory, and he has not received a salary increase during his ten years of employment, indeed, due to the economic crises it has actually decreased. This has forced Virginia into the informal economy to earn additional income. By selling prayers and blessings to pilgrims at the pilgrimage site of the Virgin of Urkupiña, she earns around 20 bolivianos (BOB), or 2 euros, a day. According to Virginia, every day she needs 2 BOB for the return trip by bus to the Calvary Hill, 5 BOB to buy bread in the morning, 4 BOB for her lunch on days she could not prepare one beforehand, and an average of 5 BOB for incense and coals each day, leaving her the meager sum of 4 BOB, or 40 eurocents, for her other needs. A kilo of potatoes costs 5 BOB, five kilos of rice is 14 BOB, a kilo of meat is 14 BOB, and vegetables are around 5 BOB a kilo. Luckily she does not have to pay rent, as they own their house, but electricity for her family unit costs about 40 BOB a month, water about 20 BOB.

When arriving in Quillacollo, Virginia's family could not find a house and had to live in a little rented shack at the outskirts of Quillacollo. With the help of an Italian nun she met while praying in church, at the end of the1980s they managed to get a piece of uncultivated land in what nowadays is called Siglo Veinte, a migrant district. Virginia's niece, who also came to Quillacollo and lives next door, says:

> It was so awful, there was nothing but snakes and *vinchucas* [large beetles that transmit Chagas disease]. Lots of infections and diseases. All houses in Quillacollo were made from mud. There was not even a road to Cochabamba! Quillacollo has changed a lot. I'm happy to have a house, but I would have preferred it in another district. They still treat us as dirty and poor. That's why the municipalities never want to construct

> street lighting or paved roads. I preferred the mines, because there I could feel safe. I did not have to think all the time that someone might kill me or my children. There is so much criminality here. Police have even given up our district; they don't come when you call them. Then they say: "Oh, Siglo Veinte, whatever." My husband was murdered; I have four little children and don't want anything to happen to them. But I'm scared in this crazy world of Siglo Veinte.

It is clear in this account by Virginia's niece that the state does not offer her family any facilities or protection. 'Self-help security,' a term coined by Goldstein (2005:391), is the key word.

Virginia's quarter is inhabited by migrants, most of them former miners, and it is treated as a backward area. Since 1999 they have had access to water and electricity. A little tap is installed on the patio of the house in which Virginia lives with three adult sons, their wives, and nine of her grandchildren. There is neither shower nor toilet in the house, and although there is electricity, it is used sparingly, as the family wants to keep costs as low as possible.

A total of seventeen people live in the house, all packed into four tiny rooms. Each part of the family must live in a single small room of about three by three meters. For nearly twenty years they have been trying to build two more rooms. The walls have been erected, but there never seems to be enough money to construct a roof. Two of the three sons living in the house have never completed secondary school. Their irregular work as masons is not based on a contract, so they do not have a stable income. Disputes and quarrels about money are a feature of their daily life.

The family units do not operate absolutely independently. During my fieldwork I was invited to several social occasions with the family, such as birthdays, marriages, and religious feasts, and I noticed that a supportive kinship net exists. For example, when one of Virginia's 27 grandchildren had his birthday, Virginia bought a useful present, a new school uniform. In this way she also helps the parents. However, within the family direct financial exchanges are not made, only help in goods is provided. For larger expenses such as health costs, they cannot depend on the family unit but have to make do with the minimal state provisions.

In 2007 Virginia told me that her daughter had uterine cancer, but that they could not afford the 700 dollar operation. After a few weeks I asked Virginia about her daughter's health and she answered that everything was fine. The situation had not changed, they just ignored the topic of her illness: as long as there were no complications, there was no cancer. Another example of the day-by-day vision was Virginia's reaction to my offer to buy her new teeth. She does not have a single tooth left and she complains a lot about it, because it makes her look years older than she is. I found a clinic in Cochabamba and obtained information about the prices. Excited, I went to Virginia to tell her the good news and to make an appointment to go there together. However, she did not show up for the appointment, because as she said: 'I could not afford not to make money that day.' Her daily profit was so essential for her survival that she could not forego it for long term benefit.

For those who grew up in a socialist orientated system, in which the state offered social security, the shift to a neoliberal system, with its emphasis on self-responsibility, is difficult. Virginia's story demonstrates the harsh living conditions of the poor in modern Bolivian society; they face unemployment, individualization of society, and decreasing social security. Virginia's way of coping with these problems is to both work and pray at the site of the Virgin of Urkupiña.

Praying for money

In order to survive, Virginia works at the pilgrimage site of the Virgin of Urkupiña: seven days a week she is there to sell blessings to pilgrims who pay her to pray to Mary to grant their petitions. The ritual of selling blessings started about twenty years ago, according to the local historian Alba Fernandez (2001: 208) and the sellers who told me their life stories. Victoria, Virginia's older sister, was one of the first two *sahumeras* of the Calvary Hill. The word *sahumera* refers to a woman who performs rituals with burning incense, and is derived from the Spanish word *humo*, or smoke. When pilgrims come to the Calvary Hill to perform their rituals, they can approach a *sahumera* to ask for an additional prayer and ritual to reinforce their requests. While singing and praying for the pilgrims, a *sahumera* drops incense into an iron bowl filled with glowing coals. The sweet-smelling smoke rises to the sky to please Mary and induce her to intervene. The *sahumeras* also sell *k'oa* material, and if people ask, prepare the ritual by putting all offer ingredients, such as herbs, cigarettes, coca leaves, and sweets on the glowing coals in their iron bowls. Virginia's sister told me that years ago a nun in the church advised her to go to the Calvary Hill during the *fiesta* of Urkupiña and to charge one boliviano to pray for the petitions of pilgrims. There she met Nathalie, another woman who did the same thing. Victoria tells:

> At the beginning we were not friends. We were competitors. Nathalie was very ambitious and did not want me to make a few *pesos* at all. Nathalie started to make a show, by burning incense, so more pilgrims came to her. Then I started to do the same. Every morning we took wood to burn. Later I found out that coals could be bought at the market in town. So we started this profession.

'Selling religion' is a serious and sincere business. As Virginia tells me:

> Victoria did this job before me, and she asked permission from the Virgin to let me do the same job. As I always pray to the Virgin, I could do it. I pray from my heart for other pilgrims.

According to Virginia, the Virgin Mary knows this and acknowledges Virginia's tremendous faith in her. 'Because of the Virgin, I earn my money.' Virginia says. The sincerity of Virginia's actions is exemplified by the following account. One day a family asked Virginia to perform a *k'oa* for the Virgin, but they left while all ingredients were still burning. Most of the elements were still intact, so I said to Virginia: 'Why don't you put back this *k'oa*, then you can sell it again.' She was indignant: she said: 'No! I cannot do that! This is an offering for those pilgrims. Otherwise the prayer will not work!' Virginia's reaction shows that she is not only interested in the lucrative aspect, but also has a sincere concern for her clients.

Like the *sahumeras*, the majority of pilgrims come to the Calvary Hill to pray for money. While the vendors are paid to pray by the pilgrims, the pilgrims pray to ask Mary for money. The title of Martha Giorgis' book (2004) on the *fiesta* of the Virgin of Urkupiña as celebrated in a migrant community in Cordoba also demonstrates the capitalistic character of the Virgin. She entitled the book '*La Virgen Prestamista*' or 'The Virgin Moneylender'. The requests that pilgrims make show how they are influenced by the effects of the neoliberal system. Mary is approached especially by pilgrims attempting to escape the effects of the recession, and their requests reflect what is lacking in their daily lives. The needs of the poor are immediate, pressing, and often vital. They come to Mary to ask her for protection in their daily economic hardship, and they ask for money, jobs and *pan del día* (daily bread). Others urgently need a house. Richer people come to ask for status articles, ranging from gas stoves to motorbikes. The next chapter will examine further class differences in pilgrims' requests. Many of the pilgrims interviewed said they asked first of all for health, but this was immediately connected with its economic aspect. Virginia explains: 'Without health you cannot work, you cannot make money. Therefore the first thing to ask for is health.' Health is usually requested as a means to make money: money is needed in order to survive.

There are two ways in which the material requests are visualized and symbolized at the pilgrimage to the Virgin of Urkupiña. First, miniature objects, called *alasitas*, can be bought from the numerous stalls in front of the entrance to the Calvary Hill. These are direct representations of desired articles associated with upward mobility, such as paper money, computers, diplomas, houses, and cars. The miniature replicas symbolizing the requests are taken to the Virgin as offerings and then taken home as reminders of the Virgin's blessings. The great number of miniatures that represent articles associated with consumption reflect the appreciation of economic goods.

Second, the requests pilgrims make are given form by the dislodging of stones from the Calvary Hill. With big, heavy hammers people cut stones from large rocks on the hill. During the year the hammers can be rented from Doña Gregoria, the guard who lives at the Calvary Hill, and makes the hammers herself. She loans them for a small 'voluntary' gift, as an extra source of income.

At the time of the *fiesta*, numerous people set up a small business, renting out hammers and offering access to a particular site at the Calvary Hill to hammer out the rocks. The stones pilgrims dislodge symbolize their requests. Many pilgrims refer to the stones as 'money from the Virgin'; to them, the stones represent wealth, to others, they symbolize health or a house. Some pilgrims explain that the stones symbolize the strength and effort that they will need to obtain what they ask: from the ease or difficulty with which the stones were dislodged, they can judge how easy or difficult it will be to obtain what they requested.

According to Cano Galvarro (2001: 222), the custom of taking stones from the Calvary Hill was started by a woman who had seen how devotees of the Virgin of Copacabana took stones from Lake Titicaca home as a reminder of their pilgrimage. During the *fiesta* of Urkupiña in 1944, she handed out flowers to the pilgrims who came to bring alms or ask for blessings, and told them to take a stone with the blessing of the Virgin. From then on, year after year, the custom took a more definite form, and has increased to the proportions it has today. To understand the rapid adoption of this form of devotion, it must be realized that stones have always been important in the Andean *cosmovisión*. Because they cannot be burnt or destroyed easily, stones are seen as objects with special powers. Therefore they were already used in rituals (Thomas, 1995), symbolizing vital powers of Mother Earth they were especially utilized in fertility rituals (Lagos, 2001).

Most pilgrims have their stones blessed through offering a *ch'alla*. The *ch'alla* is a pre-Inca libation offering that consists of sprinkling drink on the ground, the corners of the house, over rocks, or over every object recently acquired. Usually these drinks contain alcohol, such as beer, wine, *chicha* (an alcoholic corn drink), or *singani* (strong liquor). The offering of a *ch'alla* is motivated by the desire for luck, blessing, endurance, gratitude, or purification (Delgado Morales, 1999). Before starting to hammer out a stone a *ch'alla* is also performed on the rocks. The stones are parts of Pachamama, or regarded as being owned by Mary, her successor, and by giving alcohol to the earth, the pilgrims ask permission to take them away. It is part of the reciprocal relationship with Mary: in order to receive the favors they request, they have to give something in return.

Alcohol is not only offered and shared with deities, but also consumed in large quantities by the pilgrims. The church frowns on the high rate of the consumption of alcohol as part of the pilgrimage. However, 'a *ch'alla* is not a *ch'alla* without alcohol, and a good *ch'alla* has to be performed!' as a man from Santa Cruz told me once, while opening the fourteenth liter bottle of Taquiña. For most of the pilgrims, there is no conflict, as in Andean religiosity alcohol has always been present in religious celebrations.[3] The Andean custom of *ch'alla*

3 Celine Geffroy, an anthropologist from France, who lives in Cochabamba, presented a paper titled: Beber con la Pachamama: Los usos sociales del alcohol en los Andes, at a conference held in Cochabamba in August 2007. She described the pre-Incan roots of the use of alcohol in religious rites in the Andes.

is deeply embedded in the culture: often devotees even invite the priests to perform a *ch'alla* at religious *fiestas*. Most church leaders do not necessarily disapprove of this custom, as they respect the Andean religiosity. Their criticism is usually directed at the consumption of alcohol by pilgrims. Performing *ch'allas* goes hand in hand with drinking alcohol, and the over-indulgence in alcohol is the focus of the church's disapproval.

The dislodging of stones is an offering, because it is heavy work to break the rocks with a weighty hammer, and so are the *ch'allas* and prayers said by *sahumeras* and by the pilgrims themselves. According to the believers, the petition will become reality within a year. To give thanks for the petition fulfilled, pilgrims return their symbolic favors, the stones, after a year. Once having returned their stones, they can again make a petition by dislodging new stones. The returning of the stones makes this pilgrimage a continuous affair, rather than a once-in-a-life time experience.

Virginia, too, goes up the mountain every year to dislodge stones for herself and make a request. However, she has another view on the extracting of stones: 'I don't want to dislodge stones with a hammer; I just take little stones home. Lots of little ones, so I will also have a lot of money.' According to Virginia, if you have to work hard to extract the stones, you also have to work hard to make your wish come true. 'I want to get money without working!' Clearly, her view is not in line with reality. Virginia is at the pilgrimage site every day, where she puts in long, heavy hours, quarrels with the other vendors, and can hardly make enough money to cover her expenses.

While Virginia was collecting stones, I asked her what the stones symbolized for her. She answered: "The stones symbolize my wish that pilgrims will come from all parts, from Argentina, the United States, and from everywhere in Bolivia. The stones are my clients." She started to perform a blessing with incense, kneeling, her knees bare, on the rocks and praying:

> *Virgen Maria de Urkupiña*, I come to salute you, *Mamita*, to your feet, your plants, Pachamama, Holy Earth, for your blessing. At this moment I take stones from your mine, from your bank, you are the owner of this incredible treasure. I take these stones so pilgrims will come to you and money will come to me, *Virgencita*.

Later she took her stones to the statue of Urkupiña, showed them to the image, and whispered a few Hail Marys. In her house she keeps the stones in a drawer where she also puts her money.

Virginia's prayer to the *Virgen* reveals the capitalist language that is used. In this highly economic vocabulary regarding the stones of Urkupiña, the earth is seen as a metaphor for a financial bank. Stones are referred to as money, and all these stones together are of course an immense treasure, of which, as Virginia says, 'the Virgin Mary is the owner.' Pilgrims refer to the places from which they dislodge stones as 'mines'. As every year so many people come to extract stones, the back of the Calvary Hill has been shrinking. Big holes have been made that do resemble mines, and over the years have been cut deeper and deeper by the numerous pilgrims. They call them 'mines' because the holes are situated below the mountain surface, and because mines are the places par excellence where minerals and wealth can be found. As in the mine, the labor is heavy, and pilgrims offer their effort to Mary by breaking stones with huge hammers they can hardly lift. This working in the mine is a sacrifice to the Virgin. In the reciprocal relationship, Mary pays a symbolic salary in the form of stones that are taken home. Especially when they ask for large amounts, the metaphor of capital is used, rather than talking of an exchange of small gifts. If stones are taken as capital, the pilgrim has to return the stones after a year. When returning the stones, the pilgrims have to pay interest in the form of *ch'allas* and *sahumas*. While making a *k'oa* and drinking and offering beer and wine, a middle class couple from the lowlands confirmed:

> Last year the Virgin lent us a large amount of capital. We hacked big rocks and we have taken the money home. Because of the Virgin we were able to start a shop. Today we came to pay her back the interest. Therefore we make prayers of gratitude, we bought bottles of beer and perform a *k'oa*.

If pilgrims need a large amount of capital to make an actual purchase, they speak of taking a symbolic loan from Mary's bank. Pilgrims who come from distant regions can also leave their money in a 'bank account' by leaving most of the big stones behind directly at the place where they dislodged them. A *mestizo* woman in her forties from the city of Sucre explained how this worked:

> I cannot carry all the money the Virgin has given me. Therefore, after working in the mine, at once I made my deposit at the Virgin's bank. I have heaped up all the stones at the Calvary Hill, burnt a candle. Here, with Mary, my money is safe.

The economic terminology around the stones is well-known and is employed by most of the pilgrims. The metaphors of the Virgin of Urkupiña's bank and Mary's mine are a familiar ones for Virginia and many other Bolivians.

Thus, at the pilgrimage site of the Virgin of Urkupiña, pilgrims come in order to deal with the results of neoliberal policies in daily life. At the same time, they reproduce the neoliberal model in the capitalist vocabulary that is used around the ritual of stones. Moreover, market activities and the selling of religion are another form of appropriation of the neoliberal model. Vendors act according to the neoliberal principles of self-responsibility, market negotiations, and competition.

In neoliberal terms, Virginia's job of 'praying for money' reflects labor flexibility. As the state does not provide jobs, people have to invent their own private micro-businesses to survive. As a consequence, the pilgrimage to the Virgin of Urkupiña is highly commercialized, and the vendors act in accordance with the open-market principle. When pilgrims arrive, they are harassed by numerous women trying to sell blessings, drinks, candles, souvenirs, and the constituent elements of offerings. In their attempts to make a sale, the vendors can be very aggressive, both to each other and to their potential clients. For example, they often perform expensive services without asking permission, leaving the pilgrims no choice but to pay after the ritual. Interestingly, at the pilgrimage site, the vendors, marginalized migrants and victims of the neoliberal model, become themselves powerful agents who act according to the neoliberal rules (see also: Albro, 1998: 136). This is in line with the observations of Scheper Hughes and Bourgois (2004: 1) who note that violence is a slippery concept that is nonlinear, productive, destructive and reproductive. This is confirmed by the vendors and pilgrims at the shrine: they reproduce the violence in society at the shrine. Paradoxically, at the same time most pilgrims criticize the neoliberal model.

Competition among vendors is keen. At least twelve women other than Virginia, sell blessings. Arguments between the *sahumeras* are a daily occurrence, sometimes even accompanied by physical violence, such as pushing or hitting. Occasionally the fights get out of hand, and the participants are taken to court. In 2007, Virginia had to appear in court on two different counts for attacks on other petty traders. Since all vendors have their own private businesses, it is difficult to organize themselves and come to some form of agreement, but in order to decrease the numbers of fights and to lessen the worst effects of competition they sometimes manage to make a few rules, such as a schedule of turns based on age, or a fixed price for their services. For only praying with incense they ask pilgrims, 'Twenty bolivianos and your voluntary gift.' Twenty bolivianos, around two euros, is quite a high price for a blessing, but, outside the *fiesta* period, each vendor has only one or, if she is lucky, two turns a day.

During *fiesta,* chances are better, but then the competition becomes keener. During the *fiesta* of Urkupiña in August, *sahumeros* and *curanderos* - Andean medicine men - from different Bolivian Aymara regions come in great numbers to Quillacollo to obtain money from the many pilgrims. *Sahumar* is a particularly Aymara practice, performed by Aymara migrants and *campesinos* from the *Altiplano* who travel to the festivities of Urkupiña (Alba Fernandez, 2001). On these busiest days in August, the rules of the all-year-round-vendors are suspended for the time of the *fiesta*. All vendors can enter the gates and sell at the pilgrimage site itself. For a few days the vendors do not leave the Calvary Hill, spending the night sleeping in the open air or under plastic sheeting. The *sahumeras* are able to perform their blessings directly at the mines. They do not work in turns, and just try to sell to whomever they can find. As Virginia says: 'The one who shouts the loudest, will make the most. I always make a lot during the *fiesta*...' According to Virginia, it is the only time in the year she can save a little money, a necessary reserve, so as to have enough money during the less frequented months from January to April.

The priests of the parish in Quillacollo disapprove of the business mentality of the petty traders and competitive atmosphere they generate, as it scares off the pilgrims when they arrive. When the traders argue too much, the priests threaten that they will have them and their businesses moved to a place before the bridge, an extremely disadvantageous place for selling, as the buses and cars that transport the pilgrims stop after the bridge. In addition, not all priests countenance the *sahuma* rituals. According to Virginia: 'The priest speaks of paganism, he calls us witches.' When I interviewed a former parish priest in 2005, he simply denied the existence of these rituals, demonstrating his negative attitude towards them.

Virginia does not like her work on the Calvary Hill. There is too much competition with other vendors, and she never knows beforehand how many pilgrims will come, or whether she will have more than one turn. Moreover, she is at the mercy of the weather, working in the burning sun, the harsh wind, or pouring rain with only a little plastic sheeting to protect her. The daily inhalation of smoke from the coals and incense affects her throat and eyes. However, her need for every peso means that she cannot afford to stay at home.

Virginia's story shows how the neoliberal model is adapted to, and even appropriated and reproduced, at the pilgrimage site of Urkupiña. The rituals performed by the pilgrims, their conceptualization, the religious market economy, and behavior of the vendors are shaped by neoliberal structures and vocabulary. As will be seen in the next section, although pilgrims seek a solution from Mary for the consequences of neoliberal violence in their daily lives, in the exchange relationship with Mary they are subjugated to another form of violence.

Violent Mary

When Virginia took the little stones from Mary's mines, she smiled at me and said:

> I take the money as a gift from Mary. I do not usually take them as a capital loan. It is safer to take the stones as a present. It is also better not to take too many stones, because if you take a lot, it is even more important that you fulfill your promise. I have seen so many pilgrims who failed to return what they promised to Mary. It scares me.

Since Mary's gift is small, Virginia does not have to promise the Virgin of Urkupiña something in return. For Virginia it also implies that she cannot be too ambitious; she only asks for 'enough, nothing more than I need.' According to Virginia, when pilgrims ask for large amounts of money or investment capital they become seriously indebted to Mary. Making a promise to Mary also means one has to keep the promise, because receiving Mary's help is not without obligations.

The exchange relationship with Mary is structured by the reciprocity principle. When pilgrims take stones away as capital they promise Mary to bring them back after a year and pay interest in prayers, *ch'allas*, and candles, analogous to taking a loan from the bank, implying that you have to pay back the borrowed amount plus interest. Even if pilgrims take the stones as a small gift, they often promise the Virgin something in return, such as bringing flowers to her statue, or dedicating a Mass to her. Virginia, while kneeling on the rocky hill, whispered: 'I don't know how to repay you, *Virgencita*,' in her prayer.

What happens when pilgrims do not keep their promises? According to the majority of the Bolivian pilgrims, Mary is not just a generous, giving divinity, she can also be demanding. Most of the pilgrims were convinced that Mary could also punish and destroy when they do not keep their promises to her.

Because the Virgin Mary is partly conflated with Pachamama by the Andean people, certain characteristics of Pachamama have been transferred to Mary. This occurs regardless of whether they perceive Pachamama and the Virgin Mary as one and the same or as two different entities. Reciprocity is a rule applied to all entities in the Andean *cosmovisión*. Reciprocal relations between people and their gods, goddesses and spirits are not limited to the Andean world. Throughout the world, there are several examples of reciprocal relations established between people and the supernatural world (e.g. Mauss, 1990; McCarthy Brown, 2001; Taylor, 2004). In Bolivia the principle of reciprocity forms the basis of the exchange relationship with Mary. Another principle that is in force is complementarity. Like all supernatural spirits, Pachamama has a complementary character: she integrates both good and bad qualities. In the Andean *cosmovisión* there are no entities that are absolutely and only good or only bad. Mary also is perceived this way, and is seen as an entity who integrates opposite characteristics (Van Kessel, 1992; Estermann, 1993). As a pilgrim explains: 'The Virgin of Urkupiña can give and she can take; she can be peaceful and she can be angry.' In the reciprocal relationship, pilgrims are able to influence the outcome, as Virginia explains: 'If you treat her well, she will be good to you; if not, you will be punished.'

During the Spanish colonization, several aspects of the Andean *cosmovisión* were incorporated into the Catholic religion. The principle of reciprocity - to receive, one should give something in return - (e.g. Mauss (1990) structured the relations between the Andean people and Pachamama. Because of the integration of Pachamama with the Virgin Mary this principle was also applied to Mary, and forms the basis of the relationship pilgrims establish with her.

Another important consequence of the integration of Pachamama with the Virgin Mary is that pilgrims attribute independent powers to Mary. Pachamama is an independent deity who does not act on behalf of an hierarchically higher deity. Therefore the Virgin Mary is often also perceived as having independent powers. The pilgrims make their petitions directly to Mary, without taking into consideration that, theologically, she would only be a mediator who acts on behalf of one of the persons of the Trinity. According to most pilgrims,

Mary decides by herself whether intervention is necessary and how to intervene, whether to bless and forgive or be angry and punish.

Mary's punishments are not moderate. She can punish in an economic fashion, by making people lose their job, by causing large bills, or creating debts, as the story of one pilgrim demonstrates. He credits Mary for the taxi company he started three years ago. He went to the Calvary Hill to dislodge stones, asking Mary for her help in buying a car and starting work as a taxi driver. He promised Mary he would bring back the stones after a year, but, as he recounts:

> I forgot. I just didn't think about it. Before, everything went really well. Thanks to the Virgin, my capital increased and I already had three cars. However, I didn't keep my promise, and one car after the other broke down. In the end I was worse off than when I started, because I ended up in debt. It was Mary's punishment for forgetting her. This year I came back to the Calvary Hill to ask forgiveness. Although I need capital for opening a new business, I don't dare to ask for it. I just have to make it up, so I will wait one year, and take only a few stones as a gift. If she will forgive me, I will come next year to ask her for capital.

Mary can also punish in several other ways; she can let the harvest fail or cause accidents and illnesses, even with fatal consequences. Virginia recounted how her son had refused to go to the Calvary Hill one year. Three weeks after his decision not to go, his firstborn child died. His daughter's death was associated with the punishing power of the Virgin. Now he always goes with Virginia to the Calvary Hill and obeys the religious rules. Virginia continued:

> He knows now that Mary will punish him if he neglects her. Urkupiña is a demanding lady and we don't want to risk her punishments. Since that time, my son goes every year to the Virgin, and you see, all his children are healthy and full of life!

Listening to pilgrims' stories every day of the year, the *sahumeras* knew many tales of pilgrims who had been punished. They told me many stories of weeping pilgrims who came to beg Mary to stop punishing them: they told me of people who were too ambitious, who asked too much from Mary, and were chastened by misfortunes; and I heard about ungrateful pilgrims, or those who just forgot to thank Mary. I heard tales of people going bankrupt or getting into debt, about pain, suffering, illness and death.

According to the pilgrims I spoke to, Mary punishes when you do not keep your promise, if you make the mistake of behaving badly and committing sins, or if you forget her. Like Virginia, who said that she would not be able to keep her promise and would be punished, or the man who did not dare ask Mary for new capital, as he was afraid he would lose it because of her anger, many pilgrims told me to be afraid of the potential violence of Mary. A market woman told me:

> She is so powerful that it scares me. Once, I couldn't get pregnant and went to Mary to ask for a little boy. Directly after my visit, I got pregnant. Since then I don't really dare to go to her anymore, as she gives everything with so much violence!

Although her wish was granted, she was shocked by the straightforwardness of Mary's behavior. All pilgrims told me that the Virgin of Urkupiña is "*muy poderosa*" – very powerful. She always gives what you ask her, if you have faith in her.

The relation between pilgrims and Mary is shaped by a conditional relationship: Mary forces pilgrims to obey her rules. For example, they have to show Mary that they think of her by bringing flowers to the church or burning candles at their house altars. Mary demands respect, attention, and acknowledgement of her authority. If they are negligent about thinking of her, or do not show their gratitude and respect by prayer, living virtuously, or returning the material symbols of her blessings, Mary will remind pilgrims of her power. She enforces the pilgrims' veneration in a violent manner. In addition, if they behave badly, such as being too ambitious or egocentric, Mary will summon them back. As such, Mary is not just a generous, giving divinity, but also a goddess of vengeance. Her punishments can be drastic and violent, and can cause enormous suffering. In fact, it seems that pilgrims are bound in a violent religious straitjacket in their relations with Mary.

Conclusions

This chapter showed how neoliberal structures in Bolivian society are reproduced at the pilgrimage site of the Virgin of Urkupiña in Quillacollo. Neoliberal policies can be seen as a form of structural violence, as it expands social inequality and poverty on a systematic and institutional level. Neoliberalism has a severe impact on several aspects of the daily life of the majority of Bolivians. Through the detailed case of Virginia, I showed the impact of the social and economic forces on an individual level. Virginia represents the individual embodiment of economic suffering, as one among the many Bolivian victims of the neoliberal policies of the past decades.

The consequences of neoliberal policies shape the material petitions that pilgrims make to Mary. Most petitions have to do with upward economic mobility, demonstrate the appreciation of material goods, and reflect the economic needs of pilgrims. The individual requests that people make are embedded in their daily lives and their struggles to survive. Economic suffering is privatized, as the state does not offer protection for the poor. However, at the pilgrimage site they can find social and, in particular, economic security with Mary. We have seen that through the exchange of gifts pilgrims establish cogent relations with her in order to cope with the problems that are generated by the neoliberal political structures.

Paradoxically, despite severe political and social resistance to the neoliberal model in society, it is actually reproduced at the pilgrimage site of the Virgin of Urkupiña. In their vocabulary of mines, money, payment, capital, and interest, and in their ritual acts of borrowing capital and returning it with interest, pilgrims reproduce capitalism at the Calvary Hill. The religious market, as conducted by the vendors, also reproduces the neoliberal model. Virginia, as a *sahumera,* prays for money in her job of selling blessings to pilgrims. In a neoliberal world of self-responsibility, labor flexibility, individualism, and competition, people have to be inventive to survive. For Virginia, her faith in Mary provides an opportunity to gain additional and necessary income. In her small private business she is subjected to the neoliberal rules of competition, supply and demand, and survival of the fittest. At the same time, Virginia herself applies these rules, and becomes an active neoliberal agent at the pilgrimage site. This shows how structural inequalities are reflected in the religious domain of pilgrimage. Looking for empowerment to deal with the devastating neoliberal structures, the pilgrims themselves actually reproduce these structures.

So to what extent are pilgrims and vendors like Virginia actually empowered by Mary? Although pilgrims and vendors feel themselves empowered socially and economically by the Virgin of Urkupiña, she does not resolve the structural inequalities of Bolivian society for them. In fact, one can argue that the Virgin is actually part of the social and economic mechanisms that maintain structural inequality. Neoliberalism is reflected in the capitalistic mode of engagement among vendors, between pilgrims and vendors, *and* between them and Mary. When pilgrims and vendors engage in a relationship with Mary, they 'sign' a contract for an enduring reciprocal relationship with her. For those who do not obey her demands and rules, Mary turns into a vigorous entity who can be violent in her punishments. Thus engaging in a reciprocal relationship with Mary binds pilgrims a forceful religious straitjacket. In this way, pilgrims and vendors subject themselves to yet another form of violent power in their lives. While the dire economic consequences of the neoliberal model may result in financial problems, debts, poverty, and related social repression, one's economic and moral debt to the Virgin of Urkupiña in fact may be a more severe burden to carry as her interest rate is the highest and deadliest.

Photo 5: Stones and miniatures returned to the Calvary Hill

5

MINIATURES AND STONES IN A SPIRITUAL ECONOMY[1]

'I buy *alasitas* and chop stones to promise Mary that I will work hard'
- Yomar Suarez Riveyro, Calvary Hill, 15-8-2007

The ironing board in the corner of Yomar's rented room was transformed into a personal house altar. Next to a large image of the Virgin of Urkupiña, stood a miniature suitcase open to reveal a tiny university degree, a small identity card, a little plane ticket, and a bundle of fake dollars decorated with a picture of the Virgin. Sticking out of the case were colorful festoons into which a few stones had been rolled. On the left side of the suitcase a toy car was displayed, and on the right side a miniature house. On the other side of the image of Mary stood a vase of flowers. The stones and miniature objects, or *alasitas,* were the material reminders of the requests of Yomar, a 25 year old medical student in the city of Cochabamba, made during the pilgrimage to the Virgin of Urkupiña at the Calvary Hill in Quillacollo, Bolivia. Standing in front of her ironing board, Yomar smiled and explained:

> The stones symbolize health, strength, and work, all necessary to obtain in reality what I bought in *alasita*. Chopping out the stones each year is my promise to the Virgin that I will work hard. In return she blesses my wishes. I would like to have a house with a garden and a jeep to drive to my work in the hospital. But before gaining money, I have to get my degree in medicine. When finished, I need the identity card and the plane ticket to leave for Spain, where I will be able to make even more money. That's why I bought so many dollars.

1 Part of this chapter will appear as: Derks, S.W., Jansen, W.H.M. & Notermans, C. (forthcoming). Miniatures and stones in the spiritual economy of the Virgin of Urkupiña in Bolivia. In: *Things: Material Religion and the Topography of Divine Spaces,* edited by D. Houtman & B. Meyer, New York: Fordham University Press.

In this way, Yomar revealed her requests and goals at her personal house altar. In this chapter I look at how pilgrims' requests are given material form, and focus on the *alasitas* that are bought at the shrine and stones that are hammered out of the Lady's hill, as the material religious expressions at this Bolivian Marian shrine. Bolivians use the word *alasitas* as an equivalent for the miniature representations. The etymological origin of the word is derived from the Aymara word '*alathaña*' that means 'to buy'. *Alasitas* means 'buy me' (Cuentas, 1984). Another possible explanation might be that the word is derived from the Arabic word *al-asyd*, which means mediator. The Spanish language uses several words that are Arabic in origin, dating from the Moorish conquest of Spain in the 8th century, and it is possible that the word spread to Bolivia during the colonization. However, the word *alasita* is not known in present-day Spanish.

This study of the 'biography of the objects', as introduced by Kopytoff (1986), and pilgrims' interpretations of these things, will confirm that the material expressions of religion are an important dimension of the spiritual practices of pilgrims. Therefore, this chapter argues that the frequently mentioned dichotomy between spiritual and material does not hold when studying religious objects. The view that the spiritual and material conflate helps to understand how these particular objects function in the relationship between pilgrims and Mary (Mc Dannell, 1995: 6). In particular, by following the objects I will argue that the stones and *alasitas* circulate in a spiritual economy, in which pilgrims negotiate with Mary in order to create what they want in reality.

I employ the term 'spiritual economy' that David Morgan proposed to me when discussing my work (personal communication with David Morgan, 29-4-2007). I use this term to refer to the exchange relationship that is built up between Mary and pilgrims, a reciprocal relationship that includes both the supernatural world of Mary and the everyday lives of pilgrims. In this relationship the pilgrims trade vows and offerings for Mary's support. The term spiritual economy is to be found in a few other studies; for example, Sweetinburgh (2004) employs the term to describe how hospitals in medieval England generated gifts such as money, land, or goods from rich patrons in exchange for prayers from the poor and sick. Burns (1999) uses the term to refer to the dense network of interests and investments between rich Peruvian convents and the material world outside. Both studies refer to the exchange relations between the spiritual and the material. Although I also look at an exchange relationship, I use the term in a different way. In my study, it does not denote the monetary transactions, but the economic symbolism of the way in which pilgrims negotiate with Mary to improve their daily life. Through this study, better insights can be gained into how the objects are part of the symbolic means of exchange and how they function in the lived religion of the pilgrims.

I use the term material to refer to tangible physical matters, and the term materialistic to refer to people's wishes for upward mobility and their desires for money and possessions. I will explain that the pilgrims do not perceive it as contradictory to mobilize the spiritual world for materialistic ends. In this they build on the Andean *cosmovisión* in which material things were always exchanged between the people and the supernatural world in an attempt to improve life. Based on this structure, the Andean people also established a reciprocal relationship with Mary when Catholicism was introduced (Estermann, 1993). Nowadays, pilgrims still make their requests in a reciprocal form: they promise Mary something in return for her help. Also money is perceived in a discourse of fertility, necessary to improve existence. As fertility is a key-value in the Andean *cosmovisión*, it is still related to religion (Harris, 2000). As the majority of Bolivians live in poor circumstances, where the state provides little in the way of social security, turning to the divine world for increasing their economic mobility is one of the options available to deal with poverty, as we have seen in the previous chapter.

This chapter will go especially into the construction of a spiritual economy with Mary, and shows that pilgrims at the same time negotiate and collaborate with Mary to improve their material existence. Again class inequality is dealt with, as people from different classes make differing requests. In the previous chapter it was emphasized how class inequality is implemented at a macro-level by the neo-liberal policies. This chapter looks at what happens on a micro-level, and focuses on the exchange relationship that pilgrims establish with Mary. It literally studies the micro-politics of making requests through micro-objects.

After an outline of the theories on religious objects and their meanings I will continue with a description of the miniature objects, the stones, and their trajectories. Next I will introduce the case of Escarlent, a female pilgrim who visits the shrine every year on or around Calvary Day, to follow the biography of her requests. Finally, I will analyze these data in terms of class differences and the collaborative contract that is established with Mary.

Religious objects and their meanings

Material religion sets out to consider religion through the lens of its material forms and their use in material practice. During the nineteen nineties Colleen Mc Dannell (1995) and David Morgan (1998), among others, signaled the shift in anthropological studies of religion away from verbal/textual doctrine toward the visual and material artifacts of religious practices. For example Mc Dannell (1995: 2) writes:

> The symbol systems of a particular religious language are not merely handed down, they must be learned through doing, seeing, and touching. Experiencing the physical dimension of religion helps bring about religious values, norms, behaviours and attitudes.

Thus, studying the material objects that are used in religious practices can also give insight into the meanings of religion for the believers. The senses are important tools in the construction of meaning around objects, as thoughts are inextricably linked to the handling, smelling, seeing, and manipulating of these objects (Stoller, 1986, Venbrux, 2007). Applied to religion, both the ideological and material are aspects of a single interactive process (e.g. Durrans, 2000: 64). Studying the religious practices of the devotees shifts the focus away from the doctrinal and ideological dimension towards the lived religion of the devotees (e.g. Plate, 2002; Hermkens et al., forthcoming). Such religious practices do not necessarily correspond to the ideas of church authorities, but for the pilgrims these practices give them an important discourse to express their own religiosity and construct meaning in their lives. Morgan (1998: 172) also emphasizes the extra dimension of ritual practices when he says:

> Rituals and their material culture are powerful practices that create meanings that people experience together as groups and as individuals within groups. Rites enact in the lives of their participants meanings that outside ritual exist only as spoken discourse.

Rituals and practices add an extra dimension to the expression of religious ideas. Although the importance of studying material objects in religion has been emphasized only since the 1990s, the 1980s already showed a revival of interest in material culture in general (e.g. Appadurai, 1986; Reynolds & Stott, 1987; Stocking, 1985; Stoller, 1986). A new approach was proposed by Appadurai (1986) in his book *The Social Life of Things* in which he suggests that the meanings of objects are inscribed in their uses and trajectories. Kopytoff's (1986), contribution to the book takes the trajectory a step further by introducing the 'cultural biography of commodities', by asking questions about the thing's life similar to those one asks concerning people's biographies. For example, where does the thing come from? What is its career so far, and what do people consider to be an ideal career for such things? How does the thing's use change with its age, and what happens to it when it reaches the end of its usefulness? The biography of things can also be applied to 'religious' objects to discover their meanings. I will use Kopytoff's biography to understand the relationship between Mary, the pilgrims, and the objects, as it reveals when the things come into contact with Mary, what happens with them afterwards, and what meanings people attribute to the objects, and, through them, to Mary.

Studying the biography of things also shows that the objects can transform from a commodity state into a religious state and back again (Appadurai, 1986: 14). Also Freedberg (1989: 83) points out that rites are performed with objects to attribute powers which transcend the purely material aspect of the objects. These practices are consecration acts that bespeak the transition from human product to sacredly endowed object. As we will see, in Bolivia consecration acts are frequently performed with the miniature objects. Furthermore, it will be shown that these revert to a commodity status after having had a religious meaning for the limited period of a year.

Material things do not have a value in themselves, but derive their meanings in a context of human and religious acts. Following the objects draws us to the 'human transactions and calculations that enliven things' (Appadurai, 1986: 5). The biography of the objects provides insights into the personal stories, conflicts, and biographies of the pilgrims, as the objects also derive their meaning from the interaction between persons and these things (Hermkens, 2005: 10; Hoskins, 1998: 2; Venbrux, 2007: 5). Stones and *alasitas* follow similar typical trajectories, but the personal perceptions and interactions of the believers give the objects their singular biographical elements, and therefore their meanings. This also underlines Hoskins' (1998: 8) view that it is the relationship that a person establishes with an object that gives it an identity that is localized, particular, and individual. Therefore, later in this chapter, I will follow one particular individual with her miniatures, to discover the personal meanings ascribed to these objects.

As Dubisch (1995: 38) already pointed out, the traveling of objects blurs the boundaries of the pilgrimage site, as the pilgrims take the sacred home with them. By displaying the objects imbued with the sacred on their house altars, the spiritual is re-materialized in another place. In a similar fashion, Mc Dannell (1995: 4) contests the association of the material expressions of religion exclusively with the profane and mundane, and instead points out that objects embody the sacred and spiritual. Therefore, the dichotomy does not hold when looking at material religious objects. This classification into sacred and profane is derived from Durkheim, who wrote in 1912 that all religions classify things into the two opposing and distinctive categories of the sacred and the profane. The sacred consists of an ideal and transcendental world that is set apart from the ordinary life. The profane is the everyday and the utilitarian (Mc Dannell, 1995: 4). In history the material has become subjugated to the ideological aspects of religion (e.g. Mcguire, 2003). I follow Dubisch and Mc Dannell in criticizing this dichotomy.

Breaking the dichotomy between these two spheres, however, does not yet reveal how people experience religion by using objects. This study takes previous insights a step further and aims to demonstrate that the Bolivian pilgrims use the objects to combine the supernatural powers of Mary with their own forces in a spiritual economy to realize their requests. The miniatures and stones serve as the tangible mediators in this spiritual economy, and come to symbolize the contract agreed with Mary.

As already shown in the previous chapter, pilgrims establish an exchange relationship with Mary, in which they make a promise - *promesa* - to Mary in return for the granting of their request. They can promise to do something, for example dedicate a mass in church to Mary or bring back the stones and *alasitas* after a year: or they can promise Mary to work hard to realize the requested goals.

The reciprocal relationship between pilgrims and Mary is in line with what Mauss (1990) has argued in his famous book 'The Gift' on the reciprocal exchange of things in several societies. He argues that in all societies gifts, which are supposed to be given voluntarily, are actually obligatory as the receiver has to reciprocate in one form or another. Exchanging gifts between people and the supernatural world also means a social contract in which the sacrifice of, in this case, buying miniature objects and dislodging stones is exchanged for Mary's help and protection. As Mauss noted, a time delay might occur between the time of sacrifice and the time of Mary's intervention. In addition, Taylor (1999: 149) pointed out that since people created networks for exchange, so they established economic bonds with their gods. As already shown in the previous chapter, on the pilgrimage to the Virgin of Urkupiña economy and religion are interwoven.

In this chapter I argue that during pilgrimage, people make Mary a witness of their sufferings and aspirations. With Mary as witness, many pilgrims felt motivated and empowered to continue their own efforts to reach their goals. The exchange relationship shows how pilgrims do business with Mary in a spiritual economy. The objects are in fact the currency of the transactions.

Alasitas, stones and their trajectories

From market stalls in front of the Calvary Hill and a few in front of the church San Ildefonso, pilgrims can choose from all possible miniature objects, and buy those items that symbolize their material aspirations. Most pilgrims analyze thoroughly the various objects, as all are convinced that 'the Virgin will give exactly what you asked'. Little packets of paper money, either in bolivianos, dollars or euros, are the best-selling *alasitas*. In Bolivia, bolivianos are used for the daily expenses of food, clothes, and small items. Dollars are used for expensive articles, such as cars, houses, televisions, and sometimes rent. Although the euro is not used for real payment in society, miniature euros have also entered the miniature market. As the euro is strong compared to the dollar, and, as in Yomar's case, brings about associations with emigration to Europe, a pile of miniature European bank notes have become the most purchased item (*Los Tiempos*, 17-8-2005). The surveys held with pilgrims at the Calvary Hill showed that 49 out of 86 pilgrims bought *alasitas* during their pilgrimage. Of these 49 people, 41 had also bought miniature money.

With the widely heard phrase: '*Mil dolares por un peso*' - Thousand dollar for one Boliviano - the 'money changers' call out to their clients to sell them their wares. The phrase implies that just a tiny investment of only one *peso* has to be made in order to achieve great results, like thousands of dollars. The *alasitas* of paper money are usually sold in bundles, and vary in size from a few centimeters to the real size of dollar bills. When the bills are of the same size as real US dollars, they bear a printed phrase to distinguish them from the real notes and to prevent confusion, such as *banco de alasitas*, or *alasitas* bank, *billete de la fortuna*, banknote of fortune, or *sin valor legal*, without legal value. In Bolivia, where everyone is acquainted with the custom of *alasitas*, people will note the difference, but in foreign countries, the *alasitas* can be used as false money. I was told the story of a tourist who took a quantity of *alasitas*-dollars to the United States and used them for payment. When he was caught, he was jailed for forgery.

Sometimes the paper money is packed in plastic, together with a little picture of the Virgin, or with many other tiny symbols. One of the vendors explained the meaning of the symbols:

> Those two little dolls are a symbol for marriage; the frog represents Pachamama, and she protects you from sinfulness. The horseshoe is a symbol of good luck. The hand is the powerful hand so you will never fail to have work. The lock is for security. The little red nut means plentitude and the yellow spiral thing means that all the bad energy directed at you returns in greater amounts to the person who sent it to you. The little flag symbolizes our *patria*, or fatherland, and the little stone is a stone of Urkupiña, to bless you.

Next to money, miniature credit cards of different companies, certificates for bank accounts and lottery tickets can be purchased. Also flight tickets of different airlines, passports and identity cards are sold frequently. For many of the pilgrims these *alasitas* express the desire for migration, as many Bolivians want to emigrate to another country to obtain a better standard of living. In particular, I liked the identity cards of the Virgin of Urkupina. These plasticized miniature cards of about 2.5 by 3.5 centimeters have a picture and a fingerprint of the Virgin on one side. At the other side is written her name: 'Virgin of Urkupiña', her date and place of birth: 15th of August 0001, in Quillacollo. Her civil status is 'single' and her profession is filled in as 'the director of miracles'.

All types of little houses, cars and motorcycles are also sold. Some of the houses are plain, others are large and palatial. Some have gardens, some even have a swimming pool, so everyone can find something that fits his or her personal wishes. Those wanting to build their own house do not have to feel neglected: all the materials and tools for the construction of houses are there, along with other luxury goods such as microwave ovens, computers, and cell phones, all are for sale in tiny format.

All types of certificates and documents can be bought in miniature, like birth certificates, health papers, bureaucratic forms necessary to open a new business or to buy a car, house, shop, or plot of land, university titles including specializations at different Bolivian universities, marriage papers, and even divorce certificates. Although divorce is contradictory to the Catholic ideology, these little replicas reveal that pilgrims also approach Mary to aid them in getting a divorce. This demonstrates that all possible demands are given material form in miniature. Every need can be wished for, and this connects the lived religion of the pilgrims with their everyday life. I would like to state that pilgrims do not approach Mary with exclusively material and materialistic requests. Some of them also make spiritual wishes, such as love, harmony and luck. Some of these wishes are also given material form in miniature. For example, little images of a bride and groom that are usually put on the wedding-cake can be bought to express *una pareja*, a couple or 'love'. Also different little stones, herbs and nuts are sold as symbols of 'luck'. However, the material petitions were predominant, and in this chapter, the focus of research. In addition, the majority of the miniature objects is linked directly or indirectly to economic matters. For example, pilgrims who bought health papers emphasized that they needed health in order to be able to work and earn money. Diplomas, too, are bought in the light of the socio-economic wishes of pilgrims, and symbolize the possibilities they will have of making money after graduating. Cars are often bought as an investment to make money; cars and vans often symbolize the requests for a job as taxi-driver or transporter.

The custom of *alasitas* reportedly comes from the Aymaras in La Paz, where in 1781 the first *alasita* market was held in honor of *Ekekho*, an Andean deity associated with abundance and economic productivity (Martinez Espinoza, 1995). The custom has been taken out of its Aymara based context and has been slowly transferred to other religious festivities in the Bolivian highlands, and even to *fiestas* outside Bolivia, such as Peru (Arnillas, 1996). Previously, the custom of *alasitas* at the *fiesta* of Urkupiña existed in another form: a bank of *alasitas* was installed on the Calvary Hill, where in exchange for a small amount of money, pilgrims got a certain number of Calvary stones. With these stones the pilgrims were able to buy the *alasitas* on the miniature market (Berramendy Orrelana, 2001). Interestingly, at that time the *alasitas* and stones interacted together in a ritual. A few decades ago the custom transformed into that of trading *alasitas* for actual money, as elsewhere at Bolivian religious feasts, and was no longer connected to the ritual use of stones.

During the recent decades, the miniature objects changed from purely agricultural rural products, such as potatoes and animals, to commercial urban products such as paper money, cars and houses. The offerings parallel the transformations in society from an agricultural to a commercialized urban society (Aguilo, 1985). According to a Bolivian priest, Javier Baptista, the *alasitas* have expanded greatly in recent decades as a result of increased mobility of the Bolivians.[2] In addition, *alasitas* have been incorporated more intimately in the department of Cochabamba in comparison with other departments. Javier Baptista explains this intensification in terms of the commercial character of the Cochabamba department. Because of its fertile climate and central location in Bolivian society, Cochabamba developed into a commercial area where large

2 Interview with Javier Baptista during fieldwork in Cochabamba, 7-4-2005.

markets are held and most people live from commercial activities. According to Baptista, the *alasitas* relate mostly to economic purposes, in accordance with the commercial mentality of the *Cochabambinos*.

There is still one tradition of agricultural *alasitas* alive and characteristic for the *fiesta* of the Virgin of Urkupiña on the 24th and 25th of August. The main streets of Quillacollo then change into a market of all possible kinds of real foodstuffs in miniature. Devotees go around the market to buy, for instance, hamburgers, carrots, potatoes, onions, and salt. Also miniatures of domestic articles can be bought, such as toothpaste, rolls of toilet paper, and corn flakes. With their baskets full, they enter the church where the priest blesses the food in the name of the Virgin. The miniature food is taken home, cooked and eaten by all the members of the family. The emphasis is on the familiar basket of food, and it is commonly believed that people who observe this tradition will not lack food in the coming year. In the Catholic calendar the 24th of August is the day of Saint Bartholomew, one of the apostles of Jesus (Beramendy Orellana, 1999: 35).

A week before, on Calvary Day at the 16th of August, the stones and non-food miniature representations take a central place. That day the Calvary Hill is transformed into an ant-heap when hundreds of thousands of pilgrims come to Mary to dislodge stones and buy *alasitas*. The two kilometer long road between the church in Quillacollo and the gate of the Calvary Hill is packed with stands, selling all types of *alasitas*, souvenirs, and ingredients for offerings. Even when entering the sanctuary, hundreds of vendors approach the pilgrims to offer them hammers, bags, and *ch'alla*-sachets - containing alcohol, confetti and festoons - to offer when hacking out stones, and miniature houses, cars, and health certificates to physically underscore their requests. Andean ritualists offer pilgrims their blessings for the objects, and priests consecrate collectively pilgrims and their objects by sprinkling holy water over the crowd.

As described in the previous chapter, people symbolize their requests by the dislodging of stones on the Calvary Hill. Pilgrims refer to them as 'money' and see them as a form of wealth. For others they symbolize health or a house. In return for the sacrifice of their effort in extracting stones, devotees expect the Virgin to help them realize their petitions. Most pilgrims also buy a direct representation of their request in *alasitas*, such as paper money, a house, or health papers, and many explained the relation between *alasitas* and stones in this way: 'The stones symbolize the strength and effort I have to make in obtaining what I want.' From the energy it costs to dislodge the stones they can read how much energy it will take to create what they want in daily life. The objects can be seen as the currency of the reciprocal relationship. In return for having their wish granted, pilgrims firstly offer Mary their labor by breaking the rocks with a heavy hammer. The stones are the tangible profit. Secondly, the pilgrims invest in *alasitas* and offering ingredients.

The stones are part of the earth, and therefore of Pachamama and the sacred domain. Mary is considered the owner of the mine where the stones are obtained. As stones are initially already related to the supernatural world, they are often seen as more powerful than the miniature objects. Stones have to come from the Calvary Hill of the Virgin of Urkupiña, and cannot just be purchased anywhere. The place is seen as a sacred spot, owned by the Virgin Mary. This is also to be seen in the great number of *yatiris*, or Andean medicine men, who come with their clients to the Calvary Hill to perform their rituals. A *yatiri* explained: 'I come to the Hill of the Virgin as I need the Virgin's powers to be combined with my powers to heal. The power and energy is strong here. I cannot go just anywhere.' For the pilgrims too, sacred power is already attributed to the stones, as they are derived directly from the pilgrimage site. The *alasitas* however, start their biography in shops and markets, and do not gain any religious status until they are blessed. For example, the miniature cars are still toys that have not yet any religious value. Angelica, one of the candle vendors at the square in Quillacollo told me that she displays the toy cars on Sundays when baptisms are held and many families with children stroll around the church square. These days she also sells the miniature cars as simple playthings for children. However, when the miniature objects are bought to symbolize the materialistic aspirations of pilgrims, from that moment they follow a similar trajectory and ritual to that of the dislodged stones.

First, a *ch'alla* is performed in which the rocks and *alasitas* are sprinkled with pure alcohol, wine and beer, and wrapped into colorful festoons. The *ch'alla* is a pre-Inca libation offering for blessing and purification. The miniature objects and stones, usually in the same bag, are taken to the chapel on the Calvary Hill that houses the Virgin, and people pray while they burn candles. Next, pilgrims often obtain another blessing by asking a *sahumera* - seller of prayers and blessings - to pray for them. Afterwards, the pilgrims take their objects to the church for yet another blessing be carried out by a priest, who sprinkles the objects with holy water in the name of the Virgin of Urkupiña. The several blessing acts, such as *ch'allas*, prayers, *sahumas,* and sprinkling with holy water in the church, can be seen as religious acts that invoke consecration and serve to give a religious meaning to the objects (e.g. Freedberg, 1989: 83-84). During these trajectories blessings are heaped upon the objects, and with each blessing they become more valuable and spiritually loaded for the believers.

Afterwards the objects are taken home. Many pilgrims put the stones and *alasitas* in the same place they keep their money, in a drawer for example. Others display them on their house altars, and put them close to a statue or picture of the Virgin, as Yomar did. Some pilgrims put flowers and burn candles on their altar throughout the year. After a year, the pilgrims have to return the stones and miniature objects to Calvary Hill. They again perform blessings in the form of *sahumas* and *ch'allas,* and then destroy their dollars, cars, houses, and papers, and leave their stones behind. By destroying the miniatures the devotee shows that the life-time of the symbolic request has terminated. On the same day the pilgrims make new requests for the coming year. Even pilgrims who do not return their miniatures told me that the objects lose their religious status after a year.

Thus the religious life of the objects is limited to a certain time period. They are included in the spiritual economy established with the Virgin for a year only. After that, a new cycle begins with new offers and new requests. The old miniatures and stones lose their religious status, when the ties with Mary are not re-established through a new pilgrimage and offering. Furthermore, the trajectory of *alasitas* and stones shows that all kinds of things can be given by the Virgin, so all material representations of them can participate in the spiritual economy. All that has to happen for an object to be incorporated into the symbolic exchange, is to be bought, offered, blessed, displayed, and prayed over.

Escarlent's pilgrimage to the Calvary Hill

The biography of things does not consist only of a trajectory, but also of the human interactions that give significance to things. Up to now, I have described only the general trajectory of all objects. The following account of a particular case illustrates how the personal perspectives of pilgrims add meaning to every individual object. The personal interpretations give the thing its biographical data.

Escarlent is a 25 year old woman from a middle class family from the city of Cochabamba. Every year since she was very young she has gone to the Calvary Hill to perform her rituals. She explains that the pilgrimage is both a social and a religious ritual:

> I have grown up with the Virgin of Urkupiña. When my grandmother was alive, every year she invited all her children with their families to go together on pilgrimage. The Day of the Calvary was one of the happy occasions that the whole family was together. I also liked the *fiesta*, but more because that day my mother gave me her old *alasitas* of the previous year, so I got presents to play with. I still like to go. Over the years my faith in the Virgin has increased and this special day gives me the opportunity to reflect on my life, on what is missing, on what I want to change and to find new directions.

Escarlent still makes the pilgrimage together with her mother's family, and they turn it into a annual entertaining daytrip. In 2007 I joined them during their pilgrimage.

At the entrance of the Calvary Hill Escarlent bought a little bar, a pack of dollars and a university title from two different stands. She explained:

> This year I want to open a bar. This tiny one has beer on every table, it has a huge fridge and they have a food-menu. That's exactly what I

> would like to see in my real bar! I will change it, and also the name. Now it is called: San Lorenzo.

While scratching off the n of San, she continues:

> I will call it Sas, as my friends used to call me Saskaya. I need a lot of money to invest in this bar, so I bought these dollars. The university title is not to graduate, as I have at least two years to go. For me it symbolizes that I will enroll for next year and study.

After lunch at the picnic space at the Calvary Hill, the group went up to the road to the hill behind the chapel, to hack out new stones and return the old ones. Everybody had to dislodge their own stones. Escarlent's mother, who went first, had some trouble chopping off parts of the rocks. She laughed about it and joked: 'I don't need that much, I'm not too ambitious.' For her, extracting only tiny fragments of the stones meant that in real life she would have only a bit of 'money and luck' in the coming year. Escarlent, on the other hand, smashed powerfully down on the same rock, and with her first blow she had a big piece of rock. She smiled proudly and said relieved: 'Yes! That is exactly what I need! Now I know I can stop being so stressed, everything will turn out all right!' She continued until she collected so many stones that her big bag was half filled.

When all had 'worked in the mine', as they call the dislodging of stones from the holes, all started making *ch'allas* to their stones. Escarlent enrolled her stones with colorful festoons, put confetti on top, sprinkled pure alcohol on it, and lit some fire crackers. According to Escarlent 'the bangs will call Mary's attention to my wishes. The festoons and confetti show that it is a *fiesta,* and the alcohol is to please Mary.' After making her own blessing, she went to the bags of her family and sprinkled beer while saying prayers. While doing her *ch'alla*, a piece of stone from another mine fell into Escarlent's lap. She smiled and joked: 'Look, the money is just falling from the sky', and she put the little stone in her bag. One of her uncles called a *sahumera* to perform a blessing on their stones and *alasitas*. Escarlent said: 'I usually do not do a *sahuma*, as I do not trust other hands with my wishes.'

The old stones had not yet been returned to the Virgin. They moved to a place away from the mine, and all the bags with the old stones were emptied out on the same heap. The big stones were taken out, and together the family started building a little house with a fence around it. 'It is our own custom. Every year we construct a house together, it is just for fun.' When the house was finished another *ch'alla* was performed by the family members. Afterwards everybody turned to go down the hill. I walked with Escarlent a little behind the rest, chatting. When we finally arrived at the picnic spot, the group had not yet arrived. 'Ay', Escarlent said, 'I forgot to take my stones and *alasitas* to the Virgin. Well, I am not going back. I will let them be blessed next week in the *fiesta* of *alasitas* in church.'

A few days later the miniature food market took place in Quillacollo, and together with her mother Escarlent collected the necessary miniature foods. Escarlent explained: 'We have thrown away the old, rotten and discolored packages from our *alasitas* provision cupboard, and we made a list of all things that we need.' At a stand of plastic and paper packages they bought about 30 pieces, such as toothpaste, washing powder, cornflakes, tinned tomatoes, and oil. While shopping for real potatoes, meat and groceries, Escarlent discovered a stand with miniature alcoholic beverages. She did not hesitate and bought two little bottles for the bar. After the purchase of little loaves and sugar, they entered the church. Both Escarlent and her mother had also brought their stones and *alasitas*. They put all their things on the ground, lit candles, and prayed to the image of the Virgin. After a few minutes they asked the sacristan to bless their objects. Escarlent wanted to be sure that all objects would be blessed so she clutched all her items in her arms, the dollars and university papers in her left hand, the bag of stones around her wrist, the bar tucked under her arm, and the bag of packages in her other hand. Her mother had put her car and dollars on top of the vegetables in the basket of food. After the blessing they sat at a table at the miniature eatery stand where a miniature meal was shared. Escarlent explains:

> There are always days that you cannot eat at home and you have to eat in the streets. Therefore we have this meal, so we will always be able to find food easily on these days. We will eat the vegetables, meat, and bread we bought during this week. We do not make a special meal with it, but just use the ingredients when we cook. The other things are just symbolic, we do not eat them. But really, it works. One year we did not observe this tradition, and the whole year we had problems. We forgot to buy sugar for example, or when we wanted to buy bread, there was no bread left, things like that. Always something was lacking. But now, with the blessing of Urkupiña, we can be sure that everything will turn out fine.

In her house the *alasitas* are placed in different spots. One shelf of the provision cupboard was dedicated to all *alasitas* from the food market in Quillacollo. The miniature bar was put on her desk in her bedroom. She had drawn a new name and signboard, and also changed the menu. Her bag of stones, together with the university title and dollars, was put in the living room, under a little table that served as a house altar. Under a picture of the Virgin, her bag was placed next to those of her brother and mother. Escarlent explained: 'So Mary can watch over our wishes.'

Class and materialistic aspirations

The pilgrims who come to the *fiesta* to dislodge stones and buy *alasitas* are a heterogeneous group, from all socio-economic and ethnic backgrounds. As Lagos (1993: 64) pointed out, the pilgrims 'learn to ask for gifts they may reasonably expect to receive.' Rich pilgrims ask for luxury articles such as cars, big houses, and swimming pools, objects they would be in a position to buy anyway before going to the *fiesta*. Poor pilgrims ask for basic things, according to their needs. For example, presidential candidates ask to become president, students ask for higher grades, shopkeepers ask for improved trade, young couples come to ask for babies, a house, or land, and petty traders ask for '*pan del dia*' – daily bread. The pilgrims adjust their petitions according to the possibilities afforded by their circumstances, and in this way everybody can receive something from the Virgin. For example, for years Escarlent dreamed of opening a bar in the city, during which time she had saved an investment capital and was already looking for a place. She bought a bar in miniature to ask Mary for her blessing on her new project. Sometimes pilgrims buy *alasitas* of many more things than they actually expect to receive. Of the many miniatures Yomar bought, only a few will become reality, but by buying so many miniatures, she can give direction to her life. Yomar also explained that it was the fourth time she asked for a car: 'Sometimes the Virgin does not make it possible the first time you ask for it, but she wants you to put more effort in it.'

Poorer pilgrims see that others ask for impressive luxury goods. Because of the class differences in society they accept these distinctions in requests at the pilgrimage site. Virginia, the poor petty trader who was introduced in the previous chapter, legitimized this attitude:

> Some pilgrims are too ambitious and ask too much. They ask for more than they need. However, if you have more, your life is also more complicated, as you cannot be satisfied anymore. You always want to have more. This can be dangerous, because the Virgin will know when your requests are not sincere anymore.

On the other hand, the rich justify their requests in terms of the faith they have in the Virgin and the hard work they have put in to reach their material goals. The rich also have more money to invest in rituals, in the miniature objects, *sahumas* and *ch'allas*. For them bringing bigger offers legitimizes their large requests. For example, the miniature bar of Escarlent was 30 BOB, around a day's salary for people from the lower class. Escarlent bought a bundle of 50,000 dollars for 5 BOB: poorer pilgrims can buy 10,000 dollar for 1 BOB. They offer less and so receive less. The *alasitas* also promote a sense of well-being. By buying 10,000 dollars in miniature for one boliviano, the poor people can feel rich for one day in the year. This way they are able to give expression to their desires and aspirations to have access to large amounts of money.

The resemblance between Pachamama and the Virgin Mary explains why the pilgrims experience no incongruity in approaching the spiritual world with materialistic requests. Pachamama is a goddess of fertility, and the petitions to Mary are derived from the Andean view on fertility. In the Andean *cosmovisión* the key value of fertility is experienced as reproduction and prosperity. In a changing world where money is needed for a fertile life, the initial requests for fertility have expanded into petitions for health and the multiplication of wealth (Harris, 2000: 51-57). As materialistic requests are viewed in terms of fertility, for most Bolivians, there is no sense of incompatibility to call upon the supernatural world for upward mobility. This has also been demonstrated by Taussig (1977; 1980), who explains that in the Andean interpretation of money, supernatural power should be invoked to obtain the increase of money as capital. He showed that in Bolivia during the beginning of the capitalist era the economy was interpreted in a religious discourse. This illustrates that Bolivian pilgrims are used to appealing to the supernatural world to obtain money and material goods. With 60 per cent of the Bolivians living in poverty and 37 per cent in extreme poverty, it is common for pilgrims to ask for material things that contribute to meeting their daily necessities (INE, 2007: 389).

It is hard to draw a line between material necessities and merely materialistic desires. In general, pilgrims from a lower class tend to take the rituals more seriously. For them there is more at stake, and they hope to obtain what they need so desperately in their daily lives. Pilgrims from the higher class are more likely to parody the rituals when performing them: they joke about it, but just in case, they perform all the necessary steps in the right order to make sure they are able to receive what they want. For example, Escarlent's mother joked when she did not manage to dislodge big pieces from the rocks, but still followed the entire trajectory with her objects. It also demonstrates that those people who already have most things they need, confirm their relationship with Mary in order to maintain the status quo or to improve their fortunate situation.

Pilgrims also often feel moved emotionally on seeing those beautiful colorful imitations in miniature of all possible goods. Richer pilgrims especially are amused by the miniatures; some see it as a game and search around for the most original objects. As Harskamp et al. (2006) point out in the book *Playful religion*, religion can also have a playful dimension. Playing is part of how people are involved in religious practices, whether they explicitly call their spiritual practices play or not. The miniature objects obviously have a playful dimension. This is also exemplified in the story of Ronald, a 38 year old bar-owner from a higher class family in Cochabamba. One afternoon we talked extensively about his pilgrimage to the Virgin of Urkupiña during Calvary Hill 2005. He stood up to take a Mexican *sombrero* - hat - that seemed to be a decoration on top of the cupboard. Holding the hat, he came back to my table and told me:

> I will explain to you. Here I keep my *alasitas* during the year. First thing you need is health. Therefore I bought this health certificate. After that, you need a job, don't you? I have a business, so I need a license of operation and an individual working contract. Besides, I bought this little thing with all symbols of luck. If everything goes well and I am lucky, I will gain a lot of money. That's why I bought miniature euros, dollars

> and bolivianos. I need the dollars to buy a house in Cochabamba; with the bolivianos I will buy a car; and with the euros I will go on holiday. I bought my miniature air ticket, a passport, a money belt and a Visa card for my holiday already. It is all symbolic. Ha ha, funny, isn't it?

Although Ronald laughed loudly about his 'funny things', he did keep them and had serious reasons for doing so: they symbolized his goals for the coming year.

The church takes an ambivalent attitude towards the materialistic requests of pilgrims. On the one hand, every year during the *fiesta* of Urkupiña, an article appears in the newspaper that calls upon the devotees to 'leave behind their materialistic interests' and preaches about 'spiritual values' of love, respect, and harmony. In a similar fashion, not all priests agree with the rituals of dislodging stones. One of the priests in charge in 2005, denied completely the existence of such a ritual. Another priest that worked in the parish in 2007 spoke of 'pagan rituals that have to stop'. This priest explained:

> These rituals will stop in a few years as we have already started to build a large basilica at the top of the Calvary Hill. We have already closed more than half of the mines, by putting sand in them. We want to change the sanctuary into an absolutely spiritual one, like Lourdes in France or Guadalupe in Mexico. When the basilica is there, there will be no mines left and the pilgrims will stop dislodging stones. They will only come with spiritual intentions.

On the other hand, the majority of the priests does not have a problem with blessing the objects. One priest explained: 'What can I do? If I make these people feel better by blessing their items, why not?' Another priest explained: 'Well, they make materialistic requests, but all people come together with their families to buy the paper money and other *alasitas*. The practice of *alasitas* contributes to the unity of the family, and therefore it is not a problem at all.' Thus, the practice is variously condemned or condoned by representatives of the church. The varying social positions influence the meanings given to these religious artifacts and the practices that surround them. While for some the meanings are related to survival, for others they represent general feelings of security, or a mere joke or toy.

Collaborative Mary

The miniatures symbolize the requests people make. As symbols they are used for communication (e.g. Droogers, 1980: 119). They not only help in giving material form to the requests for each individual personally, but they also communicate a message to others. When buying miniatures, carrying them around at the pilgrimage place or church and displaying them on a house altar, also makes the goals and wishes public. Others can see what project you have in mind.

The tangible miniature objects and stones make the requests more vivid and solid, and their materiality makes them appealing. The senses play an important role, as people touch the objects, decorate them, for instance by festooning them and putting confetti around and on top of them; people burn incense around them, put flowers close to the objects on their altars. These acts also help to make the objects more personal. As we have seen in the case of Escarlent, all members of the family make their personal requests, hack out their own stones, buy their own *alasitas* and even personalize them, like Escarlent did by changing the bar's name and menu. The personal relationship with the objects symbolizes the intense, unique and personal relationship between Mary and the pilgrims. The case also showed how the trajectory of the stones and *alasitas* turns into a personal biography, as every person decides what steps to take and in which order. For example, Escarlent and her family extracted new stones before returning the old ones. Escarlent did not find it necessary to perform a *sahuma* or return for a blessing, but her relatives did. Still, Escarlent prays, burns candles, makes numerous *ch'allas,* and takes her objects to be blessed by the priest. Despite numerous variations, a dominant line can be discerned in investing objects with religious meanings.

In fact, faith is invested in the objects. But what role do the objects play in the relationship between pilgrims and Mary? What are pilgrims' perceptions of the objects? All pilgrims who bought the *alasitas* explained: 'You have to have faith, otherwise it will not work.' Just buying the miniature objects is not enough, you have to believe in the possibilities and pray. Escarlent's aunt explains: 'Miracles won't fall from the sky. But because we cannot make it in daily life, we look for other possibilities. Religion is one of them. It is the only hope we have!' She continues:

> The people have to make the effort. For example, if one wants to buy a house, someone can buy the miniature of it, but he also has to search and earn money to buy land and a house himself. It is the Virgin who makes the person continue his search.

This is in line with what Karen McCarthy Brown (2001: 254) wrote about spirits in voodoo religion. The spirits function as a catalyst in formulating the problems to yourself and making your own goals clear in your mind. Also Escarlent explains:

> For example, the university title symbolizes my wish to enroll at university. Together with the effort of dislodging stones it functions to encourage me to study. Of course, if I do not study, I will not pass. But I don't want to disappoint the *Virgencita*. When I asked her help in front of her image, I also promised her that I would do my utmost in studying.

Interestingly, pilgrims use the objects to remind them of their own goals. By displaying them on the house altar and renewing them after a year they are again and again confronted with their ideals and aspirations, and the need to work towards fulfilling them. After a year they are able to evaluate their projects and, if necessary, adjust their aims. With Mary as witness, pilgrims feel empowered to work towards their goals. The pilgrims do not attribute success to Mary's powers alone, but also to their own powers. All emphasized that they themselves have to make an effort. In the reciprocal relationship with Mary, the pilgrims have to promise something in return for her help. As Escarlent said: 'It is not an unconditional gift of the Virgin. No, I promise her to study, to work, and make money and search for a bar.' This quotation makes evident that pilgrims expect the Virgin to work with them in the realization of their requests. Before Mary, the pilgrims create a spiritual economy in which they promise her, and themselves, to continue their steps in striving for upward mobility.

If their requests are not realized after a year, the relationship with Mary is not affected. The pilgrims always blame themselves for failure. They say they did not have enough faith in Mary, or explain it by the way they performed their rituals. One day, however, I spoke to a man at the Calvary Hill who said he had lost confidence in Mary. For four years in a row he had asked Mary for a stable job and during these years his job prospects got worse and worse. He was convinced that he did not want to make his requests again: 'as it is all *tontería* - foolishness - to believe in a Virgin who sends help from heaven...' Nevertheless he was there and performed carefully the rituals for bringing back his miniatures, explaining that he had to fulfill his part of the bargain as promised, otherwise he could be punished. This account shows that he still attributes miraculous powers to Mary, even though he denies them in his speech. The relationship with Mary remains largely unaffected when the desired results fail to be realized.

Sometimes the pilgrims make the requests over many years. The objects function as continuous reminders, both for the pilgrims and for Mary. A pilgrim's account illustrates this:

> In our house we have a little shelf with a painting of Mary. I put the miniature house in front of her, so she won't forget about us. She will see the house and that will remind her to help us. At the same time, we see the little house. It reminds us what we are working for.

This way, the objects are not only used as a tangible reminder to Mary to help them, but also functions as a reminder for the pilgrims to keep their goals in mind.

Most pilgrims were willing to tell me their stories of success. For example, an Argentinean couple told me:

> Five years ago we went to the *fiesta* of Urkupiña in Salta. I bought a miniature house, and with the house came also a car, as a miniature car was parked in the garden. At that moment we were living in the house of my mother, but my mother wanted to throw us out. She bought us a field and gave us 45,00 dollar, on the condition that we would leave in two months. We borrowed another 70,00 dollar from the bank. Although it seemed impossible, we were able to construct a new house in two months! It was a miracle. Without too much sacrifice we bought it.

> And you know what? I went to a garage to look for a car. The guy said: "Try this one. If you like it, you can have it." That afternoon he gave me the keys and I drove home. Again, without effort we found a car. Therefore we have a lot of faith in the Virgin of Urkupiña. Today we came to Quillacollo as a pilgrimage of thanksgiving.

Interestingly, the Virgin of Urkupiña is not directly mentioned in the success story, but these pilgrims emphasize that it is due to the powers of the Virgin of Urkupiña that they were able to realize, without too many difficulties, a house with a car in their garden. Both Mary's effort and that of the pilgrims are necessary to convert the miniatures into what they represent. It demonstrates that the pilgrims take a collaborative approach in their relationship with Mary. The term 'collaborative approach' is derived from the study of Pargament (1997), a psychologist in the area of religious coping, who developed a classification of religious coping styles. The pilgrims do not take a 'deferring' approach, in which the outcome of their request is passively handed over to Mary's judgment, but pilgrims expect Mary to shape the circumstances for them to realize their goals. The pilgrims take the steps necessary to finish a study, buy a car, or construct a house, and the Virgin intervenes in the conditions necessary to achieve the specific goal. I would like to state that pilgrims do not change the structures of inequalities that underlie their petitions, but in the sacralization of things, they can find the stimulus for their own actions, creativity, and inventiveness to change what is in their power.

Mary makes it easier for pilgrims to accomplish what they want. When Escarlent was able to dislodge a big part of the rock in one stroke, she felt reassured that in real life it would also be easy to obtain what she wanted. Pilgrims' belief in Mary's help offers them trust, patience, and confidence in their actions. It gives them self-confidence and faith in the feasibility of their projects. By making Mary part of their struggles, pilgrims actively try to change their situation. By engaging in a public act of extracting stones and offering miniatures, a sense of control is experienced: they are no longer the victims of circumstances, but the director of them (e.g. Orsi, 1996: 136). Furthermore, the objects show that the relationship with Mary is not limited to a few moments at the pilgrimage shrine, but continues at home. The objects function as a vehicle of empowerment in a spiritual exchange economy between pilgrims and Mary.

Conclusions

In this chapter, I looked at the materialization of pilgrims' requests in stones and *alasitas* at the pilgrimage site to the Virgin of Urkupiña in Quillacollo and tried to give more insight in what these objects reveal about the relationship between pilgrims and Mary. I have employed Kopytoff's notion of the biography of things to do so, as the trajectory of the objects, together with the human interactions with them, construct meaning in the objects and thus can reveal much about pilgrim's relations with Mary. The biographies of objects show that the Bolivian pilgrims construct a spiritual economy in which they appeal to the spiritual world to improve their chances of upward mobility. To do so, they collaborate with Mary. Stones and *alasitas* embody not merely a simple wish for divine intervention in one's economic distress, but a complex intertwining of the religious, social and economic domains whose joint forces allow the pilgrims to cope with the difficulties of life, and motivates them to work towards their solution.

For most of the pilgrims, there is no contradiction in approaching Mary for materialistic improvement. In line with the conflation of the Andean goddess of fertility Pachamama with the Virgin Mary during colonization, the material is conflated with the spiritual domain. The investment in objects and offerings is exchanged for Mary's intervention in the necessary conditions to accomplish their goals. The objects function, in fact, as the currency of these transactions, but, like modern currency, their real value lies in the faith held in them.

In fact, a spiritual economy is established, in which pilgrims negotiate with Mary for intervention in their daily lives. The pilgrims work together with Mary in a collaborative relationship, in which Mary has the power to shape the possibilities, and empowers the pilgrims to continue their own steps towards their economic aspirations. Therefore, this study shows the empowering function that religion can have for people. Through making Mary part of their problems, they become active agents to change their class position within the boundaries of their personal possibilities.

The stones and *alasitas* function as reminders and daily constants in the relationship between pilgrims and Mary. The biographies show how the objects are the tangible mediators between Mary and the pilgrims. Back home, the objects are displayed at house altars where they serve both as reminders for Mary to help them, and for themselves of what goals they had in mind. The use of miniature symbols and stones offers the pilgrims trust and confidence in the feasibility of their projects, and in them they find spiritual encouragement to take the necessary steps to realize their economic aspirations.

At the same time, however, this chapter shows that the pilgrims ask for things they can reasonably expect, and when they cannot turn their requests into reality in the coming year, they do not lose trust in Mary, but rather readjust their goals and wishes. Literally and figuratively, objects and wishes keep 'moving'. To a certain extent, they have to accept their own economic limits and their class situation in the relationship with Mary. Poor people cannot ask Mary for villas, nor do they have the conditions to find, buy or build a villa. Although the pilgrimage provides a space to reflect on realistic goals to advance in daily life, it does not take away the inequalities. Even more strongly, they are encouraged to accept their own poor economic situation and the differences between theirs and that of others. Their negotiating power in improving their individual class position is not really able to bring about changes in structural inequalities. Accepting the boundaries is part of the 'play' of religion.

Both forms of empowerment exist next to each other. With the *alasitas* and stones pilgrims motivate and activate themselves, but at the same time they keep realistic considerations in mind when confronted with inequalities, and accept the limitations of their circumstances. As we have seen, the rich justify their class position by the hard work they have done to achieve their goals, whereas the poor accept the inequality and look for the necessary tiny investments of Mary to keep their heads above water.

Photo 6: Margarita praying at her mountain looking out at the Cochabamba Valley

6

DOMESTIC VIOLENCE, *MARIANISMO*, AND THE ANGER OF WOMEN

'I prefer to have boys, as they suffer less than girls.'

- Margarita, Quillacollo 2-10-2005

Margarita, a mother of a twelve year old boy, told me many times that she preferred to have boys rather than girls. She used to say: 'Girls will only suffer in Bolivia. I want the best for my children. That's why I prefer boys.' According to Margarita and the other women I spoke with, girls suffer more than boys because of marriage and motherhood. To be considered a good and respectable woman in a patrilineal society Bolivian women have to be married and have to bear children. The numerous conversations with women from diverse social backgrounds taught me that marriage was a very unequal relationship. What struck me was there were so many stories of Bolivian women about violent men who abused them physically, psychologically, and sexually. The topic of domestic violence came up constantly as a dominant form of gender-related suffering for these women. I wondered why motherhood was venerated to such a degree, while at the same time women, even if they were mothers, were degraded.

Domestic violence is one of Latin America's most pressing social problems. According to surveys in the region, almost half of all women suffer from psychological abuse, and one to two women in five experience physical violence (Buvinic et al, 1999). In comparison, according to a study in the Netherlands five years ago, only 4 percent of the Dutch women has been the victim of psychological, physical or sexual violence (Movisie, 2007). As domestic violence appears to be a systematic form of violence in Latin America, like economic poverty, it is a form of structural violence. In the case of domestic violence, the family is the violent institution of suffering.

Although the attitude of women towards men is rather negative, most women come to live with a man at some point in their lives. According to the Bolivian census of 2001, more than 56 percent of all people over 15 years old lives in union, that is married or living together (INE, 2003: 90). In Latin America it is common, especially among the poor, to live together for years without the formality of marriage in order to save for the expenses of a formal celebration. Living together as a way of life, has its roots in the colonial period. In that period, questions of honor, female sexuality, and illegitimacy became inextricably linked. Women who engaged in premarital or extramarital relations not only lost their personal reputation and honor, but could also affect the honor of other family members. The double standard characteristic of a patriarchal colonial society meant that similar sexual behavior by males did not threaten personal and familial honor. To a certain extent, honor could be saved by a 'promise of marriage.' In such cases unmarried women who had exchanged a promise of marriage lived openly for years, and even decades, in public monogamous relationships with prospective husbands. Couples who exchanged a marriage promise customarily recorded the names of both mother and father on the baptism certificates of their illegitimate children (Twinam, 1989: 123-137). Nowadays most Bolivian couples engage in multiple forms of ceremony, including a betrothal, civil marriage, and a Catholic wedding. Often people state publicly that they 'have a husband' or 'have a wife' after their parents legitimate the relationship in the betrothal ceremony, even if it takes years before they have saved enough money to afford their Catholic wedding ceremony and *fiesta* (Van Vleet, 2008: 130).

In 2001 about 13 percent of the population over 15 years old was living together and 43 percent was married. Eight percent of the population over 15 was separated, divorced, or widowed, and 36 percent was single (INE, 2003: 90). According to data of the 43 household surveys that I held in three different districts of Quillacollo, in 26 households there were a husband, wife and children, and in 16 houses lived a divorced, widowed, or separated woman with her children. Only one household was that of a single man living alone. In Bolivia it is not common to live alone. Often a single niece, nephew, brother, sister, or acquaintance also lived in the households. This is in line with what Van Vleet (2008: 63) points out about households in Andean communities. A household is typically composed of many members, not necessarily direct kin. An older and more established household, for example Virginia's family, may consist of three generations. Parents and unmarried children may live with at least one married son, his wife and children. When the household compound becomes too crowded, a married son moves his family into its own house, forming a nuclear family household in place of the extended family household. Occasionally, a family takes the children of relatives or *compadres*, or godfathers, into their house, as in Margarita's family. As we will see in this chapter, many Bolivian women suffer from their violent husbands, but stay married in spite of continuing quarrels and fights rather than leave their husbands and live alone with their children.

Many studies on domestic violence in Latin America relate this suffering to the dominant gender notions of *marianismo* and *machismo* (e.g. Ellsberg et al, 2000; Flake & Forste, 2006; Sagot, 2005). Women's suffering is often explained in the notion of femininity, *marianismo*, in which women are said to embrace the values of the Virgin Mary as a passive and submissive role-model, as a mother who makes sacrifices for her child (e.g. Ellsberg et al, 2000; Flake & Forste, 2006; Sagot, 2005; Salyers Bull, 1998; Stevens, 1973). However, these studies seldom look at women's actual interpretations of Mary. It is merely assumed that women venerate Mary for her submissiveness, suffering, and passivity. Several studies have already shown that the *machismo-marianismo* complex gives a too simplistic and dualistic view of the gender relations in Latin America (Bachrach Ehlers, 1991; Guttman, 1996; Navarro, 2002; Steenbeek, 1986, 1995), but it has not yet been shown what is Mary's actual role in problems of domestic violence, nor whether battered Latin American women really do have this perception of Mary. This chapter looks at Bolivian women's experiences of domestic violence and relates this to their interpretations of the Virgin of Urkupiña. I will argue that women do not suffer as passively in their marriages to violent husbands as the literature suggests. Rather than imitating Mary in showing submissiveness and accepting suffering, my respondents experience a profound rage that cannot always be expressed in their marriage. They approach the Virgin of Urkupiña to transfer their rage to her. These battered women do not refer to Mary as a symbol of endurance in their suffering; on the contrary, they perceive her rather as a powerful, vicious goddess of vengeance.

The next sections will describe the theoretical concepts of domestic violence, and *marianismo*. After that I will introduce the case of Margarita, a 46 year old religious Aymara woman who suffered from domestic violence during her marriage. Subsequently I will look at women's experiences of suffering and rage, as a predominant reaction to violent husbands. After that I will continue with women's approaches and perceptions of the Virgin of Urkupiña.

Domestic violence

Domestic violence is a complex phenomenon, as it includes a range of physical, sexual, and psychological acts within the family. As defined in a report of the Secretary-General of the United Nations (2006: 37):

> Physical violence involves intentionally using physical force, strength or a weapon to harm or injure a person. Sexual violence includes abusive sexual contact, making a woman engage in a sexual act without her consent, and attempted or completed sex acts with a woman who is ill, disabled, under pressure or under the influence of alcohol or other drugs. Psychological violence includes controlling or isolating the woman, and humiliating or embarrassing her. Economic violence includes denying a woman access to and control over basic resources.

Violence does not usually take only one of these forms, and women suffering from one form usually suffer others as well: often physical violence is accompanied by verbal humiliations, sexual violence, and/or economic violence (Sagot's 2005: 1299; Ellsberg et al. 2000). In Latin America, domestic violence often occurs when alcohol is involved (Flake & Forste, 2006).

Numerous studies from around the world have suggested that violence against women is most common in societies where gender roles are rigidly defined and enforced, and where the concept of masculinity is linked to toughness, male honor and dominance, as in Latin America and the Middle East (Ellsberg et all, 2000: 1598; Flake & Dorste, 2006: 20). As the World Report on Violence and Health (World Health Organization, 2002: 94-95) notes, in these societies, wife-beating is largely regarded as a consequence of a man's right to inflict physical punishment on his wife. Cultural justifications for violence usually follow from traditional notions of the proper roles of men and women. In many contexts women are expected to look after their homes and children, and show their husbands obedience and respect. In these countries, women often agree with the idea that men have the right to discipline their wives, if necessary with force. Significantly, one of the reasons that women most often cite as a just cause for beatings is refusing a man sex. These ideas are also derived from church teachings on proper gender roles in society (Hamington, 1995; Maeckelberghe, 1991).

On the website of the English NGO Womankind Worldwide (2007) the shocking statement that 'seven out of every ten Bolivian woman are victims of physical violence' is made, but there is no explicit source given on which these high figures are based. A report of the Health Ministry in Bolivia also notes that domestic violence is a common problem in Bolivia, encountered in 55 percent of the population of economically active men and women of fertile age. Victims are almost exclusively women (Ministerio de Salud, 2004). Violence of husbands against wives is especially common. Van Vleet (2008) shows in her book *Performing Kinship: Narrative, Gender, and the Intimacies of Power in the Andes* that in the Bolivian village where she carried out her fieldwork, domestic violence is not limited to the behavior of the husband towards the wife, but that violence between mothers-in-law and daughters-in-law also occurs.

A study carried out in the tropical area of the Cochabamba department in Bolivia (Defensor del Pueblo, 2006) again demonstrates the high level of domestic violence; 67 per cent of the women interviewed stated that violence exists within their family unit; 27 per cent reported physical violence, 23 per cent psychological violence, 8 per cent economic violence; 6 per cent reported physical and psychological violence, 2 per cent physical and economic, and 1 per cent reported physical and sexual violence. In total, 36 per cent reported physical violence. The World Report on Violence and Health (2002:90) gives lower statistics for Bolivia. Their study carried out in three departments of the country in

1998 notes that 17 per cent of women above 20 years old reported being physically assaulted in the previous twelve months.

A study of Revollo Quiroga (1995: 13) points out that the largest numbers of the incidence of domestic violence are reported in the city of Cochabamba, together with the cities of El Alto, La Paz and Santa Cruz. It also mentioned that in Cochabamba most reports are made by cohabiting and married women, whereas in Santa Cruz more single women report gender related violence. Victims often experience physical aggression not only once, but many times (e.g. World Health Organization, 2002). The reports of the Cochabamba police over 2005 and the first semester of 2007 show that often the same woman reports several incidents by the same offender (Las Brigadas de Protección a la Familia, 2005-2007). According to the Bolivian National Institute of Statistics (INE, 2007), 48 per cent of the reported cases of domestic violence in the entire Cochabamba department is committed by a registered offender.

There are various factors that affect the quality and comparability of data on domestic violence. There are inconsistencies in the way violence and abuse are defined; variations in the selection criteria for women being surveyed or interviewed; differences resulting from the sources of data, and the willingness of respondents to talk openly and honestly about experiences with violence (World Health Organization, 2002: 92). Besides, in some societies, like Bolivia, domestic violence is seen as a justifiable way to resolve problems in the family. When domestic violence is 'normalized' many women do not perceive it as a crime and will not report it as such (Defensor del Pueblo, 2006: 33-34; Van Vleet, 2008: 136). As a consequence, the figures presented often vary greatly between different sources. Moreover, the figures might also diverge from the actual situation, as in reality the numbers could be higher. What all the sources have in common however, is that they note a considerable degree of domestic violence, and regard it as a serious social problem and a sign of unequal gender relations.

In the past decade, gender-based violence became one of the topics on the political agenda. In 1994 the National Plan for Prevention and Eradication of Violence against Women was approved in which the necessity for adequate legislation to prevent, take sanctions against, and eradicate violence against women was defined, together with the necessity of methodologies to measure the magnitude of this violence, for public institutions to effect this, and the need for a different mentality. The same year departments of gender and municipal offices for women were created in every department. One of the first results of the Plan was the approval in 1995 of Law 1674 against domestic violence, which aims at the physical, psychological, moral, and sexual protection of any members of the nuclear family unit. Established sanctions include a fine (20 per cent of the minimum national salary up to twenty times this amount, depending on the circumstances), arrest (maximum of four days), and alternative measures such as community work. From then on, several other Decrees and Laws were approved to optimize Law 1674 and extend the efforts to eradicate gender based violence. Also *Las Brigadas de Proteccion a la Familia* - Brigades for Family Protection - were developed, departments at the major police stations, where cases of violence can be reported and claims for protection can be made (Comité de America Latina y el Caribe para la Defensa de los Derechos de la Mujer (CLADEM), 2005; Gumucio Hinojosa, 2005).

Although laws and services have been developed in recent decades, there are still problems with the implementation of the Law, especially with regard to indigenous women. For example, the normalization of violence in societal standards, and the rigid gender prescriptions are difficult and slow to change; women know of neither the law nor of the services, and often feel embarrassed or fear revenge, and do not want to report the violence with which they are faced (CLADEM, 2005; Daarte & Doerge, 1992).

Another problem is that battered women frequently lack an extended social network. They have to take care of the children, and often their husbands monitor their movements jealously (e.g. Levine, 1993: 98). Especially when women have children, they do not know where to go if they were to leave their husbands. Several Bolivian women told me that when they went to their mothers for protection, they were sent back to their husbands. According to the societal norms, married mothers should stay married, no matter what happens to them. The fear of gossip and social rejection is also an important reason to stay with a violent husband (Ellsberg et al, 2000). As Favret-Saada (1980) shows in her book on witchcraft in a rural region of France, *Deadly Words*, words can have a tremendous power on the lives of the persons to whom they are addressed. Gossip, as a spoken discourse, can influence the lives of the beaten women to a great extent. Women are supposed to behave in certain ways and will be 'punished' by gossip, if their behavior differs from public expectations. Therefore, women often want to behave according to the prescribed gender notions. The societal norms play an important role in Bolivian women's decisions to stay with their husbands, as do economic reasons. For poor women it is almost impossible to leave, as they cannot provide for themselves and their children, and need their husband for economic support.

Marianismo, a contested term

The gender notions of *marianismo* and *machismo* are often used to explain the high levels of domestic violence in Latin America. *Marianismo* developed as a scholarly term to refer to the capacity of women to suffer in unequal gender relations. The term was introduced to Latin American literature by Stevens (1973) to refer to a sacred notion of motherhood. Stevens defines *marianismo* as 'the cult of feminine spiritual superiority, which teaches that women are semi-divine, morally superior to and spiritually stronger than men' (Stevens, 1973: 91). Stevens notes that *marianismo* is not a religious practice such as Mariology, but that from the central figure of Mary beliefs and practices have been derived that are related to the subordinate position of women in society. Among the secular edifice of beliefs and practices Stevens (1973: 94-95) mentions:

> Over the characteristics of this ideal are semidivinity, moral superiority, and spiritual strength. This spiritual strength engenders abnegation, that is, an infinite capacity for humility and sacrifice. No self-denial is too great for the Latin American women, no limit can be divined to her vast store of patience with the men of her world... Beneath the submissiveness, however, lies the strength of her conviction –shared by the entire society- than men must be humoured, for after all "they can't help the way they are".

Marianismo has become a popular concept to describe notions of femininity in Latin America. After Stevens introduced the term, numerous studies have used the concept (e.g. Ellsberg et al, 2000; Flake & Forste, 2006; Hubbell, 1993; Salyers Bull, 1998; Upchurch et al. 2001). Although these studies do not emphasize the aspect of moral superiority as Stevens did, but instead highlight women's suffering, they take over the concept uncritically. For example, Salyers Bull (1998: 3) defines *marianismo* as follows:

> *Marianismo* refers to a concept that incorporates female gender-roles. The term is derived from the Virgin Mary. Embodied in this term are the concepts of virginity, chastity, honor and shame, the ability to suffer and willingness to serve.

Flake & Forste (2006: 20) neither refer to women's superiority in their description of the term:

> Male dominance is reinforced by women's role in Latin American society. *Marianismo* refers to the expectation that women embrace the veneration of the Virgin Mary in that they are capable of enduring any suffering inflicted upon them by males. Latin American women are to be submissive, dependent, sexually faithful to their husbands, and are expected to take care of household needs and dedicate themselves entirely to their husbands and children.

From these studies it becomes clear that the term is used to emphasize women's capacity to suffer. All authors emphasize that these characteristics are derived from the Virgin Mary as a role-model of submission and suffering that embodies the ideals of maternity and chastity (e.g. Ellsberg et al, 2000: 1604). Although Stevens referred to women's moral superiority, the term is generally used to refer to women's inferiority. *Marianismo* is understood both as the explanation of women's subordinate status and the legitimization of their sufferings.

Opposed to this cultural concept of femininity is the gender notion of masculinity, or *machismo*. The stereotypical ideal of Latin American masculinity, *machismo*, emphasizes a man's personal control of people and things, and the ideal image of a man is of someone strong, virile, and in competition with other males. In the general view of *machismo* free sex and extramarital relationships are signs of social prestige and personal attractiveness for the Latin *machos*, whereas for females monogamy is socially expected, imposed, and preserved. Men frequently behave in a domineering and oppressive way towards women, and at times do not hesitate to coerce them physically and morally (Gutmann, 2006; Hardin, 2002; Morales-Gorecki, 1988; Salyers Bull, 1998). Interestingly, this generalized gender notion of *machismo*, in its turn, is used in literature to explain the high levels of domestic violence in Latin America.

Both *machismo* and *marianismo* behaviors are regarded as having their roots in the Spanish Conquest. According to Hardin (2002: 20) *machismo* is a legacy of the Spanish *conquistadores*.

> It was the product of the rape of indigenous women, the response to indigenous imperial ritual, and the sublimation of indigenous male sexualities and genders. It was a response to social and religious control of the male body.

Bachrach Ehlers (1991: 3) describes how *marianismo* or 'the fatalistic acceptance of women suffering at the hands of men' is rooted in the colonial period, when women were taught to emulate the virtues of the Virgin Mary.

Machismo, as a term, has passed into the vocabulary of the general public throughout Latin America, whereas *marianismo* has only spread in the scholarly domain. During my fieldwork I noticed that the term *macho* was omnipresent in conversations and jokes. Most women employ the term *machismo* when speaking about their husbands or Bolivian men in general. They talk about proud men who enforce obedience from their women. They speak of violent drunken men, about unequal relations, about different standards in daily life: women have to stay at home, cook for their husbands, are not allowed to speak about their desires or needs, they have to serve his ego. Their stories reveal the negative perceptions they have of men, including their husbands.

A short conversation I had with a few young Quechua girls of around eight years old in the main square of Quillacollo struck me forcibly. The little girls all said firmly they did not want to marry later. 'Men are lazy, they steal and they lie', one of them said, referring to the three commandments of the Andean *cosmovisión*: *Ama suwa, ama llulla, ama qella*, which mean 'you are not allowed to steal, you are not allowed to lie and you are not allowed to be lazy.' It showed me clearly that women's negative views about men have been transmitted to the next generation of Bolivian females at a very early age. Interestingly, when I spoke with men about *machismo*, most of them denied the existence of *machismo* in their mentality. They said women were equal to men nowadays, and that they prefer to love one woman rather than have numerous girlfriends. Economic factors also play a role, as the majority was also poor. They said that maintaining one family is difficult enough, so it would be impossible to maintain girlfriends on the side.

The concepts of *marianismo* and *machismo* have not only been taken over, but have also been widely criticized. In her article 'Against Marianismo' Navarro (2002) severely criticizes Stevens' article. She concludes that '*marianismo* is an a-historical, essentialist, anachronistic, sexist, and orientalist fabrication.' In addition, Bachrach Ehlers (1991: 1) notes that the stereotypical concepts of *machismo* and *marianismo* are applied indiscriminately to an entire continent. This generalization has resulted in criticism, as it does not leave much space for the different cultural contexts to which they are applied. *Marianismo* is often considered as a complement to *machismo*, where the passive, long-suffering woman acts in response to male irresponsibility; without *marianismo*, *machismo* could not exist (Bachrach Ehlers, 1991). In the general descriptions a one-dimensional approach is revealed, in which *machismo* and *marianismo* are seen as two opposites, reduced to a dichotomy. However, both Villarreal (1996: 204) and Steenbeek (1986: 62) suggest looking at the multidimensionality of gender concepts. For example, Steenbeek (1986) notes:

> Femininity and masculinity can have more meanings; the concepts cannot be separated; they belong together to an ideological complex that is appropriate for both sexes. Between the components *machismo* and *marianismo* exists an ambiguous multidimensional relation. Women are both inferior and superior, in need for protection and with the ability to give protection. The same multidimensionality is in *machismo*: superior and inferior, powerful and weak.

Steenbeek criticizes the suggested equilibrium between *machismo* and *marianismo,* and underlines that this superiority and inferiority of men and women is related to different domains. The superiority of women is only applied to the sphere of morality, whereas the superiority of men is omnipresent, except in morality. The inferiority of women and men is also valued differently. The superiority of men is accepted, whereas that of women is not. Another point of power inequality is related to the means that are available for men and women to impose their will. The power that women possess is manipulative and can be overruled by the formal and/or physical violence of men. Therefore, the power of women is limited.

When looking at studies that consider Latin Americans' actual behavior in their unequal marriages, we see that women's behavior is not as passive as suggested in the literature that uses the concepts of *machismo* and *marianismo*. A study of Bachrach-Ehlers (1991: 2) illustrates that Latin American women's behavior is not merely a response to *machismo*, but a survival strategy emerging from female economic, social, and sexual dependence in a society where men hold economic, political, and legal power. Another study reveals that Latin American working-class women see marriage as a fundamentally economic exchange, and evaluate a husband's worth primarily in terms of his ability and willingness to meet the material needs of his family. Marriage allows Latin American women to meet their own material needs while bearing and raising the children they desire (Browner & Lewin,1982: 65-70). Many Latinas get married in order to have children, and in the long run the children are more important than being or having been someone's wife. In Bolivia I also found that women married in order to get legal, thus respected, children. Bolivian laws distinguish among legitimate offspring, illegitimate, and 'natural' children. Legitimate children are born of a civil and a church-sanctioned marriage ceremony; illegitimate children are the offspring of an unmarried couple prohibited from marrying, while natural children are the offspring of an unmarried couple that may marry in the future (Sanabria, 2001: 141). Sanabria (2001) explains that the formal distinctions in Bolivian law between legitimate and non-legitimate birth status are significant for inheritance laws and surname transmission. Birth status is closely bound up with inheritance: legitimate and legitimated offspring can claim equal shares of inheritance from their fathers, while illegitimate and natural offspring can claim inheritance only from their mothers. Collier (1986: 106) notes that the virtue of chastity is related to this, as a mother's chastity guarantees her children's right to inherit. Also in case of surname transmission questions of legitimacy are relevant, as often legitimate offspring are entitled to both paternal and maternal first surnames, while illegitimate and natural children carry only their mother's surname (Sanabria, 2001). Only a few women told me they married because they fell in love. It is necessary to take these attitudes towards marriage into account in order to understand women's experiences of domestic violence in Bolivia. It is also necessary to understand why, even in violent relationships, women seldom leave their husbands.

Despite the high cultural value attached to marriage and motherhood, women often behave differently from the established norm that says that they should be faithful, submissive and caring to their husband and self-sacrificing for their children. As Brown (1975: 334) shows for Dominican women, their behavior goes against the established gender norms. As a way to cope with poverty, these women often enter several sequential relationships with different men, so all men have to provide what is necessary for all their children. Economically the women were better off in not behaving according to the societal norms for contracting a monogamous marriage. Although it is less common in Bolivia to change relationships frequently, many women continue a marriage with a violent partner, not only because of the societal gender norms that prescribe submission and 'purity', but also for economic reasons, as we will see below.

In this chapter I will show that the physical violence of men towards their wives is not merely accepted in a 'marianistic' way. I will contribute to the critical studies on the *marianismo*-complex from a different angle. Studies that make use of the concept of *marianismo* to explain women's suffering in Latin America generally just assume that women venerate Mary especially for her suffering qualities. Researchers borrow the term from other scholars, but do not carry out their own research to see if women do indeed perceive Mary as a submissive and suffering mother, and emulate these characteristics. Therefore, in this chapter I will base my argument on the interpretations of Bolivian women of the Virgin Mary, as these interpretations are often neglected in studies of *marianismo*.

Vuola (2006) is one of the few authors that relate *marianismo* to women's interpretations of the Virgin Mary. She argues that Latin American women see Mary as a suffering sister or mother, who knows the pain of childbirth, raising the child, and then losing the child to death. This is why they prefer talking and praying to her, not because she is the model of chastity and subservience. Vuola looks especially at the recognition of motherhood in Mary. But in line with other scholars, Vuola also emphasizes that the Latin American believers approach Mary for her suffering qualities, whereas I will show in this chapter that the Bolivian devotees not only approach Mary because of her suffering qualities but also because of her abilities to articulate rage and anger. The Virgin of Urkupiña has a vicious side and is able to take revenge on violent husbands.

Hermkens (2007; 2008), one of the researchers in *The Power of Marian Pilgrimage* project, also studied the way Catholic women in Papua New Guinea use the symbol of Mary to deal with domestic violence, however without using the term *marianismo*. Mary enables these Catholic women to endure their suffering, while according to Hermkens (2007: 7):

> at the same time, Mary's submissive image falls in line with pre-existing gender relations and gender hierarchies, in which women are constituted as submissive to their husbands, their primary role being that of caretakers of the families, as mothers.

In another article (2008: 158-160), she shows that the women cope with domestic violence by submitting themselves to Mary and their husbands. By submitting to Mary, the women often gain the necessary strength to keep going, that is, to stay with their husbands. With Mary as a role-model, women imbue themselves with such virtues as humility, obedience and patience. By changing themselves they change their anger in humility.

Although we should expect a similar picture in Bolivia, because the church presents Mary as a submissive role-model and because of the pre-existing gender roles in Bolivian society, the data below will show she is not merely perceived as a submissive role-model by the majority of the battered women. Mary can be venerated for other qualities, even qualities in direct opposition to acceptance of suffering. The meanings given to Mary are culturally constructed and are embedded in historical and cultural values of a society. The synthesis with Pachamama, or Mother Earth, has profound consequences for the interpretation people have of Mary. In order to analyze women's interpretations of Mary in connection with gender related suffering, I will present the case study of Margarita and demonstrate that women do not necessarily accept the violence against them, even though they do not always have many options available to actually change the situation.

Margarita's case

I met Margarita when I visited the Calvary Hill for the first time. A woman in her forties, in an old and dirty layered skirt, a bowler hat and two long thick black braids approached me on flip-flops, to offer me *ch'alla* ingredients - materials for offerings, such as a little bottle of pure alcohol, festoons, confetti and firecrackers - in a plastic bag. Although I felt uncomfortable at being hassled by all the women who came running towards me to sell beer, blessings and *ch'allas*, at the same time I was curious about their lives and the rituals that they performed on the Calvary Hill. As I was not yet familiar with these rituals, I accepted Margarita's offer to accompany me up the hill to explain to me how to make an offering and dislodge stones. As a guide she walked in front of me and directed me to the chapel to pray to *la Virgencita*. When she asked me about my request, I answered jokingly that I was looking for a nice and loyal boyfriend. Margarita laughed and answered: 'You better not look for one in Bolivia!' Attentively, she helped me offer all the elements in the right order. Afterwards, she took me to a good viewpoint to look out over the outskirts of Quillacollo and the mountains. When drinking beer - part of the ritual - on top of the rocks she answered all my questions and was not shy in telling me some of the personal details of her life. Out of the blue she said she had been waiting for me for hours already. How could she know I was coming if she had never seen me before? She told me she had had a dream in which a blond young woman arrived at the Calvary Hill. In the beginning, I was a bit suspicious, as I classified her revelation as a selling strategy; I still had to pay her for the *ch'alla* ingredients and her prayers. However, during the following year I felt ashamed of this suspicion, as I got to know her as a pure, honest, and sweet woman. She even became like a mother to me.

Once I spoke with Margarita about her childhood and the environment in which she was raised. She said:

> Look at me now! I'm a real city woman, with my bowler, *pollera* and jersey. I even have tight shoes, although I don't like to wear them. Until I was eight years old I did not have shoes at all, not even flip-flops. All my clothes were made by hand, from the fleece of sheep and dyed in hard colors. Green, pink!

Margarita grew up in a rural village in the La Paz department, among sheep and llamas. She had four sisters and five brothers. One of her brothers died when he was young. When she was seven years old her father died. Her mother could not take care of all her children, so when she was eight years old Margarita moved with her older sister and brother-in-law to a miners' town. In the town of her birth she had followed two years of primary school, but in the miners' town there was no school, so she helped her sister in the household. When she was eleven years old she started working in the mines, and at the age of seventeen, she moved with her sister to Vinto, near Quillacollo, where she started to sell food and drinks, and later on she started selling *ch'allas* on the Calvary Hill. When one of Margarita's other sisters suddenly died of an illness, Margarita took her sister's baby daughter Dayana into her house to care for her, as Dayana's father was still young and did not want to take care of his daughter. In Bolivia it is common practise that when a mother dies the children move to a natural and female family member, or to the godparents, even if their father is still alive. Women are seen as nurturing and caring, whereas men are generally viewed as not capable of caring for children. Generally men are held responsible for the generation of income in the family, and they cannot care for children at the same time.

Margarita told me she has always had a negative idea about men and that she had never in her life fallen in love:

> I knew how to live alone. I was flattered by Juanito, a man I knew from selling fruits, because he always had a crush on me. But I always told him: "I will die single". I did not want to marry. I did not want children. I just hated men. I had seen so many examples of women treated badly by their husbands. My sister was always being hit, and all the women in the market with wounds and black eyes...

When she was around thirty, Margarita was pressured by her brothers to get married, although she did not want to. She recounts:

> My brothers wanted me to marry. According to them, a good and respectable woman should be married. They found a man, a friend of theirs; I did not know this man. I had to live with him in a room of my brother's house for a month before we gave the word and married. I just slept with little Dayana in a bed, I did not want to sleep with him in a bed. He wanted to play with me, but I didn't want to. Then we gave the word, and they left him in my house. I told him: "You are young, I'm older, what are you going to tell your friends? Leave me, there are plenty women for you." But he stayed with me.

I asked her whether she started to love her husband after a while, but she said: 'No, nothing!'

Her marriage lasted three years and two months, and during this time, Margarita became pregnant twice and had a son and a daughter. Her husband's violent behavior started shortly after her marriage, after a trip to the lowlands:

> I was married with my husband for only one month. I had to travel to the Chapare region to buy fruits to sell. In the *campo* I knew Juanito. I knew him for three or four years already. We were eating in a *comedor*, when my son's father appeared in the doorway. He looked at me. I didn't know he was coming. I was scared when I saw him. He said: "Let's go outside to eat", so I went with him outside. Scared, we did not talk. Then

> Juanito came towards us and hit me with his fist in my eye. All little stars! He said: "You are married!" My husband stood up to defend me and said: "That's my wife" and he started fighting with Juanito. In the end the owner of the *comedor* came to intervene.

I was surprised at this story, but Margarita could only laugh about it: 'Can you imagine! Two men fighting over me, whereas I preferred to be single!' She continues:

> Next we went back together, in the car. But the car broke down on the road. I wanted to sleep alone, but all other passengers insisted that I would sleep with him. They said: "How can you reject this poor little boy? You are his wife." There, in the road it was my first time with him. We played, we played it all. I was so scared, but I did not dare to say no. Since then he got jealous about me.

For Margarita, the trip to Chapare marks the beginning of the violence. Two elements are important: during that trip her husband had seen that other men were interested in his wife and second, they had their first sexual experience, which gave him a sense of ownership about his wife.

Since then her husband became violent more often. She tells me:

> Terrible. Then he arrived late. The dirty smell of *chicha*' [corn drink with alcohol]. "Don't come close to me" I said. But he said: "For something you are my wife." And I could not say anything. I just shut up, so at least he wouldn't beat me.

I said: 'But that is sexual abuse, that is terrible.' Margarita replied: 'After a while you get used to it. You just let time pass. I can be happy that there was only one man in my entire life.' For Margarita it is important that she was with only one man, first of all, to be a respected woman in society and to avoid the punishment of gossip. Secondly, because in her view, suffering is related to being someone's wife: As she only had one husband in her life, she only has suffered because of one man.

Margarita did not know her husband well. He had seemed to be a good man, but after only one month of marriage he changed and started hitting her. Once Margarita showed me her mouth and said: 'Look, these three teeth are gone, because my husband hit me with a shoe. In another fight this one has been knocked out with a fist. And on the other side I also lost three teeth because of my husband was beating me up so much.' However, Margarita told me that she did not want to divorce. 'How could I divorce? I had children by him...' Having children was for Margarita, as for many other Bolivian women a major reason to stay together. Economically, it was easier for her to stay with him. Besides, she explained that it is important for children to have both their mother and their father around because they have different areas of authority. She was also afraid of the disapproval of society after separation. According to the societal norms, it is not acceptable for women to leave their husbands.

One day, Margarita's brother was visiting her, and her husband came home with a girl in his taxi. According to Margarita her husband was a '*cholero*, like most taxi-drivers.' *Cholero* is a term for men who want to go out with many Indian women, or *cholitas*. Her brother asked: 'Why are you driving this girl?' and he answered: 'Because I'm young'. Her brother started hitting Margarita's husband. Margarita tells:

> When my husband was hit, a lot of blood flowed out of his nose. My brother told me to drink it, so I drank his blood. This is against a potential curse. People always say you have to drink blood, so if someone wants to perform a ritual against you, the curse does not fall on you.[1] After the fight, my husband left with the other woman. The father of his new woman, who was a *yatiri*, performed a ritual against me and my son. She wanted me to die, and my child too, because she did not want him to pay alimony for my son. But the curse did not come to me, because I drank his blood. The curse went to my husband. After a few years my husband died.

From the day of the incident with her husband and her brother she was alone again. Her husband started living with the other woman and even had a child by her. At that time Margarita was in debt, because her husband had recently had an accident with his taxi. To replace all the broken parts, they had borrowed money from Margarita's brother. As her husband had left the scene, Margarita was held responsible for paying back the money. I asked why she could not reclaim the money from her husband and she said:

> We never had an official ceremony. We were married *así no más*, - just like that -. Since he was kicked out by my brother, he was not my husband anymore. I did not want to see him ever again. And it was money from my brother, so I was responsible for that money. It was a tough time, as I also had to provide for my son, Carlos, and my daughter.

Carlos is the only biological child she has left, because her own daughter died after having lived for only fourteen months. The cause of death was *susto,* or soul shock, one of the common forms of *nervos* that Schepers Hughes (1992: 173) also gives as the reasons for premature child death in Brazil. *Nervos* is a common complaint among poor and marginalized people in many parts of the world, but especially in the Mediterranean countries and in Latin America. *Nervos* became a large and expansive folk idiom of distress in which emotional stress is somatised (e.g. Cartwright, 2007). *Susto* is a form of *nervos* in which the soul in the body suffers shock and can have deadly consequences. Margarita had accompanied a family of pilgrims on the Calvary Hill, and her child was

1 The practice of 'magic' rituals is common in the popular religion in Bolivia. Mostly this 'black magic' is performed by *yatiris*, or Andean medicine-men. There are several types of *yatiris*, not all of them dedicate themselves to the practice of harming others, most of the *yatiris* are approached for healing rituals.

sleeping there on top of the mountain. When one of the pilgrims threw the firecrackers they landed right next to the sleeping child, who woke and cried. From then on, Margarita's daughter got sick. Margarita took her daughter to a *yatiri*, to cure her. 'The *yatiri* tried his best, but he found out that because of the shock, her little soul had escaped from her body.' She died four days after the incident. When she referred to her daughter in the quote above, she meant her foster daughter. Margarita treated her foster daughter as her own. According to Van Vleet (2008: 64) in the Andean kinship perception, families are not necessarily bounded by birth relationships. Those who share food and space with each other constantly reproduce and reinforce relatedness and become a son or daughter by receiving food.

In the week of *Todos Santos*, or All Saints, I went with Margarita to the cemetery in Vinto where her daughter was buried. Margarita walked in a direct line towards the grave, next to that of a daughter of her sister. During a previous visit that week, Margarita had marked the graves with a rusty tin and a stick in the ground. Sitting on a tomb, she told me: 'When I came here with Carlos, it was nothing but sand. Now she has a grave': she pointed at the stick. 'We want to make it like this one' and she knocked on the tomb on which she was sitting. Marking of the grave of her daughter is a ritual act that shows that people cannot easily take leave of the dead. They want to make a last act to honor their loved one (e.g. Venbrux et al., 2008). Margarita continued:

> When my daughter died, my husband had left already. I went alone with little Carlos to the cemetery. I dug the hole to put the coffin in. There was nobody here, just me and my son. We worked hard, but the coffin didn't fit in. We rested a while and worked again. The whole day we were busy here digging the hole. At night I came back to my house. I couldn't stop crying.

I asked Margarita if there was a funeral. 'No, I went to the *alcaldia* - town hall - to tell that my daughter died. After that I went to the priest. The father cut her hair. It's like that. Hair is holy and cannot go into the grave. The priest gave a blessing, that was it.' I sat down next to Margarita, with tears of dismay in my eyes. Digging the grave of your own daughter... Not a single sign, no cross, no name, *nada*! I asked her if she wanted a picture of her sitting next to the grave. That was the only thing I could do for her at that moment, and I felt so embarrassed. Taking pictures, was the only ceremony I could think of to empathize, to show her I shared her feelings.

Nowadays Margarita lives with her foster daughter, Dayana, and her son, Carlos, in an adobe house on her sisters' property. Margarita did not want to remarry. 'I want to be alone, *tranquillo*!' It is hard for her to make enough money to pay all expenses for the three of them by selling *ch'alla*-ingredients. Even though she says she would probably have an economically better life with a husband, she never wanted to remarry.

Religion is very important in Margarita's life. God and the Virgin come to her in her dreams to instruct or reassure her. Margarita told me about a dream she had in Vinto:

> My house had collapsed in a heavy cloudburst. Afterwards, I was afraid to sleep again when it rained, as I was afraid it would happen again. One night God came to me in my dreams and said: 'Child don't cry. I am here, in all four corners of your house, I will protect you.' Since then, I could sleep again.

The dreams in which the Virgin Mary appears are mostly related to economic struggles. In relation to domestic violence, Margarita only remembers one dream she had in the time she was still married:

> The Virgin Mary came out of the ground near the Calvary Hill. She had such a beautiful face. She wore the *Cochala* clothes, a short lilac *pollera* and a white blouse.[2] She came to me, and I was too shy to look her in the eyes. She had the most beautiful face I ever saw. But she insisted, and when I looked into her eyes, she opened her arms. I couldn't do anything else than embrace her. She said: "Don't cry, *wawitay* –child." When she was holding me, my husband passed by on a dirty, dusty road. He carried a very heavy bag. The bag was so heavy that he almost collapsed!

According to Margarita, she knew from this dream that sooner or later he would be punished. When I asked whether her husband died because of the curse or because of the Virgin, she answered: 'Because of drinking the blood the curse did not fall on me, and because of the Virgin the curse fell on him!'

Margarita often prays on a mountain close to her village Vinto. She tries to go there every Wednesday, as according to Margarita, 'That is the day that God and Mary have most time. For example on Sundays they are too busy and might not hear your wishes.' In the Andean *cosmovisión* mountains have always been associated with supernatural powers, as the souls of the ancestors were believed to live there. According to Margarita: 'The mountain is closer to heaven. The mountain is peaceful and quiet. Besides, there are no people on the mountain. Therefore the energy is more pure. There are no people, so there is no sin.' On the mountain Margarita kneels for hours on her bare knees and pours incense on a fire, while making her requests. She prays for herself and her family, but also for clients who bought her *ch'allas*, that their wishes may be heard. She also prays 'for the poor in general, for people who don't have a house, for abandoned women and children, for married people who fight, and for the people in the hospital.'

2 From the clothes that indigenous women wear, one is able to see from which department or area someone comes. The Virgin of Urkupiña is located in the Cochabamba department, where the indigenous women wear relatively short skirts and white blouses. According to Margarita, the Virgin always appears out of the earth; probably this is derived from the synthesis between Pachamama and the Virgin.

Suffering

As Margarita's case shows, she suffered from domestic violence during her marriage, but did not separate. As the *marianismo* complex assumes, the Bolivian women do suffer in their marriages, but do they endure their suffering because they take Mary as a model of self-sacrifice and submission? To answer this question I want to take a closer look at why these women continue to suffer in the abusive relationships with their husbands.

Even if a husband treats his wife badly, most battered women are not willing to divorce their husbands. An important reason is connected to status. For example, one woman said: 'I'd rather stay with this dog, than leave him and be looked at askance by my family and acquaintances in the street.' Many women are afraid of the gossip that they can expect to arise if they leave their husbands. A woman leaving her husband is regarded differently from a man leaving his wife. After divorce women are afraid to deal with the social stigma of having failed as a wife and mother (Ellsberg et al., 2000: 1905). Margarita, for example, is proud to be a respected woman. Her husband left, which society considers a fair reason for separation. After that, she has never had another relationship with another man. One day we walked through her village and she said: 'I know the man who is living in this house for twenty years. He always tells me I am a good woman.' By chance, that day she had told me and the other vendors about the lumps in her belly. One of the vendors suggested that she get pregnant; with the child, the lumps would go out of her body. Margarita did not like the option of being cured by being pregnant, but the idea was still in her mind. She said: 'What would he think of me if he saw me suddenly with a big pregnant belly?' It shows how the opinions of others and the established norms in society are important considerations for women to behave the way expected of them. Natalia, one of the *sahumeras* at the Calvary Hill, also recounted how she got married to her violent husband:

> I was still living in La Paz. I met him when I was 18. Now I am 62 years old. Can you imagine? All these years I have been with this old guy. I did not know him very well, only a few months. I fell in love with him. He invited me into his house, but once I was in, he closed the door and did everything by force. I was so afraid becoming pregnant. After that happened I was not in love anymore, but I was scared. I got pregnant and my parents made me marry him.

According to Natalia she had to stay with him in order not to lose the respect of her family. Even after her parents died she stayed with her husband, as she feared the reactions of society. Like Natalia, many women preferred to suffer from domestic violence rather than suffer the social stigma that is attached to them after a divorce initiated by a woman.

Another reason often mentioned is 'for the sake of the children', as in Margaritas case. The women explained that their children would not be treated with respect if they did not have a father around, so women try to keep their husbands at their sides. Sylvana, mother of seven children, explained: 'Because of the *machismo*, women are considered as the weaker sex. Children need their father to guide them, to tell them what is right and what is wrong. If I am on my own, my children will not listen to me.' According to many women, children need an authoritarian father figure in their upbringing. Societal norms also play a role, as the children are *mal visto* (literally: seen badly), if there is no father around. This reason is related to the fear of being blamed for lack of respect by society.

'For the sake of the children' can also imply economic reasons. In Bolivia it is very common that the children stay with the wife. In general women have few prospects of getting a full-time well-paid job, and these are even less if they have several children. They need the financial support of the father. As Dayana, Margaritas foster child, explains:

> Although he beats you up, at times he works and gets the money to provide for the children. So many women stay with a violent husband. They know that if they are alone, they almost have to beg for money.

Men also often do not want to divorce for economic reasons, as, technically, they have to pay alimony. The price depends on the income of the parents and the needs of the children. Men with an absolute minimum of salary (around 1000 BOB per month) have to pay 150 BOB per child per month. According to a lawyer the amount of alimony can range from 150 BOB per month to 300 US$ per month for each child. Although these arrangements can be made about alimony, I heard numerous stories in which the men did not fulfill their obligations. Women therefore, are also often anxious about the decision to divorce, as they do not see many alternatives for economic survival. For Margarita too, it was hard when her husband left. Before she had children, she was a market trader and had to travel; with children this was no longer possible. Besides, now she had to earn for herself and her children. Many women have even more children to feed. They desperately need the income of their husbands in order to provide for their children. In addition, couples often do not want to divorce as they have to divide the house and their belongings, and will always end up with less than they had initially. This is in line with Browner and Lewin's (1982) findings that Latina women see marriage as a fundamentally economic exchange. Marriage gives women the opportunity to behave according to the expectations of society: the women can be mothers, and the father can generate the income.

Another economic motive to stay together as a couple is the price of the divorce formalities. Money is needed for the divorce papers, and often families cannot afford to pay for the separation. An official divorce cost around 2000 BOB, 200 euro, and in addition the lawyer has to be paid the amount of 5 to15 per cent of the value of the goods possessed. The price is even higher if one of the two does not want to separate because then it goes to an expensive court case.

Another reason for continuing a marriage with a violent husband lies in psychological factors. Some women told me they were afraid of what happened after making such a decision. For example Natalia explained:

> If he is capable of attacking me with shoes, sticks, and knives only for tiny reasons, such as not cooking what he likes, what will happen with his frustration when I leave him? I will be in danger. My children will have to live without their mother...

A 21 year old student explained about her parents:

> After one of those fights when my father beat up my mother, there always came a short period of peace and tranquility. After a while tensions increased again and another drama occurred with my mother. However, she always hoped he would change. Somehow, she managed to love the bastard.

Also Margarita explained: 'It is not only the physical violence, it is also the humiliations and words that affect you. After hearing every day you are bad, you start to feel bad about yourself.'

The reasons women have to stay with their husband (status, economy, and fear), demonstrate that often the women are not able to leave their husbands. Their behavior is not derived from the *marianismo*-complex; it is not that they want to suffer at the hands of men, but choose suffering because the other options are perceived as worse. Especially the economic motives show that suffering is a 'survival technique' as proposed by Bachrach Ehlers (1991). Thus the reasons the women give for staying with their husbands is not that they want to be passive and submissive in an effort to emulate Mary, and feel morally superior, but that they do not have a better option.

Although not all women feel capable of leaving their husbands, sometimes they do separate. Most separated women did not mention domestic violence as the main reason for their divorce or separation, although they mentioned it as an important reason for other women to separate. According to a number of lawyers I visited, domestic violence, together with adultery, were the main reasons for women to separate. For a sensitive topic like domestic violence, the women needed to have confidence. After a while, when they had learned to trust me, they were willing to talk about their negative experiences with men. Still they felt embarrassed sometimes, and many women told me their stories as if they were history, as if their husband did not use violence anymore, even if he did. One still married woman in her thirties told me: 'Mostly we are too proud to admit what is wrong in our marriage. We just tell everyone that everything goes well.'

One of the main reasons mentioned by women to divorce is their partner's alcohol use. Men often spent their money on alcohol at the expense of food. Next to the economic problems it triggers, it is often seen as the main social and family problem, including being the cause of violence. According to Margarita, alcohol use was one of the causes of the domestic violence she suffered. From the women's stories, men change their behavior drastically when drunk, and start to quarrel or even hit their wives and sometimes their children. Both Levine (1993: 86) and Ellsberg et al. (2006) show alcohol consumption as a determinant for domestic violence. However, from the perspective of men, drinking gives status. Excessive drinking is one of the characteristics of a real *macho*. The generalized ideas about Bolivian *machos* are very common in Bolivian society; women especially, use the *macho* concept in a stereotypical way. However, this concept also has to be viewed critically. As in *marianismo*, studies that use *machismo* should leave room for individual differences between men, and to the multi-dimensionality of behaviors (e.g. Gutmann, 1996).

The stereotype of the *macho* also prescribes that a man is not faithful to his wife. The term *cholero*, as used by Margarita to refer to married men who pick up several women, also refers to this stereotype. Adultery and a man leaving his wife for another woman are often mentioned reasons to separate. Interestingly, almost never did I hear about a woman leaving her husband for another man. I heard many stories of women who told me that their husband abandoned them when he migrated to another country or city to work. Often the women just speak bitterly, not even angry or sad about it. Remarks as: 'He went to Argentina and there he forgot about us' are common. When someone tells a story like this, most women respond with other stories of acquaintances or family members who were in a similar situation.

After divorce, many women do not want to remarry, especially if they have children. Margarita also does not want to remarry. She does not trust Bolivian men and prefers to stay single. Women are often afraid their new husbands will not accept the children from a previous marriage. For example, Rosa, a market woman, has eight children; three from a previous marriage and another five by her present husband. When her husband was not around, she told me she had eight children, but when her husband was there she mentioned only five. Her husband does not want to know anything about her other children. One of the three children from the first marriage has been adopted and taken to the United States, one moved in with the biological father in Santa Cruz, and the other one is at a boarding school run by nuns.

At times women who stayed in an abusive relationship told me that the physical violence had stopped, sometimes because their husband stopped drinking. Others said they were able to explain to their husband that what he did was wrong. One woman explained: 'As women, we can influence the behavior of our men. We need to have patience, and explain to them that what they are doing is wrong.' Others told me their men changed as their children grew up: children often confronted their fathers in an attempt to correct them. Carlos, Margarita's son, went to eat at the house of Margarita's sister and her husband. During the dinner, the uncle hit his wife in the face. Carlos stood up and said: 'Why do you hit your wife? She is the one who makes you a dinner every day! Stop that!' By defending Margarita's sister, Carlos was in fact also defending his mother. In a patriarchal society like Bolivia, men's power is accepted to a greater extent than the power of women. Margarita's story also shows how her brothers played an important role in her life: it was her brothers who made her marry, and also her brothers who, in fact, threw out her husband the day he came home with another woman in his taxi. As Van Vleet (2008: 175) mentions, brotherly protection does not end when their sister marries.

This analysis shows that for women domestic violence is often not a reason to separate. As the concept of *marianismo* describes, suffering is part of women's experiences. However, studies that use the concept of *marianismo* assume that the women suffer because they follow Mary's example. Reality shows that women suffer because they want to behave according to the societal norms, because of economic factors, because their gender inequality intersects with class inequality. Women's experiences of domestic violence, do not only have a suffering and accepting side, but also a reactive side.

Rabia

Although suffering seems to be an important part of the violent marriage relations, in the stories of the women the word *rabia* arose time and again. *Rabia* means fury, rage, and anger. First of all, *rabia* was mentioned by women as a reason for men to hit them. Margarita told me:

> He usually hit me when he was drunk. Unfortunately, he started to drink more and more, because he was frustrated with his life. He felt *rabia* for not be able to be rich. He felt *rabia* for being married to me, whereas he wanted to play around with other women.

She also told me that sometimes he hit her out of jealousy, another form of *rabia*. Other women also gave *rabia*, frustration, powerlessness, and jealousy as the reasons for the aggressive behavior of their husbands. An Aymara woman from La Paz explained: 'He hit me for nothing, just to let me know he was more powerful'. A woman who owned an eatery in Quillacollo said: 'He could not stand it that I made more money than he did.' Others explained that their husbands were afraid they would leave them for another man. In many conversations the word *rabia* came up as a reason for the violence. One day I found Natalia, one of the *sahumeras* crying in front of the gate of the Calvary Hill. She told me about her violent husband:

> My husband, yesterday when I came home, he kicked me in my belly. Because I was late. He was jealous. But I just came from this mountain, I didn't go anywhere. I think it was his *rabia*, because he cannot see anymore. He was a tailor, so he cannot work anymore. Every day I am so scared to go home. He can always find a reason. I might be late, or I don't have enough money, he always feels *rabia*.

As well as referring to anger and rage, *rabia* is also the word for rabies, the canine disease. Infected dogs attack without any reason, because of their illness, just as their husbands do. Bolivians use the term *rabia* often to refer to the anger they experience for the inability to change the unbearable circumstances of life.

Rabia was not only the reason given by women for being hit, but also the most frequently mentioned reaction of women to the violence. For instance, Margarita told me: 'I felt an intense *rabia*. I hated him, but I could not change it, I had to stay with him.' Natalia recounted: 'This *rabia* sits inside and swallows you up.' Natalia was a big and robust woman. When I met Natalia's husband I was surprised to see such a tiny man. I asked her if she had ever hit him back and she responded:

> Only once, with a stick. He came home drunk and couldn't find his key. Then he started to break all the windows with stones and he tried to force the door. He was out of his mind, and then I took a stick and smashed him on his head. Also on his knees. It was only the one time. Normally, he is very quick, and when he hits me, I fall down quickly. Usually he starts punching my face, next my belly, and afterwards I don't know because I cannot remember. This time I attacked him before he could do anything. Only one time... And I have known it; I can better keep my *rabia* within me...

Women are often not in the position to express their rage.

In the Mexican context *coraje* is a term described in scholarly literature as similar in the meaning to the word *rabia* in Bolivia (e.g. Behar, 1990; Cartwright, 2007; Steenbeek, 1995). Behar notices *coraje* as a key word in the life story of Esperanza, a Mexican indigenous market trader (Behar, 1990: 240-241). *Coraje* is translated as a very deep anger or rage; 'an emotion and illness state especially common to women that is sparked by strife between spouses or between mother and child, *coraje* forms part of a feminine ontology of suffering and despair' (Behar, 1990: 241). According to Behar, Esperanza views her married life as the embodiment of a constant, suppressed rage. Also Steenbeek (1995: 231) speaks of *coraje* as a powerful emotion experienced by Mexican women. According to Steenbeek, *coraje* means both courage and fury. It is a word that women use to refer to the injustice that has been done to them as women. That requires courage. That is why it is not just an emotion but a form of consciousness. That is also the reason why men, although they might suffer to a certain extent, will never reach this power. *Coraje* is an experience that is developed amongst women together.

In the Bolivian context, I never came across the word *coraje*, but *rabia* was the most commonly used form to express this emotion. According to Margarita '*Rabia* is frustration, an emotion felt when someone ignores your rights. You want to hurt the other, because the other hurt you before.' Margarita associates the emotion directly with the suffering in her marriage, but explains that the emotion is not restricted to marriage issues.

> I can also feel *rabia* when I work but do not gain enough money to buy food, or when I quarrel with the other vendors. But the *rabia* I felt in my marriage was the strongest and worst anger I ever felt.

Both Behar (1990) and Steenbeek (1995) emphasize that *coraje* is restricted to women's experiences. Instead, the word *rabia* is used to refer to a state of defenselessness and frustration that can happen to both men and women. However, the circumstances in which the word *rabia* is used, differ for each sex. According to the stories, men hit women out of *rabia*, whereas the women experience *rabia* as a result of being hit by their husbands. As *rabia* is part of an ontology of both men and women's suffering, it is a useful concept to break the dichotomy between *machismo* and *marianismo*. Although women often stay in an abusive relationship, they do not simply accept their suffering. Instead, *rabia* was one of the most important reactions of women to the physical violence to which they were exposed. *Rabia* is not a passive emotion that encourages the women to endure their suffering lot, but is a powerful and belligerent attitude. *Rabia* does not fit into the *marianismo* perspective, that prescribes only submission, passivity, and suffering.

Interestingly, both Behar (1990) and Cartwright (2007) emphasize that *coraje* can manifest itself physically in the form of an illness. Symptoms include diarrhea, headaches, lethargy, and stomach aches. Cartwright (2007: 530) classifies *coraje* as a Latino folk illness, like the illness *susto* that was used by Margarita to explain her daughter's death. These folk illnesses consist of both physical and emotional sensations, and are usually cured by *curanderos* or *yatiris*. In the Bolivian context, *rabia* was not explained as an illness and no physical symptoms were mentioned. This does not exclude the possibility that *rabia* is perceived as an illness. The emotion jealousy or *celos* was perceived as an illness that can possess people. *Celos* was, together with *rabia*, one of the main reasons that the women mentioned for being beaten by their husbands.

Coraje can be cured by *curanderos*. In the same way as the sorcerers described by Jansen (1987), the *curanderos* master the art of sorcery with its strict rules on words, sequence, timing, and ingredients. As Favret Saada (1980) showed, the spells in witchcraft can have deadly consequences: magic is a discourse in which the power of words can be tremendous. This is also evident in Margarita's explanation of her husband's death. She had blocked the spell that was directed at her by drinking his blood. The 'words' were not able to affect her, but were turned on her husband. By performing this countermeasure, she was able to send the deadly spell in another direction. The drinking of her husband's blood reflects Margarita's agency to decide whether she actually drinks it or not, whether she protects herself against a possible spell or not. As witchcraft is often seen as taboo, Margarita attributes, in words, the decision to protect herself to her brother. By following this suggestion and drinking her husband's blood, Margarita demonstrates a belief in the magical act and, even more, she is practicing it to protect herself. By drinking the blood to prevent a possible curse, she also performs an act of vengeance, as the curse turned back on her husband. As Jansen (1987: 116-117) notes on witchcraft in Algeria, it is especially practiced by marginalized women to influence unequal intimate relations. As women do not have the possibility, nor social and economic power, to change the relationships in other ways, magic gives them a powerful tool that operates as a symbolic discourse in a different kind of logic. It gives them the power to interfere in their relationships on a spiritual level and feel strong in another way, not by using physical violence, but by magic, they try to ensure retribution. It also gives them the possibility to give expression to their distress and give it a place in a magical or supernatural world. As the data below from my Bolivian research shows, Mary too can be mobilized for revenge and interfere viciously, like a magical spell.

Revengeful Mary

This section will take a closer look at the way women perceive the Virgin of Urkupiña in their attempts to deal with domestic violence and *rabia*. The Virgin of Urkupiña is not seen as Ellsberg et al (2000) indicate 'as a model of spiritual perfection and purity.' Neither does Mary reinforce 'virginity, chastity and the ability to suffer and willingness to serve' as described by Salyers Bull (1998). The Virgin of Urkupiña is not perceived merely in these marianistic terms. The Bolivians instead emphasize Mary's vicious side: Mary can also experience *rabia*. The Virgin of Urkupiña is seen as a decisive and authoritarian divinity, who can also act out of vengeance. She can direct her *rabia* against you.

Because during colonization the Virgin Mary became associated with Pachamama, she is perceived not only as an intermediary between God and the people. Pachamama was seen as a goddess of fertility with independent powers. Most pilgrims still relate Pachamama to the Virgin of Urkupiña. Therefore 'independent power' is attributed to the her. She is not merely a mediator between God and human beings, but can interfere independently. She has the power to evaluate the situation and decide if intervention is needed. As Mary is interpreted as the Earth Mother, she is seen as a powerful goddess of fertility rather than as a suffering woman, as the Catholic Church dictates.

As described in the previous chapters, Pachamama acts according to the principles of complementarity and reciprocity, and these characteristics were applied to the Catholic deities as well. As in the Andean cosmology all deities unite both good and bad qualities in themselves, Mary is also perceived as an entity who can bring punishment, as well as help. In Catholicism, Mary is described above all as a female example of obedience, self-sacrifice, motherhood, chastity, and humility (De Haardt, 2008). The church emphasizes only her 'good' side and has rejected associations of Mary with violence, anger, and vengeance. Interestingly, throughout the world there are various examples of goddesses of vengeance who unite good and caring characteristics with violent, harmful and revengeful powers (e.g. Caldwell, 2004; Grodzins Gold, 1994; McCarthy Brown, 2001). As shown in chapter four, according to the Bolivian devotees, Mary too may act violently. To please her and to make sure she will not punish them, people are obliged to bring her offerings in a reciprocal form. Therefore, the Virgin of Urkupiña enforces obedience and seems to have a strong will. As Margarita's dreams show, the Virgin of Urkupiña also appears to people in dreams. Margarita gets advice on how to sell in order to obtain the best results. The sacristan of the church of Urkupiña also declared that he got instructions from Urkupiña:

> After being in the army in Santa Cruz, I started to work with a motor-taxi. All the time I was in the army I wanted to do this. I saved my money, and together with a friend bought a motorcycle. We were so proud! One night, just before the *fiesta* of Urkupiña started in Quillacollo, where I was born, the Virgin of Urkupiña appeared in my dreams and said to me: "You don't belong in this place. Come back to the place you belong." Next day I sold my half of the motorcycle to my friend, took a plane and came back to Quillacollo. I went to church, to see my *Virgencita*. The priest came up to me and asked me where I had been and where I was going. Then he offered me a job as a sacristan in church. Now I've been working here for 24 years!

These stories show the Virgin of Urkupiña to be a demanding force, in which suffering is not perceived as her main quality. The Virgin's 'spiritual strength' as defined by Stevens (1973) as 'an infinite capacity for humility and sacrifice' is not reflected in the perceptions of devotees. Instead, her strength lies in her capacities of persuasion and command.

Her image's appearance does not emphasize her suffering qualities, but instead, she is portrayed as a rich, powerful, and authoritarian lady. As Freedberg (1989: 109) notes, in some cases, there is a perceived relationship between looks and efficacy. Pilgrims may be so impressed by how the image looks that they are filled with an even stronger belief in what it can achieve. The Virgin of Urkupiña is decked with gold and jewellery; she has a crown and a staff, which also reflect her allure as a decisive powerful woman. Her clothes, full of embroidery and brilliance, and her expensive jewellery complete the picture of power. She does not broadcast an image of a humble and sober mother, struggling for her son, but evokes an association with power and sovereignty.

This relates to a study of Herrera-Sobek (1990) who gives a feminist interpretation of the Virgin of Guadalupe in the Mexican ballad. She writes (Herrera-Sobek, 1990: 51):

> The Virgin of Guadalupe in the Mexican ballad, however, is not necessarily perceived as a frail, submissive, subservient, weak-hearted female. On the contrary, she is conceived as a warrior who can aid the various battalions to achieve victory over their enemies.

Herrera-Sobek notes that the Virgin of Guadalupe is a 'celestial aristocratic figure who had been crowned with monarchical terminology Queen of the Mexicans, Queen of the Americas and Empress of America.' Her titles declare authority instead of submissiveness. In addition, Herrera-Sobek calls Guadalupe a warrior, an association that also contradicts the notion of *marianismo*. The Virgin of Urkupiña is also perceived as a belligerent woman, with an authoritarian appeal. She has been proclaimed 'Patroness of National Integration' and on some occasions she wears a sash in the colors of the Bolivian flag. A sash is also a symbol of authority, as it is easily associated with the president. Her authoritarian, self-assured, decisive characteristics are not in line with what the *marianismo*-complex prescribes.

Presented with pictures of different Marian representations when I was working with the elicitation method, the Bolivian believers felt attracted to other highly decorated Marys that looked wealthy, proud and content. For some people, the Virgin of Urkupiña was not the same as the Virgin Mary. They explained that the Virgin Mary was simple and humble, whereas the Virgin of Urkupiña was rich and powerful. For many believers, the Virgin of Urkupiña was not perceived as being part of a pantheon with God and Jesus, but seems to stand by herself. A Bolivian anthropologist explained that this perception is derived from the pre-colonial Andean cosmology, in which a polytheistic pantheon existed in which no hierarchical distinction was made between the several supernatural deities. The Virgin of Urkupiña is also often perceived as one of several goddesses. Therefore, believers attribute different characteristics to the various Bolivian Marian representations.

As we have seen in chapter three, the Virgin of Urkupiña is feared for the power and violence with which she can give and act. The Virgin of Urkupiña seems to be dominant, strong, and she controls her relationships. In fact, she acts according to the stereotypical behavior of the *macho* man. In this way, the dichotomy between the two concepts *machismo* and *marianismo* is broken, as Mary, who is supposed to behave according to the prescribed characteristics of *marianismo*, is interpreted by the Bolivians as a feminine deity that incorporates *machismo*-behavior.

In the reciprocal relationship with Mary, pilgrims come to the Virgin of Urkupiña predominantly to make petitions. Although the majority of these petitions are material, women also take their family struggles to Mary. As described by Gemzöe (2000) on pilgrimage to Fatima, women take especially 'feminine matters' to Mary, such as issues related to mothering, dying children, pregnancy, and marriage. At the shrine of Urkupiña, sometimes devotees write letters and put these under the Virgin's dress. Most letters are from women and contain worries about children, husbands, brothers, sisters, and parents. The Virgin is approached as a powerful medium. According to most pilgrims, the Virgin does not only operate on an emotional level, but is able to change existing situations. Most pilgrims do not relate their personal suffering to Mary's suffering, but rather ask her for powerful intervention, as a fragment of one letter indicates:

> Dear Virgin of Urkupiña, I know your inexplicable powers. I trust you, that's why I want to tell you my story. I have always had faith, and you have given me so many of the things I asked. Now I would ask an ultimate favor, as I don't know how to solve this problem otherwise. You know Marcos, my husband. I cannot believe that our relationship is meant to be a good marriage. Dear Virgin of Urkupiña, can you please change my husband, so that he stops drinking, and please can you make him stop hitting me?

This letter demonstrates that women ask for divine intervention to change the relationship with their husband. Pilgrims believe the Virgin of Urkupiña to have the special powers to help and intervene in their lives. This woman does not ask Mary to help her accept her suffering, as *marianismo* would imply, but she actively asks for change. Mary is not seen as a passive symbol who only understands and consoles because of her own suffering, but is approached to intervene actively and change existing situations.

Interestingly, women approach Mary with their *rabia*, and ask her to change the personality of their violent husbands. Because of the complementarity principle, Mary can also punish. Therefore, she can act out of *rabia* and turn her anger against you. If pilgrims fail to keep their promises or behave badly, the Virgin of Urkupiña can decide to mete out punishment. Margarita's dream of the Virgin appearing while her husband passed by and collapsed showed that her husband would be punished for his deeds. Margarita also mentioned that it was because of Mary that the curse fell on him. In the perceptions of these women, Mary not only helps them to accept their suffering by consoling them, but she also gives feelings of rancor a place because pilgrims ask her to take revenge on their husbands.

According to the Bolivan battered women, the Virgin of Urkupiña can act furiously and angrily. She is not a generous and suffering divinity, but has the power to destroy. For example, Natalia, the woman I found crying at the entrance of the Calvary Hill, told me about Mary's *rabia*: 'My husband was a tailor, and now he is becoming blind. I think it is Mary's punishment for being so bad to me for so many years.' In the perception of the Bolivian women, Mary is able to exact vengeance for them.

Remarkably, the women who spoke openly about their experiences with domestic violence, often told me they asked Mary for vengeance, to translate their own *rabia* into deeds against their husbands. In the letters the requests for intervention were more moderate. Women asked Mary to put a stop to the violence, but they did not ask Mary directly to punish their husbands. Letters are part of an institutionalized discourse, as the priest might open the letter and read it. Most believers know that asking Mary for aggressive acts is contrary to church teachings. The verbal discourse, however, shows that women believe that Mary has violent powers that can be called upon.

The Virgin of Urkupiña is thus not only a suffering and obedient Mary, but can act out of *rabia*, furiously and belligerently. Heessels (2005) who studied how Mexicans employ the Virgin of Guadalupe to deal with their *coraje*, showed that the Mexicans come to Guadalupe to rid themselves of their *coraje*. Guadalupe is able to free them from their emotions and calm them. The Mexican believers emphasize that Guadalupe cannot be approached for acts of vengeance. The Bolivian women employ the Virgin of Urkupiña differently to deal with their *rabia*. They come to Urkupiña to hand over their *rabia*. They are often in no position to leave their husbands, because they need them for economic and social reasons, but they can transfer their anger to Mary. In this way they feel relieved, but they also do justice to their powerlessness and anger. After all, the Virgin of Urkupiña will decide whether she will turn her anger against the husbands who provoked the *rabia* in the women.

Conclusions

I started this chapter with an expression of Margarita: 'I prefer to have boys, as they suffer less than girls.' For many Bolivian women, suffering seemed to be related to their gender. This chapter emphasized domestic violence as a dominant form of gender related suffering as it happens on a wide scale in Bolivian society. During fieldwork I collected numerous narratives of women's experiences of domestic violence in their marriages. With this material I was able to offer an alternative theoretical approach to the study of domestic violence and female suffering in Latin America than that in terms of *marianismo* in which women are said to embrace the values of the Virgin Mary as a passive and submissive role-model to endure and accept their suffering. I have shown that previous studies failed to look at women's actual interpretations of Mary, and merely assumed that women venerate Mary for her submissiveness and passivity. This chapter studied Bolivian women's interpretations of the Virgin of Urkupiña and demonstrated that Mary has both a suffering as well as a vicious side.

Studying the domestic violence experiences of these women, it was shown that women do not only experience suffering, but also a profound anger. They do not merely accept suffering as a moral quality, although most women in an abusive relationship stay with their violent husbands. Women usually refrain from divorce for economic and social reasons, not because, as studies on *marianismo* simply assume, they accept suffering in a submissive way. Many women speak of *rabia*, or a profound feeling of rage. This state of furiousness, rage, and frustration about their inability to change situations means that women are not passive victims, but rather shows that, despite their suffering, they do experience powerful and belligerent emotions about the violence committed against them. The concept of *rabia* has been described in the Mexican context in terms of *coraje* (e.g. Behar, 1990; Cartwright, 2007; Steenbeek, 1995), but according to Behar (1990) and Steenbeek (1995) this rage was restricted to women's experiences. In Bolivia, however, *rabia* is an emotion experienced by both men and women. In relation to domestic violence in Bolivia, men beat women out of *rabia*, whereas the women experience *rabia* as a result of being hit by their husbands. Finding that *rabia* came to the fore as a predominant reaction of women to the violence they suffered, contributed to the critical studies on *marianismo* that have shown that women's suffering is not as passive as supposed by authors that make uncritical use of the concept.

In addition, my study contributed to the criticism on the concept of *marianismo* by looking at battered Bolivian women's actual interpretations of the Virgin of Urkupiña. Instead of a role model of obedience and submission, due to the integration with Pachamama, she is venerated for her ability to act out of *rabia* herself. Battered women do not approach Mary to be consoled or ask for help in accepting their fate, but instead they ask Mary to change their husbands or to take revenge on him. Instead of a submissive role model, venerated for her qualities of enduring suffering, the Virgin Mary in Bolivia is embraced as a powerful goddess of vengeance. She is seen as an vengeful goddess, something that is also reflected in her rich and powerful appearance, who has independent powers to decide whether and how she will intervene. In fact, women project their emotions of suffering and rage onto the Virgin of Urkupiña. In distinction to what the *marianismo*-complex assumes, the Virgin Mary is venerated not only for her capacity to suffer but also for her capacity to feel rage. As women themselves are not in the position to confront their violent husbands, they transfer their rage to Mary, who has the power to intervene on their behalf. These insights do more justice to the agency of women and further criticize the notion of *marianismo* and the supposed dichotomy between *machismo* and *marianismo*.

Photo 7: Dance group *Tinkus San Simon* during the *Entrada* of Urkupiña 2007 in the streets of Quillacollo

7

MEANINGS OF MOVEMENT: CONSTRUCTING ETHNIC DIFFERENCE IN RELIGIOUS DANCE PROCESSIONS

'In front of Mary and the crowd we display our indigenous roots'

- Judy, 12-8-2005

> The most intense moment is when we arrive at the church, after all those long and exhausting hours of dancing. There, in front of Mary's statue, that has been placed outside, a large crowd has gathered to welcome us and it is the ultimate time that we display our indigenous roots. The energy is tremendous, as it marks the end of the route. It evokes a feeling of victory: we made it together! We save one of our most wild and beautiful figures for this moment, and I love this part the most, as everyone gives everything, completely! We are proud of our culture; therefore we dance the *Tinkus* San Simon.

This account is part of a conversation held with Judy, a 24 years old member of the *Tinku*-dance group San Simon from Cochabamba. The *Tinku* group performed its dance at the *Entrada Folklórica*, or folkloric dance procession that is held on the 14th and 15th of August in the streets of Quillacollo during the *fiesta* of Urkupiña. Over a distance of four kilometers more than sixty dance groups perform their dances, following each other along a trajectory that starts close to the Calvary Hill and goes through the town towards the church that hosts the image of the Virgin of Urkupiña.

Dance is a bodily movement connected to the religious realm in many ways. As Guerrero Jimenez (2004: 97) puts it: 'Dance is sacred.' In various cultures, dance is an expression of devotion and is connected to the divine world (e.g. Friedson, 2005; Hanna, 1988; Jansen, 1991; Katyal, 2001; Sklar, 2001). Dance, for example, can be a bodily form of worship (e.g. Katyal, 2001); dance can elicit spiritual experience (e.g. Friedson, 2005; Tamisari, 2006); dance can embody the supernatural and the dancer becomes possessed by the divine (Hanna 1988); dance can mirror divinity in masks and movements (Hanna, 1988; Jansen, 1991), and dance can be an embodiment of vows made to Mary, as Sklar (2001) has indicated for the dancers in Tortuga. In the Bolivian *Entradas*, the dancers see themselves, and are often viewed by others, as pilgrims who embody their vows in dancing (Delgado Morales, 1999; Van Kessel, 1992; Van Laan, 1993).

In the pre-Columbian Andean world, dancing was already used in the worship of Andean deities. Theatrical dance performance was well-established in Inca times (Henrique Rojas, 1996: 41; Wilson, 2000): the Incas performed their dances in religious contexts, mostly agricultural rituals (Lautaro Nuñez, 1989: 9). When the Spaniards came, they contributed by introducing a dance drama of conquest. The Spaniards were familiar with their own, home-grown forms of Iberian church dance. These dances were considered an unquestioned part of Christian orthodoxy (Poole, 1990: 110). The missionaries also used the religious dances in order to evangelize the indigenous people by expressing the Catholic doctrine in dance. Religious dancing, therefore, became a performance that was associated with Catholicism, and Andean dances were assimilated into the Spanish idea of devotion. However, their functions were different: the Spaniards danced in order to express Catholic doctrine, whereas the Andean people danced as a tactic to express their own religiosity. Pretending to be Catholics, they could pass on their Andean religious ideas (Poole, 1990: 117). During the colonization, dance became a form of resistance for the Andean people, and one of the most important functions of dance became representation, or authenticity as Poole (1991: 309) points out: 'Pilgrimage dances were exploited as a means of expressing indigenous identity and non-submission to the foreign culture which pilgrimage and Christianity ostensibly represented.' It shows that historically, in the pilgrimage dance processions, religion and ethnicity came together. This raises the question whether and how religion and ethnicity are linked in the devotion to Mary today.

According to Van Laan (1993: 17) until the 1950s the religious dances were a relatively autonomous popular movement of the lower classes against the regime of the Catholic Church. The Spaniards associated the indigenous dances with drunkenness, disorder, and the breakdown of moral and sexual control, and the general public had a negative opinion of them (Poole, 1990). After the Agrarian Reform in 1952, in which ethnic identity was re-valued, the dances were more strictly organized, and well-organized *Entradas Folklóricas* became part of the Catholic feasts. Over time the *Entrada Folklórica* for the Virgin of Urkupiña has also developed from a regional indigenous celebration into a particularly urban *mestizo* event. Until the 1950s the *fiesta* was mostly celebrated by people from the indigenous Quechua mountain villages around Quillacollo, who saw in Mary an embodiment of Pachamama, or Mother Earth, and came with their music and dances to Quillacollo to venerate their goddess of fertility.

Since then, the inhabitants of Quillacollo, mostly merchants of mixed Spanish descent, became interested in the *fiesta* and started to organize dance performances for the Virgin by founding organized dance fraternities (Sanchez, 1992: 141). The *Entrada* of Urkupiña has increased in popularity and belongs, together with the *Entrada* of the Carnaval in Oruro for the *Virgen del Socavón* and the *Entrada* of *Gran Poder* in La Paz, to one of the three largest dance processions in the country. From the 1970s the *fiesta* also began to attract pilgrims from outside Quillacollo, and expanded into a *fiesta* of national, and even international, fame (Mendoza Flores, 1996). During the *Entrada*, dance groups from all over Bolivia come to Quillacollo to make their cultural performance over a length of four kilometers, a performance that can mean up to ten hours of dancing.

During my fieldwork in 2005 and 2007 I joined the dance group *Tinkus* San Simon and participated in the *Entrada Folklórica* of Urkupiña. This enabled me to note not only religious meanings but numerous other meanings in the dance processions. For instance, the words of Judy, quoted above, show the complex meanings of dance performance, as different elements play a role. In her account Judy mentions both Mary, her indigenous roots, and her emotions of pride, joy, and belonging.

Following Coleman & Eade (2004), who propose to study movement as a constitutive element of pilgrimage, this chapter will look at the meanings of the physical movement of dancing, and the metaphorical meanings that dance has for dancers and audience. In particular, I focus on how people deal with ethnicity in pilgrimage, and how ethnicity is linked to religious experience. The *Tinku*-dance, for example, refers to an Andean ritual fight for the fertility of the earth, carried out in the Northern Potosí region. Most other folkloric dances also represent historical and cultural events of the Bolivian ethnic groups.

When joining the dance processions, I was constantly overwhelmed by the festive and energetic atmosphere, and the combination of senses involved that increased the impact of the experience. The combination of movement, singing, colors, music, and drinking made it, in the first instance, very tempting to analyze the dance processions in terms of Turner's concept of 'communitas.' Communitas, as an egalitarian state of spontaneous bonding in which social boundaries are dissolved, focuses in particular on processes of inclusion. However, in line with Gavanas (2008:128) I argue that it is necessary to look beyond the concept of communitas, as dance - and music - can be a tool for communication and inclusion across social structures and positions, but may also be used for exclusion and reinforcing boundaries between groups. In this I follow Coleman (2002: 363) who argues that the most valuable work in the study of pilgrimage is that which looks outward, making points about human behaviour through using 'pilgrimage' as a case-study rather than focussing on the institution itself as a firmly deliniated category of action. Religion should not be seen as an autonomous isolated realm of human activity, but should be connected to the wider social context. In line with Coleman, I argue that one has to look beyond the boundaries of what belongs officially to a particular pilgrimage in order to understand what power issues are involved in the performance of ethnicity at the pilgrimage.

Since 1999 an *Entrada Autóctona* has been organized, which is held before the *Entrada Folklórica*. The *Entrada Autóctona* aims to 'rediscover the *fiesta* of Urkupiña in its origin', that is, to give space to the indigenous communities to perform their dances and show the variety in their cultures (Brun, 2007). The introduction of this 'other' *Entrada* next to the spectacular folkloric urban event, reinforces feelings of distinction, and at the same time, identity. The words *Autóctona* and *Folklórica* relate to a discourse on ethnicity and authenticity, and the fact that a distinction is made between the two made me wonder what were the grounds for such a distinction. The main question of this chapter is how ethnicity is constructed in the dance processions, and what power politics influence the centrality and marginality of certain dance groups. First I will look at which ethnic identity is expressed in each *Entrada*, and how this is done. In terms of Eade & Sallnow (1991) the competing and contested meanings of ethnicity are studied. Since processes of differentiation often lead to inequalities, I will also compare the two *Entradas* to find out if processes of marginalization take place. In addition, the dance processions are analyzed in terms of Turner's (1978) concept of 'communitas' to understand whether and if so, how, they affect the social boundaries.

The *Entrada Folklórica* and the *Entrada Autóctona* of Urkupiña

The top tier of the tribune offers a beautiful panorama of the *Tinkus* San Simon. As far as you can see the street is filled with dancers dressed in colorful indigenous costumes, the bright reds and blues standing out against the gray of the adobe-houses in the background. The red and blue plumes of the women's hats and the long yellow ribbons attached to them wave wildly in the air when the dancers jump, turn, and clap. With synchronized, lively and even wild movements the spectacle slowly approaches. Their songs and yells even drown out the brass band that enthusiastically follows the dancers, accompanying them with energetic *Tinku*-rhythms.

The dancers are lined up in rows of seven. Each row is organized the same way: at both ends, thus closest to the public lining the streets and square, dances a boy, while five girls dance in a line between them. In the *Tinku* group there are more women than men performing, and this arrangement with the boys at the ends is an attempt to protect the girls from an obtrusive public. As about 300 *Tinku*-members participate in the *Entrada Folklórica*, the group is divided into three blocks. The blocks are closed by a few so-called *Machu-tinkus*, boys that perform a different, in general wilder choreography, and who wear eye-catching clothing with spectacular decorations such as plush llamas attached to their helmets and horns in their hands. Each block is separated by a brass band, so all dancers can hear the music behind them.

In front of the group are two guides, dancers that decide and indicate which dance figure to perform. In the ideal situation, all dancers are strictly lined up behind each other, and because of the basic bent *Tinku*-position, everyone should be able to see the signals of the guides. Characteristic for the *Tinku* is a basic step in which the dancers are bent over in a belligerent posture, and wave their arms wildly over the ground. From this position, several figures are performed: these consist of a series of steps, jumps, claps, turns, and movements such as beating the air, that have to be performed by all members in the same order.

The *Tinku*-clothes resemble the indigenous clothes from the Potosí department in several ways. The models and materials look the same, but instead of hand-woven cloth, cheaper fabric is used for the dance suits. Furthermore, the colors are brighter and they are more elaborately decorated. Typical for this region are the white felt hats, decorated with mirrors and colored ribbons worn by women. The mirrors are said by some to be merely decorations: some people told me that only single women have mirrors on their hats. Another reasonable explanation was offered by one of the dancers, who said the mirrors have a function when a woman gets lost in the *campo,* or rural area: the reflection of the sun on the mirrors can be seen from a great distance, thus ensuring that lost women can be found. In the dance, the hats are more extensively decorated. The *monteros*, or leather helmets with plumes that the *tinku*-boys wear, are characteristic for men from the Potosí-region.

The *Tinku* dance refers to an Andean ritual that was performed during the harvest celebrations of the indigenous Quechua people. Nowadays the ritual is performed only in a few villages in the northern Potosí department and southern Oruro department. Gilberto Pauwels, a Belgium missionary and anthropologist living in Bolivia for the past 30 years explains:

> *Tinku* is a Quechua-word for *encuentro* or clash and encounter. The *Tinku* is a fight in which members of different communities battle with each other. The blood that flows is an offering to Mother Earth, as thanksgiving for the harvest. Actually, the one who loses is in fact the winner, as he brings the greatest offering and will get the most of protection. A real *Tinku* is practiced between two equals. Because the Andean cosmology is based on equality, you can only invite equals, of the same sex, age, height, and weight. Since 1993 women are also allowed to join.

Thus, the *Tinku* dance is derived from a fighting ritual from Andean religiosity with underlying notions of egalitarianism.

During the *Entrada Folklórica* on the 14th and 15th of August, not only the *Tinku* is performed, but also several other dances, such as *Incas, Tobas, Morenadas*, *Negritos, Caporales*, *Phujllay*, *Diablada* and *Llameradas*. It is beyond the scope of this chapter to describe all these dances in detail, but most dances represent rituals and events of Andean cosmology and history. For example the *Inca*-dance refers to the *Inca*-empire, the *Tobas* represents the indigenous warrior-population of the Southern Chaco in Bolivia (although they wear unrepresentative spectacular feather arrays, inspired by the North-American Indians). The *Morenadas, Negritos* and *Caporales* refer to the period of slavery during the Spanish colonization; the first two dances represent the slaves, whereas the latter refers to the *capataces*, the slave-owners. The *Phujllay* refers to the battle of Jumbati in Tarabuco in 1816 in which the local indigenous population was able to triumph over the Spaniards, and the *Diablada* represents both the struggle between good and evil and the spirit *el Tio* of the mineworkers, who had been given the face of the devil during colonization. The *Llameradas* refers to the Andean shepherds who travelled with their llamas through the mountains to exchange salt for other products. All dances can be distinguished by their different costumes, characteristic music and dance styles. To guarantee the variety of dances in the *Entrada Folklórica*, the *Asociación de los Conjuntos Folklóricos Virgen de Urkupiña,* the association that takes care of the dancers' interests and which is responsible for the organization of the *Entrada Folklórica*, made the rule that a maximum of eight fraternities of the same dance, such as *Tinkus*, is allowed to participate.

In the big national *Entrada Folklórica* of Urkupiña - like in the *Entradas* of the *Carnaval* in Oruro and *Gran Poder* in La Paz - not only local groups perform, but fraternities from all over the country are brought together. Most groups are from the urban areas such as Cochabamba, Quillacollo, or La Paz, and are often based on a certain profession, for example only *transportistas*, - transporters - truck drivers, bus drivers or taxi drivers - who dance, for instance, the *Morenada* or *Diablada*, or students who often perform the *Tinku* and *Caporales*. These nationally renowned *Entradas* can last for a full 24 hour day, and in these big dance processions the dancers perform on two successive days. Over the past decades the national *Entradas* have increased the number of groups performing, and the numbers of dancers and visitors have also increased. According to the local newspaper *Los Tiempos*, in 1977, the total number of dancers who participated in the *Entrada Folklórica* of Urkupiña was 2,000, divided among approximately 20 dance groups. In 2005 more than 10,000 dancers from 56 dance groups participated. In 2008 the newspaper reported 15,000 dancers and 60 groups.

The prices of the costumes in the dance groups can differ greatly, causing the economic investment for dancing to vary. For the *Tinku*-dance, the costumes are relatively cheap, costing around 200 BOB (20 euros), whereas the impressive hand-made costumes and masks of the *Diablada* - the devils dance - and *Morenada* - slavery dance - can rise to over 500 dollars! As a result, these dances especially are often associated with status. Some people save money the whole year to be able to join a dance fraternity. As well as the costumes, most fraternities also ask for a membership fee and a contribution to pay the brass band. In addition, each fraternity has to pay a registration fee to the *Asociación de los Conjuntos Folklóricos Virgen de Urkupiña* in order to participate in the *Entrada*.

Participating in the *Entrada Folklórica* can be a costly affair and so poor people are excluded from participating. Therefore, since 1999 an *Entrada Autóctona* has been organized and which takes place prior to the official *Entrada* of Urkupiña and includes the marginalized indigenous people. The introduction of an *Entrada Autóctona* has been derived from the *Carnaval* in Oruro, in which, since 1995 a dance procession is held in which indigenous groups from the tiny villages and communities around Oruro participate. Abercrombie (1998: 162) describes how in 1993 dancers and musicians from a nearby village came to Oruro to reclaim their pride in being 'the authentic possessors of the national heritage.' Two years later several rural dance groups participated in a more organized way, and every year since then an indigenous dance procession is held before the *Entrada Folklórica*. This *Entrada* is called *Anata*, referring to the indigenous harvest feasts as celebrated before the colonization. One of the organizers of the *Entrada Autóctona* in Quillacollo told me how in the *Entrada Folklórica* for Urkupiña the indigenous groups were marginalized, as they could not adjust to the strictness of the organization, nor did they have the money to pay the registration fees. Therefore the *Casa de la Cultura* in Quillacollo and a group of journalists took the initiative to organize a special *Entrada* for the indigenous groups, with the aim 'to rediscover the indigenous values.'

In the *Entrada Autóctona* the groups do not have to pay money to take part in the procession. In 2007, for the first time, the *Alcaldia* - mayor - of Quillacollo donated money for the organization of the *Entrada Autóctona*. William Brun, one of the organizers relates:

> They gave us 10,000 BOB - 1000 euros. With the money we can give money to the groups that need it for their transportation. In addition, at the end of the route we gave something that is needed in the *campo*, such as oil, sugar and rice to all the groups.

He also tells that money is collected in the street where the *Entrada* ends, to buy the food that is prepared and offered at the end of the performance. Also the *chicha* - alcoholic corn drink -that is offered in baskets to the dancing groups is paid for by the neighbors.

In the *Entrada Autóctona,* groups mostly from tiny indigenous villages around Quillacollo perform their dances. In 2007 representatives of villages further away from the lowlands (Beni and the Yungas) also participated. The dance groups, consisting of around twenty dancers, are usually smaller than the groups of the *Entrada Folklórica*. The *Macheteros*, a dance typical of a part of the Beni-department, named after the *machete* - knife for fighting and agriculture -

were present with only six members (Padilla, 1993). The *Entrada Autóctona* takes far less time than the *Folklórica*. In about six hours all groups pass through the streets of Quillacollo. Rather than ten thousand participants, only 38 tiny groups with a total of less than a thousand dancers take part (*Los Tiempos*, 2008).

The dances of the *Entrada Autóctona* are not accompanied by a brass band, but their music is performed on 'authentic' instruments, such as *charangos*, wooden flutes or pan flutes. As they make their own music when dancing, their choreographies are less complex than those in the *Entrada Folklórica*. In addition, there are no representations of devils, slave drivers, or other spectacular figures; the costumes of the dancers are more modest. Most groups wear hats and ponchos that serve as markers to indicate the origin of the dance or dancers. As Abercrombie (1998: 154) notes, the rural communities wear their own clothes and represent themselves, rather than others from more 'authentically indigenous' times or locations. Often the dances are named after the rhythms that are played by certain instruments, for example the *Sicuriada* refers to the *sicu*, or large pan flute.

The organizers of the *Entrada Autóctona* want to make the acknowledgement that the original rhythms and dances are related to Andean rites. Therefore the *Entrada* starts in the morning with an Andean ritual at the beginning of the route in which a collective offer ritual, or *k'oa*, is performed in the presence of the organizers, the dancers, and any visitors who want to attend. The *k'oa* is a ritual usually carried out for Pachamama, to ask her help in fertility issues. Several authorities that work with *campesinos* were invited to put the offering material on the coals, while saying prayers and making petitions aloud. The *k'oa* was first of all dedicated to Pachamama and the productivity of the earth. Next, it was performed to enlighten national and regional authorities in governing the country, and of course to wish good luck to all dancers. The Virgin of Urkupiña was also named in the speeches, but Pachamama seemed to be allocated a more important role. Especially the indigenous dancers from the highlands, emphasized they venerated Pachamama in their dances. In 2007 the *k'oa* was performed at the square in front of the church, but no church authorities were present.

The route of the *Entrada Autóctona* is about half the length of that of the *Entrada Folklórica*. The performance is less spectacular, and the groups do not follow each other in well-organized continuity: there are many breaks and long interruptions. A visitor recounted:

> I would like to watch their dances, but I left, because it takes too much time before the next group passes by. I decided to walk the route in the opposite direction, so I could see a bit.

As a result there is a much smaller audience in the street than can be observed during the *Entrada Folklórica,* nor is there the level of interaction between dancers and public. There is far less clapping, whistling, and yelling to encourage the dancers, fewer offers of refreshments, *chicha,* or beer, and fewer tourists taking pictures. At the end of the day, when the *Entrada Autóctona* has finished, tribunes are constructed everywhere for the much more popular *Entrada Folklórica* the next day.

Ethnicity as social identity

To analyze how ethnicity is constructed in the dance procession it is necessary first to reflect on the concept of ethnicity. Following Malešević (2004), as outlined in chapter two, I view ethnicity as a social relation that embodies culturally distinct collectivities. In addition, it is a social identity that is experienced collectively as well as individually (Jenkins, 1997: 14). Thus, ethnicity is a group-identity, as more than one person belong to a certain ethnic group. I follow Nagel (1994: 152) who views identity and culture as the basic building blocks of ethnicity. They are fundamental in the projects of ethnicity, the construction of boundaries and the production of meaning.

The two dance processions produce such meanings, and thereby express social identity (e.g. Jansen, 1997: 87; Mendoza, 1999:1; Mendoza, 2008: 1). I agree with Guss (2000: 9) who views cultural performances as

> important dramatizations that enable participants to understand, criticize, and even change the worlds in which they live. ... The public displays provide forums in which communities can reflect upon their realities.

This relates to Morgan's argument (2005: 149) that dance, as a visual practice, is a medium in which people form, transmit, and modify their self-understandings and identity, and in which they encounter other groups, and form, transmit, and convey understandings of them. The *Entradas* of Urkupiña show clearly that these identities can also be ethnic. Mendoza (1998: 165) even states that folkloric music and dance performance in the Andes are among the most dynamic and creative realms in which people shape ethnic distinctions and identities.

When looking at identity it is important to situate it in a historical context because the symbols, performances, and objects that are used to define identity develop over time (Frijhoff, 1993). In my view, ethnic identity has a fluid, situational, and dynamic character, and is continuously produced and confirmed. It is socially constructed (Nagel, 1994). As there are two *Entradas*, this could be a sign that there are different constructions of identity. In the search for the distinctions and boundaries between groups, people appeal to the concept of authenticity to distinguish themselves from 'the Other' or from the past.

The dances are often described as 'authentic' or 'inauthentic' in terms of the criterion of whether they represent, or are enacted, by local people, according to custom or tradition. The 'authenticity' is not inherent to the dance performance, but is constructed as such in terms of points of views and perceptions (Wang, 1999). To claim a dance to be authentic depends on the subjective interpretation of the person making that claim (e.g. Spooner, 1986:

221). This authentification is one of the problems of 'authenticity': who has the power to determine what should count as authentic? (Bruner & Kirshenblatt-Gimblett, 1994: 459). Discussions on cultural performance often focus on the dangers of commercialization and inauthenticity in its representation (Bossen, 2000: 127). Myers (2001: 679) also points out that 'spectacles' of cultural difference are scrutinized very critically by anthropologists and other cultural analysts on questions of authenticity. He argues that these performances might be new demonstrations - including redefinitions and rediscoveries - of authenticity, but they are no less sincere or genuine as cultural expressions in response to their histories (Myers, 2001: 680). In this case, however, it is clearly the respondents who use the term authentic without any prompting from the researcher to do so.

I adhere to the view of performance, tradition, and culture as constitutive and historically situated (Borsboom, 1998: 17; Bruner, 2005: 5; Jolly, 1992: 49; Kolig, 2005: 308). Bruner (2005: 93) notes how dance performance is often viewed as 'replicas of life in the ethnographic present, static, timeless, without history, without agency, without context', whereas he emphasizes its dynamic nature. In addition, he (2005: 93) writes:

> There does not exist a single real authentic culture, as cultures everywhere are real and authentic, if only because they are there, but this is quite different from the concept of authenticity that implies an inherent distinction between what is authentic and what is inauthentic, applies these labels to cultures, and values one more than the other.

This means that we must ask who applies the label of authenticity to the dances and why. I will elaborate on this further in the section on ethnic inequality.

Cultural performances and 'traditions' can acquire new meanings in different contexts (e.g. Steegstra, 2004: 318; Hobsbawn, 1983: 1; Jolly, 1992: 49). As Hobsbawm (1983) notes in the famous book *The Invention of Tradition*, 'traditions' that appear or claim to be old are often quite recent in origin and sometimes invented. The *Entrada Autóctona*, as a response to the *Entrada Folklórica*, is an example of where 'tradition' and 'authenticity' are actualized and invented. After all, the *Autóctona* was called into being to do justice to the indigenous dancers from the highlands who dominated the *fiesta* of Urkupiña before the fifties. However, it is a more or less organized celebration, different from the way the indigenous groups celebrated the *fiesta* in the past. I follow Grimes (2000: 4) who argues:

> Ritual is a child of imagination, but the ritual imagination requires an invention, a constantly renewed structure, on the basis of which a bodily and communal enactment is possible.

Inherent to a performance is its dynamic and transformative character. Dance performance is also constantly renewed and adjusted. Thus the representations may also change.

Over the past decades there seems to be a renewed interest in Bolivian folklore and the transmission of culture in dance. The number of folkloric events, such as dance processions at Catholic *fiestas*, or festivals organized to display the variety of Bolivia's dances, has increased. More and more dance groups are founded and their membership is also increasing. This change is linked to a revaluation of ethnic identity and 'traditional customs' (e.g. Rockefeller, 1999: 119; Janssens, 2001: 11) According to Gilberto Pauwels, the renewed interest has to do with the revival of Andean awareness because the year 1992 was a milestone in Bolivian history, 500 years after the Spanish *Conquista* of Latin America.

In 2001 the famous *Entrada* for the Virgin of Socavon, the Carnaval of Oruro, was declared a Masterpiece of the Oral and Intangible Heritage by UNESCO. As Goldstein (2004: 135) describes, this distinction is an important event with a collective national identity building function. He also notes (2005: 137) that other places in the country that celebrate a folkloric dance festival can transform their marginal *barrio* into a location of national folkloric significance, thereby contesting their own political, social, and economic marginalization from Bolivian national life. In Quillacollo, an indigenous migrant town in the shadow of the more cosmopolitan city of Cochabamba, the dance processions have grown into one of the most important to the nation. In October 2003 the Act 2536 declared the festivities of the Virgin of Urkupiña to be part of the Bolivian cultural patrimony, in order

> to preserve the traditions and customs of the religious festivity of Our Lady of Urkupiña, to protect folkloric and authentic expressions during the celebration and to preserve the religious spirit that is part of the festivity of the Virgin of Urkupiña (Reglamento de la Ley 2536, 2003).

Thus, the *Entrada Folklórica* is declared to be part of the cultural patrimony. However, it is unclear as to how far the dances refer to the ethnic groups in Bolivia. The dances are not performed by the indigenous population, but by the *mestizos* from the urban areas. As Goldstein (2004: 175) notes: 'in becoming folklore, supposedly rural cultural practices are urbanized, while continuing to stand for the countryside that is said to have produced them.' In the organized *Entrada Folklórica*, the *mestizos* from the Bolivian cities have replaced the indigenous dancers who were the protagonists of the *fiesta* until the 1950s. Nevertheless, it is the *mestizo* dances that are labeled cultural patrimony, as their dances include elements which embody indigenous identity, albeit in a stylized manner (e.g. Mendoza, 1999: 91). In addition, their dances usually do not represent those of the Quechuas, Aymaras, or other indigenous groups, but refer more generally to cultural events in a collective past.

Furthermore, with the introduction of an *Entrada Autóctona*, which can be seen as another reinvention of tradition as it is organized to 'rediscover the indigenous values' and gives back a place to the indigenous people that were marginalized in the *Entrada Folklórica*, the debate on authenticity is reinforced. In fact, another form of ethnicity is expressed in the *Entrada Autóctona*. In line with what Albo (2004) notes on the ethnic identity of the Bolivians, it is important for the indigenous people to self-identify according to their geographical region. In the *Entrada Autóctona*, it is this regional identity especially that is expressed in the dances. Hats and ponchos are markers that indicate the origin of the dancers.

However, it is difficult to draw exact borders between the dances of the two *Entradas*. For instance, while it is true that most dancers of the *Folklórica* are urban *mestizos*, and those of the *Autóctona* indigenous, there are several exceptions. A number of student fraternities from the cities also participate in the *Entrada Autóctona*. The dances are considered 'authentic' because they keep the dress, music, and dance steps of the traditional indigenous dances (Scarborough, 2005). As described before, tradition, culture, authenticity, ethnicity, and dance performance are not fixed and static, but have a fluid and dynamic nature. The dance performances are also constantly renewed; the present day *Entrada Autóctona* is not the same as the unorganized dances that were performed in the past. Furthermore, some groups are allowed to enter both *Entradas*. For example the *Phujllay*, that represents the victory of the indigenous people in the battle of Tarabuco, and the *Negritos*, that represents the former African slaves that live in the Yungas, are dances that are performed at both *Entradas*. The criterion for admission in the *Autóctona* is that they make their own music instead of being accompanied by a brass band. Even a few *Tinku* fraternities participated in the *Entrada Autóctona*, although the *Tinku* dance is a new dance that emerged a few decades ago in the Bolivian folkloric dance processions.[1] However, their costumes had fewer adornments and details, the choreography was simpler and also calmer, and the dancers played the music on large wooden flutes. According to Juan Espinosa, one of the founders, theoretically, the *Tinkus* San Simon are allowed to enter the *Entrada Autóctona* on the condition that they play their own music.

Interestingly, participants of both *Entradas* claim to express ethnic authenticity in their dances. Many people use their perception of their roots to relate to the discourse on ethnic authenticity. For example, many visitors come to watch the cultural spectacle for the Bolivian heritage and folklore that is expressed in the dances. This relates to what Schramm (2004) and Ebron (2000) have called 'roots-pilgrimage', travels in which people are looking for their 'authentic' roots. Watching the dance performances elicits memories of

1 The first *Tinku* fraternity has its origin in the student circles in La Paz, where the first *Tinku* group emerged in 1972. Since then, all over the country *Tinku*-groups have been founded that perform their dances at national and local *Entradas*. *Tinkus San Simon* was founded at the university of San Simon in Cochabamba in 1994, and grew into one of the largest Bolivian dance fraternities with over 500 members.

a shared cultural background. People are nostalgic about their backgrounds, because they want to re-live them in the form of dance procession, at least temporally, empathically and symbolically (e.g. Wang, 1999: 360). For example, an older woman who watched the *Entrada Folklórica* from a plastic chair along the route recounts:

> There is no place in the world where they dance like we do. You see, in Argentina they have the tango, in Brazil they have the samba. And in Bolivia, we have the *Entradas*. When I come here to see the dances, I feel part of my culture. It is our folklore, our past that continues in our present.

Here she refers to an overarching Bolivian folklore, she does not refer directly to *ethnic authenticity*.

The groups that are identified by the *Autóctona* are not of a national, but a local or regional character. This group identity is strengthened by a nostalgic dimension: several visitors started to recall their own dance experiences in the past. For example, a visitor told me proudly how she had been one of the guides of a *Caporales*-group. Although it was more than 30 years ago, she could describe exactly what the costumes looked like, and who had designed them. Seeing the dances, thus not only evoked memories of Bolivian cultural heritage, but also elicits memories of individual persons' youth. In their nostalgia, people express their search for meaningful existence in a shared history.

Participants of both *Entradas* often gave their reasons for their participation in terms of 'I want to demonstrate my culture.' In the 62 dance surveys 39 persons mentioned this as a reason. *Tinku* dancers told me they dance because they 'are proud of our indigenous roots' or 'to show our connection to our ancestors.' For example for Diego, one of the members of the *Tinku*-fraternity San Simon who participated in the *Entrada Folklórica* of Urkupiña in 2005, the main reason to join the *Tinkus* was the link it provided to his father and his culture. He explains:

> Actually, for me it is a tribute to my father who died seven years ago. My father was born in the Potosí department and used to tell me stories about the ritual. That's why I became a member of the *Tinkus San Simon*, to honor my father and the culture he came from.

Through the dance, Diego could connect to his authentic roots, and pay a tribute to his dead father. Nowadays indigenousness is being revalued in the public discourse. Both the *Autóctonas* and *Folklóricas* confirm this. When I walked into a little shop for a drink during the *Entrada Folklórica* 2005, the shop owner smiled at my white appearance in the indigenous *Tinku* clothes and commented:

> The world is changing. People don't have to feel ashamed for being indigenous, instead, they are proud! We already have an Aymara as president and now the Europeans come to Quillacollo to dress up like our native people!

The folkloric *Entrada* is regularly criticized for representing a distorted vision of ethnic culture, for example by performing too complicated choreographies, or by wearing stylized clothes that have never been used in history. Yet, most dancers acknowledge that their dances are inspired by Bolivia's indigenous past. In the 62 surveys that I held, only 7 persons did not know that the dance was inspired by the fighting ritual for fertility. The majority of the dancers is proud 'to keep folklore alive.' Some dancers even acknowledge the relativity of cultural performance. One of the *tinku*-dancing students explained:

> Through the dances culture is transmitted. I am active in keeping the folklore alive. Maybe our clothes are not entirely representative, but I am proud to wear them. It shows I am proud of being part of a country where an indigenous culture still exists! The *Entrada Autóctona* might also transform in the future. The ethnic groups are not static, they also change in modern times. Most of them for example sing in Spanish instead of Quechua or Aymara. And they also wear jeans!

This student defines the national identity in relation to the *Entrada Folklórica,* and feels ethnic subgroups are included despite errors in their exact representations. These errors are considered irrelevant because ethnic identities are changing anyway. Because of the existence of an *Entrada* that claims to express real authentic ethnicity, the members of the *Folklórica* also mark their identity by reflecting on authenticity. For the dancers many elements were connected with authenticity. In the surveys that were held with the *tinku*-dancers, their clothing, the *monteros* - the leather helmets -, the *chuspa* - a colorful woven little bag for transporting coca leaves - and the *abarcas*, sandals made of automobile tires worn by the *campesinos*, were mentioned. Also the *ch'alla*, pouring drinks on the ground before drinking, chewing coca, and feelings of fraternity were mentioned as examples. Also the courage and energy of the dances are mentioned as typical of their traditions. One 27 year old woman told me:

> I am proud to be a *Tinku*. For me it symbolizes courage and energy. The indigenous people from Potosí are famous for this courage and energy that is expressed in their *Tinku*. In the dance I can feel that spirit, and feel proud that I am from Bolivia, that I have indigenous blood.

For her, the courage and energy are the authentic elements of her Bolivianness that are found in the dance.

The participants of the *Entrada Autóctona*, however, claim to express greater authenticity in their dances than is to be found in those of the *Folklórica*. Sometimes the spectacular aspects of the performance in the *Folklórica* are viewed as contradictory to authentic representations (e.g. Scarborough, 2005), as the aesthetics of the spectacle are regarded as distorting the authentic representations carried out in the dance. For example, a female visitor in her forties told me:

> I don't like the *Entrada Folklórica* anymore. It is not original anymore, as you see these dances everywhere in Bolivia. It gets boring after a while. They just want to make a spectacle, a show. The skirts are getting shorter and it won't take long before it transforms into the Carnival of Rio.

Also one of the organizers of the *Entrada Autóctona* comments on the folkloric counter-procession:

> It is only a show, a choreography to show to your friends. On the other hand the *Entrada Autóctona* will show the variety of cultures that are part of Bolivia. It is authentic, whereas the *Folklórica* is not authentic.

The organizer states explicitly that the *Entrada Autóctona* is authentic, and the *Entrada Folklórica* not. Again, the authenticity of the *Entrada Autóctona* is defined by comparison with the folkloric procession. Interestingly, in this view, authenticity is seen as a given, fixed and unchanging.

As Scarborough (2005: 122) describes, the dichotomies between spiritual and commercial, authentic and modern are reinforced by the two types of *Entradas*. The *Entrada Autóctona* is associated with 'the expression of a glorification of the pre-columbian past' whereas the *Entrada Folklórica* is associated with 'the modern, the loss of values and spiritual essence.' The introduction of the *Entrada Autóctona* reinforced tensions between authenticity and spectacle around the dance processions. In general, the *Entrada Folklórica* is associated more with spectacle, as show elements play a large part in it. The dances become more stylized and sophisticated every year, the dance figures are mostly carried out correctly synchronized, and the suits, hats, and masks become more sophisticated every year, with ever more glitter, fringes, embroidery, and details. The performance is made even more spectacular by fireworks and colored smoke during the dancing. In comparison, although all 'autochthonous' dances are different, in that they play different music, wear different ponchos and make different movements, most of the visitors told me that they saw less variety in these dances.

Although Scarborough (2005) and some of the visitors create a dichotomy between authenticity and spectacle, for most of the dancers and visitors the spectacular aspects do not negate the propagation of indigenous authenticity. Both the dancers of the *Entrada Folklórica* and the *Entrada Autóctona* took the audience into account, although the former did so to a greater extent. The existence of an audience reinforces the spectacular elements of the dance processions, as the dancers want to perform as well as they are able. This was already demonstrated in the words of Judy, at the beginning of this chapter. The dancers like to perform a spectacle when expressing 'authenticity'. The spectacular display draws the attention of the audience, and thus incorporates them in the celebration of culture (e.g. Rockefeller, 1999). The existence and involvement of an audience also reinforces feelings of belonging to a dance group. In the next section I will go further into this topic.

This section showed that in the two *Entradas* different types of ethnic identity are constructed. In the *Entrada Folklórica* this identity is claimed in people's roots. It refers to an overarching national identity in which the roots lie in the indigenous past. Ethnic distinctions do not play a major role, but people claim authenticity on the basis of heritage and 'being Bolivian'. On the other hand, in the *Entrada Autóctona* ethnic identity is based on the regional differences that are expressed in clothing, music, and dances. In fact, the *Entrada* aims to show the actual differences between ethnic groups and communities in Bolivia. Thus, instead of referring to a nostalgically viewed past in which differences are subordinate to a collective history, ethnic identity in the *Entrada Autóctona* is constructed on the basis of the ethnic differences in the present. The claims of authenticity thus serve different causes and different levels of collectivity.

Ethnicity and social (in)equality

Not only differences in the construction of ethnicity are expressed, but these differences also express social inequality. Although the *Autóctona* blames the *Folklórica* for not giving an authentic representation, the *Entrada Autóctona* is marginalized in comparison to the *Entrada Folklórica*. From a dominant perspective, both the church and the local politics seem to value the *Folklórica* more: because the *Entradas* are not valued equally they therefore express social inequality. For example, in folders it is announced that the *fiesta* of Urkupiña starts at the 14th of August, whereas the *Entrada Autóctona* is held on the 13th. In the eyes of the organizers of the *fiesta*, the *Entrada Autóctona* does not count as the beginning of the *fiesta*, and is ignored as part of the celebrations. When I asked people about this striking fact, many answered: 'That is because the *campesinos* do not dance for the Virgin Mary but for Pachamama.' The dancers of the *Folklórica*, however, do not necessarily dance for the Virgin Mary either, but this comment was not made.

The priests too did not display a welcoming and open attitude towards the dancers of the *Autóctona*. One priest who commented on the opening ceremony of the *Entrada Autóctona* said:

> The *Entrada Autóctona* is an event that is not organized in accordance with the church. We allow them to perform the ritual in front of the church, and we hope that it also gives a moment to reflect on the devotion to the Virgin of Urkupiña. Before, the route started at the Calvary Hill and ended at the church. We changed it, as at the end of the route everybody arrived at the church completely drunk.[2]

The reason for changing the route is the inebriation of the *campesinos* at the end of it. At the *Folklórica* there is also a high consumption of alcohol, although the church disapproves of this practice and tries to discourage people from

2 In 2008 the route was changed again, and that year the dance procession ended at the church. This shows how different groups negotiate over these issues every year.

drinking alcohol. In 2007 the priest of Quillacollo approached especially the fraternities with many young members, such as *Tinkus*, and invited them to assist in a mass during the fifteen days of prayer prior to the actual *fiesta*. After the mass he distributed little promise-cards that the dancers could fill in to promise Mary neither to drink alcohol nor to take drugs during the entire route. Yet, the church's disapproval of drink and drugs did not seem to be a reason to change the route of the *Entrada Folklórica*. The measure therefore denigrates the *Entrada Autóctona* by classifying the participants as more likely to be drunkards than the participants in the *Entrada Folklórica,* and the event as being of lesser religious importance, with no explicit blessing by the priest.

During the *Entrada Folklórica* Mary's icon is placed outside, so the dancers can make their promises and pray when passing the church, but during the *Entrada Autóctona* she is kept inside the church, which decreases the significance of passing the church. Only once, for one day, the Virgin Mary was dressed in indigenous clothing and placed outside the church. Although the organizers have asked the church to dress Mary in indigenous clothes again, the church resists. According to one of the priests:

> We do not want to give the impression that the Virgin of Urkupiña is only for the indigenous people. She is for all Bolivians, regardless of their ethnic backgrounds. We prefer to dress her in neutral clothes, so she won't exclude anybody.

Interestingly, by refusing to dress her in indigenous clothing for a single day each year, the church, in fact, excludes the indigenous population, under the pretence of equality.

The *Entrada Autóctona* is less frequented than the *Entrada Folklórica*. The calm *Entrada Autóctona*, where only few visitors are present, is in stark contrast to the massive numbers of spectators who come to see the dances of the *Entrada Folklórica*. On the 14th and 15th along the route of the *Entrada Folklórica* tribunes are built for the thousands of spectators who come to Quillacollo. On these days travelling to another part of town is hardly possible, as there are only a few opportunities to leave the tribunes and cross the streets. Police and military are everywhere to protect the audience and guide the dancers through the crowd.

During the *Entrada Folklórica* a balcony is installed for the mayor and other notables in front of the *alcaldía*, the city hall. Although the route of the *Entrada Autóctona* also passes the *alcaldía*, the political authorities do not come to watch. Even more flagrantly, in the year 2007 they scheduled a visit of the president Evo Morales to the city hall on the day of the *Entrada Autóctona*. In first instance the presidents' visit seemed an honor to the indigenous dancers. A male dancer in his forties of the dance *Phujllay* said:

> I hope we will pass the *alcaldia* exactly when he arrives. He played an important role in the recent process of revalorization of indigenousness.

> He can be proud of Quillacollo today, as we have our biggest annual show of indigenous groups.

However, Morales did not come to watch the indigenous dancers, and the overlap of the president's visit with the dance procession distracted people's attention from the dance processions. A large crowd gathered in front of the town hall to catch a glimpse of the president and blocked the road for the dancers. I spoke to a dance group that was obliged to take a long pause as they could no longer continue their dance in the street. A dancer complained:

> I thought Evo came for us, but he seems not to bother. If he is not interested, could he not come another day? Now the road is blocked and also all journalists and people from the press are gone to take pictures of Evo.

The scant interest of the political authorities for the indigenous processions shows once again that the *Autóctona* is regarded as having little importance. Even Evo Morales, who exploits his indigenous origin politically, is not interested in the indigenous dance procession.

Paradoxically, many people say they prefer the *Autóctona* and value the dancers for the expression of authenticity. Rockefeller (1999: 118) points out that the recent interest in the *Entrada Autóctona* teaches the indigenous people that they are the bearers of a 'culture' whose value lies in being displayed. The politics of Evo Morales also propagate the *pueblos originarios* - literally the original people - and their claim on Bolivian cultural and historical patrimony (Koopman, 2008), but while indigenousness is valued more and more, the *Entrada Autóctona* is still marginalized. Fewer people show an interest in it, nevertheless, for the dancers of the *Autoctona* it is an important day. One of the organizers explained:

> Before the existence of an *Entrada Autóctona*, the indigenous people were excluded from participating. Now a place for them has been created. It marks a process of re-valorization. The indigenous people are allowed to feel proud again.

When I spoke to the six dancers of the *Machetecos* at the end of the route, one of the dancers told me:

> I am very satisfied. People paid a lot of attention to our dance. The culture of the lowlands is different from the highlands. Many people came to make a picture. We feel very proud that we had the possibility to come here and participate in this *Entrada*, and introduce people to the dances from other regions. It might not be a large crowd, but at least there is a place for us.

I have already mentioned the importance of display and audience. It is important to have an audience to whom the message can be conveyed. There seems to be a 'social contract between performers and spectators' (Wiley, 2005: 140). The co-existence of audience and performers is important for the impact of the performance (Desmond, 1999: xv). Performing ethnic identity is, in terms of MacCannell (1973), a form of staged authenticity.

Interestingly, although the dances of the *Autóctona* are generally associated more with authenticity, the folkloric dances are better 'staged' and better received. They are thus better able to convey feelings of shared identity. This is underscored by the fact that the famous dances of the *Folklórica* can be recognized by name by almost all visitors, whereas the different dances of the *Entrada Autóctona* cannot be distinguished by name. For example, Virginia's daughter, who visited the *Entrada Autóctona* because two of her children joined a dance group said:

> I liked that group best, that resembled the *Tinkus*. They had almost the same clothes and made a lively show. I also liked the group with those large feathers, I don't know the name of their dance.

Virginia's daughter does not know the exact names of the dances, but describes them according to the categories that she knows from the *Folklórica*. Because of the typical elements such as clothing, music, and masks, that differ widely between the dances, the dances of the *Folklórica* could be distinguished from each other more easily than the dances of the *Autóctona*, that resemble each other more closely. When the elements are more spectacular, they become stronger identity markers. Thus, although in the view of the organizers and promoters of the *Autóctona*, the spectacular aspects of the *Folklórica* distort the 'authentic' representation, at the same time these elements reinforce group identity, but it is more a group identity of being Bolivian, albeit by referring to traditional ethnic roots, than that of local or regional ethnicities as in the *Autóctona*.

By performing their dances, the differences between the group members, between sub-groups of each *Entrada*, are not only expressed but also overcome. As Arnoldi (1988: 87) notes, in the dance performance actors draw together visual and verbal expressive forms that act as emblems in the process of constructing a common identity. Also Myerhoff (1984: 306) notes that by dramatizing a message, the people involved often experience a profound sense of community where all manners of distinctions may be transcended in an all-embracing, sacred unity that Victor Turner (1978: 250) has called *communitas*. In the description of the term, Turner refers to an egalitarian state of spontaneous bonding. Both the collective element of dancing for Mary, as well as for the enthusiastic audience, call upon feelings of belonging and community between the members. As Judy says:

> It is fantastic to be in such a big group of people moving back and forth to the same rhythm and totally synchronized. The band plays all these tunes with this simple rhythm of the *Tinku*. And when the audience starts screaming, clapping, and whistling, we dance more and more wildly! It is impossible to describe what I feel at these moments!

Judy refers to notions of repetition and rhythm, that have been outlined as meditative aspects of bodily movement (e.g. Albers, 2007: 352). The repetitive movement, the musical beat, the colors of the dresses and other sensory aspects of the performance, as well as the existence of an audience that confirms and supports the performance, call upon profound feelings of joy, happiness, and belonging. The collectivity of the performance also plays a role in the experience. One *Tinku* dancer dancing in the streets has less impact on the audience than a group of hundreds of people in the same costumes who dance, jump and shout.

The *Tinku* is one of the most energetic dances of the *Entrada Folklórica*. Because of the enormous activity and the lively character of the dance, the *Tinku* is often the favorite of the audience. A visitor, who walked with our *Tinku*-group during the *Entrada* recounted: 'When the *Tinkus* pass, the whole energy in the audience changes. It becomes warm and happy, as if all worries drop away and the atmosphere changes.' The president of the *Tinkus* San Simon also explained the popularity of his dance group in terms of the uplifting energy of the dancers:

> The secret of *Tinkus San Simon* gaining such popularity with the public, is because we are lively. While dancing we sing, scream, and shout. This makes the audience go mad! We give them so much energy!

During the *Entrada*, the *Tinkus San Simon* could be heard from a distance because of the many members shouting the happy songs. Even during breaks several dancers kept repeating their songs. When the *Tinkus* passed, the audience revived and started whistling, clapping, and shouting words of support. The multi-sensory experience for both dancers and audience led to a spontaneous bonding between dancers and visitors, and gave both a sense of belonging.

Judy, who became a dance member three years ago, recalls that she chose the *Tinku*-group because of the memory of the feelings she experienced when watching the *Tinkus* perform:

> I had always seen the *Entradas* in the streets of Quillacollo, as I used to go with my parents to watch the *Entrada*. I liked the *Tinkus* especially, as they wear such beautiful colorful clothes and dance with so much energy. When the *Tinkus* passed, I felt this tremendous spirit of joy and freedom.

Dancing and watching the dances thus calls upon feelings of *communitas*. Not only the multi-sensory performance or the sense of history, but also spiritual connotations can add to strong feelings of collective identity. For example, Judy recounts: 'After a while it feels as if everything goes spontaneously, as if somebody else controls my body. I cannot even stop dancing at these moments.' Judy relates her emotive experiences to religion when she states:

> I look at it differently. I might not believe in a Virgin in heaven who sends her help to help me finish my studies, but the dance gives me energy to continue. I might get bored and down during the week, but after dancing I feel recharged. Dancing gives me energy.

The uplifting energy Judy experiences is compared with the religious vow. Many other dancers also spoke about the energy that dancing generated. They told me that they forget to feel pain, hunger, thirst, exhaustion, and blisters when dancing. One of the *Machu-tinkus* recounts:

> Although it is a big sacrifice to dance for ten hours in the burning sun, the shouting, the music, the singing, and the dancing make my body move. When I see the audience smiling and applauding in the street, I feel I am part of something. I don't feel the tiredness in my legs or the burning in my waist anymore.

These spiritual emotions reinforce feelings of belonging. They give an extra dimension to the sense of identity, of being a *Tinku*. As the same boy explains:

> Being a *Tinku* means being part of a group. Together we make the show. It is funny, there are people in university that I will never talk to, but once they wear a *Tinku*-dress, we suddenly are *compañeros*!

Being part of the same dance group, causes people to relate to each other, because they have something in common. Class or ethnic differences do not play a role between the members, at least during the performance. I must add that the social boundaries are dissolved only for the members who are in anyway included in the group. The poor *campesinos* are still excluded from the group because they cannot pay the registration fees nor afford the costume with all its adornments.

There are also other expressions of unity during the Virgin's feast beyond those within the dance groups. On the days of the *Entrada* many members show their empathy with dancers of other fraternities who pass by in the streets in their performance clothes. They greet each other, encourage each other, or exchange their experiences when taking a rest and buying refreshments. The feelings of competition and rivalry between fraternities of the same dance, such as different *Tinku*-fraternities, are then overcome temporarily.

The experience of communitas is not restricted to the *Entrada Folklórica*. Bonding between dancers also happens in the *Entrada Autóctona*. However, to a certain extent, they communicate these feelings differently. In the *Folklórica* the bonding element is often narrated in terms of being part of the same spectacle, making a show together, and performing in front of an audience. The members of the *Autóctona* emphasize the experience of communitas more in terms of belonging to a regional identity. For example, a man from a small group from a community on the mountains, 6 hours by truck from Quillacollo, stated: 'We all live in this town. Some work in agriculture, others in transportation and one is a lawyer even. But today we are all equal, because we belong to the same village.'

Although differences between members of one and the same *Entrada* are temporarily dissolved by the experience of communitas, at the same time the differences between the different groups are reinforced by the same concept of communitas. After all, the strong feelings of group unity and belonging that are built up in the dance groups separately also function to mark the boundaries of the group. As such, it reinforces processes of inclusion and exclusion. For instance one of the students that participated in the *Entrada Autoctona* mentioned the playing of a wooden flute as one of the most important bonding elements, that at the same time defined their group, excluding others from it:

> You know, it is quite a rare flute. We had them designed by a few *campesinos*. Together, the flutes create an extraordinary sound. Nobody else has these flutes. It is even rare to play an instrument, if you look at the *Folklórica* where every group is accompanied by a brass band, or even worse, a car with audio equipment. But even in the *Autóctona*, nobody has the flutes that we have.

In the *Folklórica* the feelings of communitas also create distinction. For example, the account of Judy about her seeing the energetic *tinkus* pass by, showed her desire to be included in that group. In the festive and spectacular elements, the groups also create differences between them and the others. In the Folklorica, for example, the members call upon the notion of authenticity, but at the same time exclude the indigenous groups from participating. By singing, jumping, sweating, and moving together, feelings of solidarity and community are reinforced and seemingly dissolve the differences, but in fact, this experience of communitas is limited as it is also used to define the group boundaries.

Conclusions

The main question of this chapter was how ethnicity is constructed, and how it is related to power, marginality, and social inequality in the dance processions that are held during the festivities for the Virgin of Urkupiña. The dance processions carry not only religious meanings, but multiple meanings are also present. Historically, in the pilgrimage processions, religion and ethnicity came together, as the dances were used to express indigenous identity. In this chapter I analyzed the differences between the *Entrada Autóctona* and the *Entrada Folklórica* to find out by which concrete means ethnicity and social inequalities were constructed.

It was demonstrated that in fact two different collective identities are constructed in the *Entradas*. In the folkloric procession ethnic identity is reclaimed and transformed into an overarching Bolivian indigenous past, whereas in the *Autóctona* ethnic identity is claimed in the present, by presenting the variety of music, dances, and clothing of different regional ethnic groups. By showing the cultural production of collective feelings of identity, my analysis underscores the view that ethnicity is socially constructed and that it has a fluid, situational, and dynamic character. Dancers of both groups claim to present ethnic authenticity, although to a different extent. The *Autóctona* criticizes the *Folklórica* for its spectacular non-representative elements, while for most dancers of the *Folklórica*, spectacle is an important element of the performance that contributes to the impact of the spectacle. As the urban folkloric dancers also claim their authenticity in the indigenous culture of the past, the dancers of the *Autóctona* are empowered to transmit and express their representations of ethnicity in the dances. By criticizing each other, feelings of identity become stronger.

Not only differences are expressed, but also inequality. By relegating it to another time, space, and status, the *Entrada Autóctona* is marginalized in relation to the *Entrada Folklórica*. Although the *fiesta* starts on the 13th with the *Autóctona*, this is not acknowledged as the official beginning of the *fiesta*. The *Autóctona* is relegated to a position that calls upon fewer emotions, as there is less spectacle and audience, and it suffers greater disapproval from the church authorities. On the other hand, by re-inventing the indigenous culture in the *Autóctona*, the indigenous culture is also re-valued in the public sphere. Instead of the marginalized actors that have been left out of the *fiesta* for years, they participate actively in the pilgrimage, and make themselves visible and valuable. It is in fact a paradox. Whereas the *Entrada* is valued primarily for being more authentic, at the same time it is marginalized for not being as spectacular as the *Folklórica*.

It has been demonstrated that the inequalities expressed, are overcome temporarily at the same time. The spectacle and emotions reinforce the experience of group identity on a higher level, and call upon feelings of belonging and community, in Turner's terms (1978), communitas. The sensory aspects of performance, the collectivity of a group, and the 'social contract' that is established with the audience all play a role. Communitas is experienced between the group members and between sub-groups of the two *Entradas*. As their identities are both rooted in ethnic authenticity, although in a different way, these emotions reinforce implicitly the construction of ethnicity. In relation to theories on pilgrimage it can be concluded that this chapter underscores Turner's theory (1978) on the experience of communitas in pilgrimage. At the same time it demonstrates Eade & Sallnow's (1991) criticism that pilgrimage is at the same time marked by the competing and contested meanings, in this case of underlying ethnicity. In fact, communitas creates these competing differences between the two dance processions, as it creates processes of in- and exclusion.

Photo 8: Devotion of a pilgrim to a reproduction of the Virgin's statue at a farewell party at Cota

8

CONCLUSIONS

The study of pilgrimage

This anthropological study has focused on the religious experiences of Bolivians at the Marian shrine of the Virgin of Urkupiña in Quillacollo, and on the ways devotees deal with different forms of social inequality at the shrine. The pilgrimage to the Virgin of Urkupiña revealed much about the power dynamics in Bolivian society, as devotees came to the shrine to express their everyday problems in a religious discourse. In this study, religious behaviors at the shrine of the Virgin of Urkupiña were used as a lens through which social inequalities were examined, as pilgrims approach Mary with the problems resulting from class, gender, and ethnic inequalities. Marian devotion gives room to express these problems, and, in its turn, influences devotees' perceptions and possibilities to deal with them. In addition, a wide range of actors, such as church authorities and believers, indigenous and non-indigenous people, rich and poor, pilgrims and tourists, devotees and traders, come together at this shrine and shape various practices and give various interpretations. Because of this heterogeneity, a multiplicity of meanings was present. I have studied pilgrimage as an arena in which the power structures in society are articulated and mediated.

Pilgrims' motives for visiting the shrine and the requests they make express the social inequalities they experience in daily life. When looking at these motives and requests it was found that economic concerns were the most frequently expressed. In particular people came to the shrine of the Virgin of Urkupiña to complain about poverty and the neoliberal politics that they held responsible for it. Their request for economic improvement could be expressed in miniature objects that symbolized their wishes. During the annual *fiesta* the two kilometer long street from the church in town to the Calvary Hill is full of stands selling miniature objects representing things that people want. Furthermore, their requests were symbolized in hacking stones from Mary's hill, a rite that in recent decades has developed to the ritual par excellence and to which the pilgrimage to the Virgin of Urkupiña owes most of its fame. Therefore, I started my analysis of this pilgrimage in terms of economic inequality, looking at both the macro-economic changes in Bolivia and at what these meant in the micro-economic life of poor women. During the period of fieldwork I established close contacts with Bolivian pilgrims, in particular women, who told me intimate details of their lives that shifted the focus to other social inequalities. Bolivian women not only suffered from poverty and economic problems, but also from gender inequality. Numerous narratives of anger and pain drew attention to the prevalence of domestic violence and other gendered suffering in Bolivian society. Furthermore, the existence of two ethnically based dance processions during the *fiesta* of Urkupiña drew attention to ethnicity as another form of social inequality in relation to this particular pilgrimage. This led me to formulate as my main question: How do Bolivian devotees deal with class, gender and ethnic inequality at the pilgrimage shrine to the Virgin of Urkupiña?

The pilgrimage to the Virgin of Urkupiña in Bolivia is relatively new, as it is only since the 1970s that it has developed from a local celebration to an event of national and even international importance. Analyzing why this devotion has grown into one of the most popular in Bolivia, we have seen in chapter three that since the nineteen seventies, especially the people from the flourishing business district Santa Cruz became interested and caused the spread of the association of the Virgin of Urkupiña with economic issues. As at that time the country was doing well economically, realistic wishes that were requested of the Virgin of Urkupiña were easily able to become reality, and the miraculous powers of Mary were affirmed and propagated. Some Bolivians also explained the growth of the *fiesta* by the booming drug trade and claimed that the devotion to the Virgin of Urkupiña was an alibi for drug runners who got rich overnight. Moreover the devotion profited from the tourist interest in folkloric processions and the increasingly important role this played in the formation of national identity. In recent decades these ceremonies have expanded into one of the three largest religious dance processions in the country. Nowadays, the Virgin of Urkupiña's fame has spread throughout the country, and every year pilgrims come from all over Bolivia, and even from foreign countries.

I based my approach towards the study of pilgrimage on Eade & Sallnow's (1991) view of a pilgrimage site as an arena where multiple meanings come to the fore and compete with each other. I looked at how the meanings that pilgrims attribute to Mary, the pilgrimage and their lives are shaped by their experiences of class, gender, and ethnicity and how people articulate, resist, or reproduce these meanings. Different groups of people, such as church authorities, vendors, and pilgrims had different interests, and these interests could change according to the context. For instance, the church tried to control and minimize the commercial activities around the shrine, whereas in order to earn a living the vendors needed to offer their goods and services to the pilgrims.

When the vendors visited the shrine as part of their annual pilgrimage, their faith in Mary and their own personal relationship with her became central. Following Foucault (1977: 98) people are viewed as 'always in the position of simultaneously undergoing and exercising power'. They adjust their meanings according to their shifting power positions. For instance, poverty in daily life made pilgrims articulate requests for economic improvement. The pilgrimage to the Virgin of Urkupiña gave them the opportunity to resist the socio-economic and political structures that were held responsible for their poverty. At the shrine they were able to express their worries and to search for solutions. At the same time, the socio-economic structures were reproduced at the shrine in narratives and performances. The focus on the multiplicity of meanings thus led to my view of pilgrimage as a way to negotiate power.

My study also connected to Coleman & Eade's (2004) suggestion of focusing on movement in the study of pilgrimage. In my study I looked at the movement of objects and rituals, and I connected the pilgrimage to Urkupiña to social movement. It is relatively new to look at the movement of things in the study of pilgrimage. Relevant for this study was how the image of Mary moves through the streets of Quillacollo during the *Quincena*, the fifteen days of prayer prior to the annual *fiesta*, and how this form of movement contributes to the personal relationships that pilgrims establish with Mary. By turning her into a pilgrim, devotees come closer to Mary. In addition, the movement of objects symbolizing the requests, such as blessed stones and miniature replicas, has been studied to understand how these objects function in the establishment of a complex of collaborative exchange relations that believers build up with Mary. The 'movement' of rituals has also been studied, not only the physical ritual movements of hacking stones or dancing in processions, but also the movements in the sense of changes in the rituals over the years and their role in identity construction.

The focus on the daily experiences of class, gender, and ethnicity at the Marian shrine, re-conceptualizes the concept of pilgrimage into a form of 'lived religion'. My view opposes Turner and Turner's (1978) view of pilgrimage as an anti-structure in which pilgrimage is seen as a domain apart from daily life. In my view, pilgrimage integrates daily life. Lived religion, after all, focuses on the way religion is experienced in the context of daily life. Following among others Dubisch (1995), Coleman & Elsner (2002), Frey (1998), and Tweed (1997), I looked at the personal interpretations and experiences of devotees, in particular their social suffering. Suffering has been related to pilgrimage before, in the sense that suffering and sacrifice were often seen as inherent and necessary conditions in pilgrimage. Later, several authors suggested that suffering was connected to pilgrimage because pilgrims went on pilgrimage to deal with the problems of everyday life (Dubisch, 1995; Gemzöe, 2005; Notermans, 2008; Schramm, 2004; Tweed, 1997). My study is in line with these studies on everyday suffering and pilgrimage, and shows how devotees are stimulated and empowered to confront their suffering in daily life.

To answer the research question, 14 months of fieldwork in Quillacollo and Cochabamba was conducted in 2005 (eleven months) and 2007 (three months). Data was gathered through a variety of research methods that included participant observation at different places and occasions (e.g. Calvary Hill, the church San Ildefonso in Quillacollo, houses of informants, religious feasts, and participation in the religious dance group *Tinkus San Simon*) in combination with informal conversations with around 200 Bolivians, and in-depth ethnographic interviews with 25 individuals. In addition, the daily lives of five people were followed extensively, and the life histories of these persons were also collected. Furthermore, photo-elicitation methods were carried out with the latter group; a set of 25 different Marian representations from all over the world was shown in order to find out the meanings of Mary for the believers, and photos that I made during fieldwork were also shown and reflected upon. Next, surveys (43 household surveys in three districts of Quillacollo, 86 pilgrim-surveys and 62 dance-surveys) have been used to provide insight into the social-economic background of the people at the shrine. Also semi-structured interviews were conducted with 22 different Bolivian specialists on religion, including anthropologists, scholars of religion, and church authorities. Finally literature study has been done in connection with the theoretical aspect of the ethnographical research data.

To understand how pilgrimage is related to inequality, special emphasis was given to the study of objects, performances, and narratives, as these were viewed as tools to express religiosity. The objects included the stones, miniature replicas and the image of Mary. Performances that were studied were the rituals of hacking stones, the blessings, prayers, *sahumas* and *ch'allas* performed over the stones and miniatures, processions with the statue of Mary, and dance processions. The stones and miniatures, and the rituals performed with them, were an entrance to the analysis of class inequality in particular, whereas the dance performances drew attention to ethnic inequality. Narratives were collected in numerous conversations and interviews. They were particularly informative of experiences of gender inequality, related to both poverty and domestic violence.

Studying how pilgrims construct meanings through objects, performances and narratives led to a focus on religious experiences outside the realm of the official church. The pilgrimage to the Virgin of Urkupiña is not restricted to the church in town, other places are also important. Most pilgrims also visit the Calvary Hill, two kilometers outside town, to pray and give material form to their requests in stones and miniatures. The streets of Quillacollo were the stage for the processions and dance processions. In general, these spaces away from the church provided more insight into the convictions and daily experiences of pilgrims. Most religious objects and performances are to be found outside the realm of the official church, and often without the approval of the church authorities. Studying religious meanings outside the dominant discourse of the church showed the power dynamics and creativity of the believers. For instance, the miniature replicas of divorce papers that are sold by vendors outside the church showed the power of believers to symbolize requests that are not supported by the ideas of the Catholic church. Devotees can give them to Mary for her blessing. It demonstrated the creativity of the devotees to employ religion for all aspects of their daily lives.

The devotees manipulate their space literally and figuratively to give their own meaning to the symbol of Mary. These interpretations do not necessarily correspond with church interpretations. The Bolivian pilgrims ascribed to Mary characteristics like violence, anger, and authority, traits that do not coincide with the church convictions in which Mary is portrayed as a humble and obedient woman. The devotees humanize and personalize the Virgin in attributing to her human characteristics such as rage, vanity, and impatience, and they establish an unique and personal relationship with Mary in such acts as speaking in diminutives, writing letters, and giving her presents. The Virgin of Urkupiña is perceived as a dominant and powerful woman. Her devotees perceive her as more than an intercessor. Most pilgrims do not approach her as the representative of her son, but believe that Mary has the capacity to decide whether and how to intervene, and the power to behave accordingly. As such, they resist formal doctrine and the meanings of the priests.

The meanings given to Mary were also influenced by the Quechua and Aymara believers whose interpretations of her have also been derived from the Andean *cosmovisión*. During the colonization their goddess of fertility, Pachamama, was incorporated with the Virgin Mary. Because of this integration the pilgrims establish reciprocal relations with Mary and use her for requests of multiplication. This way, also going against the church's views, the pilgrims do not see any contradiction in approaching Mary with materialistic goals in mind. This shows that pilgrims are creative in adjusting the pilgrimage to their needs. The vendors also influence these perceptions of the pilgrims, even of non-indigenous pilgrims. The ways that pilgrims and vendors in Bolivia transform the meanings at the pilgrimage site, shows that they are powerful agents in adjusting the pilgrimage to contemporary contexts.

Class, gender, and ethnic inequality

One of the most important findings of this thesis is that the pilgrimage to the Virgin of Urkupiña is a materialistic pilgrimage. Requests for economic improvement are the most dominant aspect of this Marian shrine. Unlike Lourdes, where the focus is on health, at the pilgrimage to the Virgin of Urkupiña the focus is on wealth. Pilgrims not only make economic requests, but also express these visually, materially, and publicly in the rituals of stones and miniature objects at the shrine. Furthermore, the rituals and performances at the shrine are embedded in an economic discourse. Therefore, I have started my analysis of the way social inequality is negotiated in this pilgrimage by looking at the economic concerns expressed and negotiated at the shrine. Class inequality was related to the pilgrimage of the Virgin of Urkupiña both on a macro and micro level.

Chapter four focused on the macro-level and looked at the neoliberal politics in society and how these socio-economic structures are articulated at the pilgrimage shrine of the Virgin of Urkupiña. Many Bolivians blame the neoliberal politics of the past decades for the increased social inequality in their society. To deal with the consequences of the neoliberal model in their personal life, pilgrims approach the Virgin of Urkupiña in search of protection and social security that the state has failed to offer. The pilgrimage, thus, provides a space to express class related problems that were generated by the neoliberal model at the level of the state. Paradoxically, at the same time, devotees appropriate the neoliberal model and reproduce it at the pilgrimage shrine in their rituals as well as in economic behavior, either as believers or traders, applying the rules of the free market. In the ritual of dislodging stones from the Calvary Hill pilgrims appropriate a capitalist jargon in which the ritual is compared to drawing money from a financial bank. Pilgrims refer to the stones as 'money from the Virgin', they speak of taking out a loan from Mary's bank or borrowing capital that has to be paid back with interest. Stones are viewed as an investment in capitalist terms: those who already have capital will be able to invest, those who are poor will only be able to ask for small amounts. When taking a gift from Mary, no interest has to be paid. When borrowing capital, the interest is paid by returning the stones and investing in offers and libations. The economic connotation around the ritual showed that the relationship with Mary is viewed as a trade-relation: in return for Mary's support they have to promise Mary to pay back the interest. The commerce around the site is also structured according to the neo-liberal rules of competition, self-responsibility and survival of the fittest. Thus, in a criticism of previous interpretations that pilgrims go on pilgrimage to deal with the disempowering circumstances created by the neoliberal politics, I argue that the neoliberal attitude and vocabulary is co-opted at the site. At the same time in people's attempts to resist the neoliberal structures in society they reproduce these structures. Thus, religion, in this case pilgrimage, can be appropriated to fight against social inequalities, but the reality is more complex, as my study shows that these social inequalities are reproduced in religion.

Chapter five focuses on the reciprocal exchange relations that pilgrims establish with Mary. It looked at the micro-level of people's economic and material requests, and put at center stage the material objects of stones and miniatures that are used in the pilgrimage to the Virgin of Urkupiña to symbolize these requests. Bolivian devotees appropriated the pilgrimage to upgrade their economic mobility and resolve their class-based problems. Both poor and rich did not experience any ambivalence in connecting the material with the spiritual, because approaching the supernatural world with material and tangible petitions was derived from Andean notions of approaching Mother Earth and asking for prosperity and fertility. At the same time, the rich had more money to invest in their faith and were able to offer more lavishly, for example by buying more miniatures or joining the more expensive dance fraternities. People from different classes adjusted their petitions to their needs and wishes.

In particular studying the stones and miniatures contributed to understanding how these material religious objects are part of the symbolic means of exchange and how they function in the pilgrims' lived religion. Pilgrims constructed a 'spiritual economy', a term proposed by David Morgan that I expanded to refer to the exchange relationship that is built up between Mary and pilgrims. This reciprocal relationship includes both the supernatural world of Mary and the everyday lives of the pilgrims. Vows and offerings are traded for Mary's support. Again the economic way in which pilgrims negotiate with Mary comes to the fore. However, my study shows that in this spiritual economy there is no automatic exchange by which pilgrims exchange prayers and faith for Mary's help. Instead, the miniatures remind people of the investment that they themselves have to make. People themselves have to work on their projects. The stones and miniatures served as tangible and powerful reminders of the cogent relationship between pilgrims and Mary. The biography of the objects revealed that the pilgrims established a collaborative relationship in which pilgrims believed that Mary shaped the necessary conditions to make their petitions reality, and empowered them to continue their own steps towards their economic aspirations. Pilgrims did not expect direct help from the Virgin Mary, but they made their requests especially to motivate themselves to work on their goals. Pilgrimage provided not only the space to reflect on life and re-direct people's goals, but also has material effects in daily life. The spiritual experience is converted into actual material consequences, as devotees are motivated by pilgrimage to work actively on their economic development. In this way, this study provided insight into the motivating character of religion that surpasses a simplified presentation of a reciprocal relation. Pilgrimage not only has a consoling function but also activates people, and thus, makes a material difference. Moreover, this study challenged the idea of a dichotomy between the spiritual and the material by showing how they conflate in people's religious experience.

Next to poverty and economic oppression, pilgrims approached the Virgin of Urkupiña for problems based on gender inequality. It was asked what gender inequality is expressed and how women deal with it in this particular pilgrimage. Domestic violence, experienced by numerous Bolivian women, came to the fore as a dominant form of gender inequality that was articulated at the shrine. Scholarly literature on domestic violence in Latin America often explains it in terms of the dominant notions of masculinity and femininity, *machismo* and *marianismo*. Latin American women's suffering is explained in this gender paradigm in which women are said to embrace the values of the Virgin Mary as a passive, submissive, and obedient role-model. However, these studies seldom look at women's actual interpretations of Mary. It is merely assumed that women venerate Mary for her submissiveness, suffering and passivity, as a symbol to endure gender-related suffering. Several studies have already shown that the *machismo-marianismo* complex gives a too simple and dualistic view of the gender relations in Latin America, but Mary's role in problems of domestic violence has not yet been studied, nor if battered Latin American women actually have this perception of Mary.

My study contributed to the existing criticism on the stereotypical concept of *marianismo*. First of all, women's suffering of domestic violence was not as passive and one-dimensional as suggested in studies that make use of the concept of *marianismo*. Although the stories of Bolivian women were full of suffering, I argued that they do not merely accept their suffering in marianistic terms. A profound rage, or *rabia*, came up as a key concept in the experience of domestic violence of Bolivian women. Rage is a reaction that does not coincide with the notion of *marianismo*. In the Mexican context this belligerent emotion of rage is called *coraje,* and has been deployed to deconstruct the *machismo-marianismo* complex. However, these studies emphasize *coraje* is restricted to women's experiences, whereas I noted that the concept *rabia* was used in Bolivia to refer to experiences of both men and women, although the contexts differ. Men became violent because of their *rabia* about the experienced powerlessness to be able to change their existing unbearable circumstances, whereas women experience *rabia* as a result of being the victims of this violence. Often the women were not able to express their rage, as they need their husbands for economic and social reasons. Therefore they endured the battering, not because they wanted to be an obedient and submissive woman like Mary, but because they were not in a position of sufficient power to have other alternatives.

My study contributed to the criticism of the concept of *marianismo,* not only by demonstrating that women's behavior is not as passive as suggested in literature, but also by asking what women themselves thought about Mary. The term *marianismo* was applied by various authors without verifying whether women actually did perceive Mary as passive and submissive. My study looked at the actual interpretations that battered women have of Mary, and showed that for them Mary had both a suffering and vicious side. Mary was also venerated for her vengeful character and her ability to interfere violently in the lives of the women's husbands. Women transferred their rage about their violent husbands to Mary, who was perceived as a goddess of vengeance, who could also put her anger at the domestic violence into play by taking revenge on the husbands. Mary was able to deploy her belligerent emotion of *rabia* on behalf of the women.

It was also asked how ethnic inequality was negotiated at the pilgrimage site. The theme of ethnic identity came to the fore most clearly in the religious dance processions that were held each year in August. During the *fiesta* of Urkupiña folkloric urban groups perform their spectacular dances in the streets of Quillacollo. Since 1999 an *Entrada Autóctona* has been held a day before the long-established *Entrada Folklórica,* with the main aim of including the indigenous people in the *fiesta*. The introduction of this dance procession reinforced the debate on authenticity and gave rise to the question of what kinds of ethnic identity were constructed in the two *Entradas*. It was demonstrated that these identities differ, as the urban *mestizos* who dance in the *Folklórica* claimed ethnic authenticity in an overarching indigenous Bolivian past, while the dancers of the *Entrada Autóctona* claimed authenticity in showing the actual ethnic regional varieties in their dances. Both make use of the concept of authenticity to justify their link with ethnicity. The folkloric dancers legitimized their dances as authentic because their dances are rooted in the indigenous past, whereas the dancers of the *Autóctona* claimed authenticity by being indigenous and showing the actual indigenous present. This case showed the complexity of the concept of ethnic authenticity. As it is a claim rather than a fact, it is a political project in which different factions with different interests participate.

In the dance processions not only ethnic identity but also ethnic inequality was articulated. A smaller audience came to watch the *Autóctona*, also because it was less spectacular, the organization had less money for organizing the event, and church authorities disapproved of it. Paradoxically, although the *Folklórica* was perceived as less authentic, it was, in general, valued more. In fact, the existing ethnic inequality in society is reproduced in the dance processions.

Furthermore, it was asked how the physical movement of dancing called upon feelings of 'communitas'. It was shown that despite the inequality between the *Entradas* the dancers in the fraternities experienced a sense of communitas when dancing, an egalitarian state of spontaneous bonding. Their group identity was reinforced by feelings of fraternity and community. In the *Autóctona* this group identity was based on regional origins, whereas in the *Folklórica* the spectacular elements created this bonding. The dancers often expressed the uplifting feelings in spiritual metaphors like 'a tremendous power and energy' or 'something else controlled my body'. This case shows that a theoretical focus of conflict and inequality, as predominates in this thesis, does not suffice to challenge Turner's concept of 'communitas' as relevant to understanding the impact of pilgrimage. In the theoretical debate on pilgrimage a counter reaction on Turner's concept of communitas came from Eade & Sallnow (1991) who looked at the contesting discourses at the shrine. My study shows that these approaches do not exclude each other. In my view communitas is part of the competing discourse: communitas on one level contributes to the construction of ethnic inequality on a higher level. Dancers of both *Entradas* experience feelings of unity, of bridging differences for the construction of their group identity. In creating feelings of unity for their own group composed of different factions, the groups also differentiate. The urban *Entrada*, for instance, calls upon the notion of authenticity, but uses such expensive costumes that the indigenous groups cannot participate. The feelings of bonding, fraternity, and communitas thus also serve to distinguish the groups from each other.

In studying religious experiences and meanings, the personal experiences of class, gender, and ethnic inequality have to be taken into account, as they shape and re-direct people's experiences. Religion, in this case pilgrimage, is appropriated to articulate, contest, resist, and reproduce the inequalities in daily life. My close analysis of these personal experiences as religiously expressed at the shrine shows that these inequalities are not given, but constantly in flux. People are continuously negotiating for space, and trying to influence their own position and these social constructions, the outcome of which they never can control.

Although in my book I have first distinguished the forms of inequality, and for ease of understanding discussed them separately in each chapter, class, gender, and ethnicity do not act separately, but interact with each other in complex ways. How they intersect was shown in several places. For example, Margarita suffers from both class, gender, and ethnic inequality. Due to the neoliberal politics, she has not completed any education and was forced to work in the informal economy. She works as a vendor of *ch'allas*, without any state protection and is self-responsible for generating enough money for all expenses. As a woman, who has to take care of the children, she was affected even more. In her earlier marriage she suffered from domestic violence, a traumatic experience that still influences her life, even though her man died years ago. Because of her experiences she does not want to remarry, not even to share in the economic benefits that the income of a potential husband can provide. In addition, as an Aymara migrant, she suffers from ethnic inequality. Sometimes pilgrims at the shrine bypass her, and thus her ethnic origin influences her income.

Also on a higher level these inequalities intersect. For instance, the prevalence of domestic violence in Bolivian society showed that gender intersects with class. Often men hit women out of *rabia*, out of their powerlessness and frustration about their unchangeable circumstances of poverty. In particular men from the lower income groups experience this frustration. Furthermore, domestic violence is normalized in Bolivian society, and especially viewed as a legitimized way to solve problems in the lower classes of society. Class, in its turn intersects with ethnic inequality, as most of the indigenous people are poor.

Empowerment and disempowerment

It was also asked whether believers were empowered through Marian devotion and if so, in what way. It was shown that the pilgrimage to the Virgin of Urkupiña provided a space to deal with the disempowering circumstances of daily life that were generated by the government's privatization of the economy and reduction of social security measures. The ritual of stones and *alasitas* gave the opportunity for empowerment by articulating problems of economic suffering, class inequality, but also gender problems like domestic violence, and at the same time, stimulated people to deal with these problems and materialize their requests. Empowerment was defined as the ability to maximize the opportunities available to people without constraints. The rituals of stones and miniature objects have empowering functions as they give pilgrims the opportunity to reflect on their goals, redirect their lives, and also activate them to make the necessary steps to reach their goals. It is a form of individual empowerment, as the use of objects makes them intervene in their own lives. By promising the powerful symbol of Mary to work hard, they are motivated to do as they have promised.

Battered women also found agency at the pilgrimage site by transferring their anger to Mary. This is a form of empowerment at the relational level. Pilgrims negotiate with Mary to cause her to intervene. As they cannot change the abusive relationships with the husbands themselves, they seek Mary's help to intervene on their behalf. In transmitting their rage to Mary they are empowered to deal with the violence used against them. By bestowing power on Mary, they feel empowered themselves, as they are relieved of their anger, and can find the faith that Mary will exact justice in the situation. In the devotion to Mary they can find a way to resist the violence that is done to them; with Mary on their side, they feel strong enough to deal with the violence, since Mary will take revenge on their behalf.

The analysis of the notions of ethnicity involved in the dance processions showed that these dance processions provide a space for the marginalized to express, in case of the *Autóctona*, and re-value, in case of the *Folklórica*, ethnicity in Bolivia. It is an example of collective empowerment, as the impact lies in the collectivity of the dance experience. In dance, pilgrims are able to show and re-value their ethnic indigenous identity by representing indigenous culture in clothes, movements, and music, or by referring to the historical roots of their performances that have also shaped self-awareness for the Bolivians. The recent increased interest in the participation of indigenous dance groups by organizing a counter-*Entrada Autóctona*, demonstrates that the marginalized are empowered to display their ethnic identity. Another way in which the dances are related to empowerment is because dancing calls upon emotions of belonging and communitas. The emotions that were summoned by the colors, the spectacle, the singing, and the collective movement while dancing and singing, also created uplifting energy that can be viewed as a form of empowerment, as many dancers, and even visitors, recounted feeling strong and energized through participating or watching the *Entrada*. In sum, the pilgrimage gave room to evaluate pilgrims' situations, what it means to be poor, battered, or ethnically marginalized, and gave space to maneuver so that they could handle the problems of everyday life.

On the pilgrimage, however, believers not only found empowerment, but also disempowerment. For instance, despite the severe resistance and criticism that pilgrims had of the neo-liberal model, they themselves reproduced it at the pilgrimage site in the economic jargon that was used in connection with the stones and miniatures and the symbolic capital to which they referred, as well as in the commercial sale of religious objects by the numerous vendors at the shrine. Furthermore, pilgrims submitted themselves to Mary's violent regime by attributing to her demanding rules of offering, praying, and investments. In this way they were disempowered, as they were exposed to Mary's powers of punishment.

Moreover, in the case of requests for intervention on issues of domestic violence, pilgrims handed over their anger to Mary and asked her for revenge. As the power to solve the problem was handed over to the supernatural, they themselves, were, in a way, disempowered to change their situations themselves. In addition, Mary does not take away the social inequalities. She does not stop the occurrence of domestic violence in daily life. In the devotion to Mary, the battered women are in fact encouraged to accept the disempowering situations of domestic violence.

The expression of ethnicity in dance is also related to disempowerment. Although the marginalized ethnic minorities were given a space to express their ethnicity during the *Entrada Autóctona*, their dance performances were marginalized in relation to the spectacular dances of the *Entrada Folklórica*, so the space to express indigenous identity during the pilgrimage dance processions was limited. Religion, thus, is able to provide empowering personal tactics to deal with social inequalities, but hardly changes or dissolves these structural inequalities. In fact, all chapters outlined the limited space for empowerment, because pilgrims could not get a car or house without working for it, battered women could not stop being beaten, and while dancing out unity, ethnic difference and marginalization was re-produced. Despite the high intensity of Marian devotion, poverty, domestic violence, and discrimination did not decrease in society. Although pilgrims come in a search of empowerment, the social inequalities people suffered were not changed by Mary. In fact, the Virgin of Urkupiña was actually part of the social and economic mechanism that maintained structural inequality. By engaging into a reciprocal exchange relation they subjected themselves to Mary's rules. In accrediting Mary with power, pilgrims were empowered, yet at the same time disempowered. That is why Virginia, who prayed with whole her heart for the empowerment of pilgrims who asked Mary for a blessing, kept seeing the shrine as a place of suffering: 'The Calvary is a calvary'.

GLOSSARY

alasitas	miniatures to symbolize requests, used at religious feasts in Bolivia
Altiplano	high plain in the Andes
Calvario	Calvary Hill: two kilometers outside of the town of Quillacollo where pilgrims materialize their requests
campesino	country person
chicha	alcoholic corn drink
ch'alla	libation, offering that usually consists of sprinkling the ground with alcohol
Cholas	indigenous market women
Conquistador	conqueror
coraje	word used in Mexico for a profound rage and anger
cosmovisión	worldview
curandero	Andean medicine man
Entrada	religious dance procession
Entrada Folklórica	folkloric dance procession performed at the fiesta of Urkupiña. Most groups are accompanied by a brass band
Entrada Autóctona	dance procession that shows ethnic regional identities. Dancers make their own music when dancing
fiesta	feast
huaca	holy places of the Quechuas and Aymaras
indígenas	self-descriptive term for indigenous people
k'oa	offering for Pachamama made by burning sweets, herbs, and incense
machismo	gender notion of dominant masculinity
Mamita	diminutive of mama, expressing an affective relationship

marianismo	scholarly term for Latin American obedient and suffering femininity
mestizos	people of mixed indigenous and white blood
Pachamama	Mother Earth
pollera	Bolivian word for skirts with layers as worn by women from La Paz
Quincena	fifteen days of prayer before the *fiesta* of Urkupiña
rabia	a profound rage, fury, and anger
sahumera	vendor of blessings
sahuma	ritual in which a *sahumera* pours incense on glowing coals while praying
Tinku	ritual fight for the fertility of the earth
Virgencita	diminutive for Virgin, expressing an affective relationship
yatiri	Andean medicine man

REFERENCES

Abercrombie, Thomas (1998). Commentary on Performance, Identity and Historical Consciousness in the Andes. *Journal of Latin American Anthropology 3* (2), pp. 150-167.

Abu-Lughod, L. (1993). *Writing Women's Worlds.* Los Angeles: University of California Press.

Aguilo, P. F. (1985). La Fiesta de Santa Vera Cruz en Proceso de Cambio. *Nueveamerica 2* (3), pp. 17-22.

Alba Fernandez, J. J. (2001). El Retorno de los Sacerdotes Aymaras. In: W. G. Valdivia & W. G. Merida (Eds.), *Historia del Milagro: Antología de Urqupiña* (pp. 205-210). Cochabamba: Los Tiempos.

Albers, I. (2007). *Heilige Kracht Wordt door Beweging Losgemaakt: Over Pelgrimage, Lopen en Genezing.* Rijksuniversiteit Groningen, Universiteit Tilburg: Ph.D. thesis.

Albo, X. (2002). *Una Casa Común para Todos: Iglesias, Ecumenismo y Desarrollo en Bolivia.* La Paz: Cipca.

Albo, X. (2004). El Futuro del Quechua Visto Desde una Perspectiva Boliviana. *International Journal of Social Languages 167*, pp.119-130.

Albro, R. (1998). Neoliberal Ritualists of Urkupiña: Bedeviling Patrimonial Identity in a Bolivian Patronal Fiesta. *Ethnology 37* (2), pp. 133-164.

Albro, R. (2005). 'The Water is Ours, Carajo!' Deep Citizenship in Bolivia's Water War. In: J. Nash (Ed.), *Social Movements: An Anthropological Reader* (pp. 249-267). Malden, Oxford, Victoria: Blackwell Publishers.

Appadurai, A. (1986). Introduction: Commodities and the Politics of Value. In: A. Appadurai (Ed.), *The Social Life of Things: Commodities in Cultural Perspective* (pp. 3-63). Cambridge: Cambridge University Press.

Arnillas L. F. (1996). Ekeko, Alacitas y Calvarios: La Fiesta de la Santa Cruz en Juliaca. *Allpanchis 47*, pp. 119-135.

Arnoldi, M.J. (1988). Style, and the Assertion of Identity in Malian Puppet Drama. *Journal of Folklore Research 25* (1-2), pp. 87-100.

Aull Davies, C. (2008). *Reflexive Ethnography: A Guide to Researching Selves and Others.* London, New York: Routledge.

Bachrach Ehlers, T. (1991). Debunking Marianismo: Economic Vulnerability and Survival Strategies among Guatemalan wives. *Ethnology 30* (1), pp. 1-14.

Badone, E. (1990). *Religious Orthodoxy and Popular Faith in European Society.* New Jersey: Princeton University Press.

Baptista, J. (1989). El Rostro Andino de Dios. *Cuarto Intermedio 11*, pp. 49-64.

Behar, R. (1990). Rage and Redemption: Reading the Life Story of a Mexican Marketing Woman. *Feminist Studies 16* (2), pp. 223-258.

Beramendy Orellana, J. A. (2001). Las Alasitas del Valle y su Perdido Encanto. In: W. G. Valdivia & W. G. Merida (Eds.), *Historia del Milagro* (pp. 129-136). Cochabamba: Los Tiempos.

Boero Rojo, H. (1993). *Bolivia Mágica*. La Paz: Industrias Offset Color.

Borland, K. (2003). Pilgrimage to Popoyuapa: Catholic Renewal and Ethnic Performance in Neoliberal Nicaragua. *Journal of American Folklore 116* (462), pp. 391-419.

Borsboom, A. P. (1998). Europa in de Pacific, de Pacific in Europa. In: A.P. Borsboom, F. A. M. Hüsken & W. G. Wolters (Eds). *Veld Winnen: Drie Redes in de Antropologie*. Radboud University Nijmegen: Oration.

Bossen, C. (2000). Festival Mania, Tourism and Nation Building in Fiji: The Case of the Hibiscus Festival, 1956-1970. *The Contemporary Pacific 12* (1), pp. 123-154.

Boyer, M.-F. (2000). *The Cult of the Virgin: Offerings, Ornaments and Festivals*. London: Thames & Hudson.

Browner, C. & Lewin, E. (1982). Female Altruism Reconsidered: The Virgin Mary as Economic Woman. *American Ethnologist 9* (1), pp. 61-75.

Brun, W. (2007). *Urqupiña de Antaño 2007: Convocatoria*. Quillacollo. Fundación Autóctona Urkupiña.

Bruner, E. M. (2005). Introduction: Travel Stories Told and Retold. In: E. M. Bruner (Ed.), *Culture on Tour: Ethnographies of Travel* (pp. 1-29). Chicago, London: The University of Chicago Press.

Bruner, E. M. (2005). The Maasai and the Lion King: Authenticity, Nationalism, and Globalization in African Tourism. In: E. M. Bruner (Ed.), *Culture on Tour: Ethnographies of Travel* (pp. 71-100). Chicago, London: The University of Chicago Press.

Bruner, E. M. & Kirshenblatt-Gimblett, B. (1994). Maasai on the Lawn: Tourism Realism in East Africa. *Cultural Anthropolog, 9* (4), pp. 435-470.

Bunster, X. & Chaney, E. M. (1985). *Sellers & Servants: Working Women in Lima, Peru*. New York: Praeger.

Burns, K. (1999). *Convents and the Spiritual Economy of Cuzco, Peru*. Durham: Duke University Press.

Buvinic, M., Morrison, A. R. & Shifter, M. (1999). Violence in the Americas: A Framework for Action. In A. R. Morrison & M. L. Biehl (Eds.), *Too Close to Home: Domestic Violence in the Americas*. Washington: Inter-American Development Bank, John Hopkins University Press.

Caldwell, S. (2004). Subverting the Fierce Goddess: Phoolan Devi and the Politics of Vengeance. In: Suthren Hirst, J. & Thomas, L. (Eds), *Playing for Real: Hindu Role Models, Religion, and Gender* (pp. 161-178). Oxford: Oxford University Press.

Cano Calvarro, F. (2001). Su Aparición y sus Misterios. In: W. G. Valdivia & W. G. Mérida (Eds.), *Historia del Milagro: Antología de Urqupiña* (pp. 138-145). Cochabamba: Los Tiempos.

Cáceres, J. S. (2001). La Basílica Neoclásica de San Ildefonso. In: W. G. Valdivia & W. G. Mérida (Eds.), *Historia del Milagro: Antología de Urqupiña* (pp. 147-152). Cochabamba: Los Tiempos.

Cartwright, E. (2007). Bodily Remembering: Memory, Place, and Understanding Latino Folk Illnesses among the Amuzgos Indians of Oaxaca, Mexico. *Culture, Medicine and Psychiatry 31* (4), pp. 527-545.

Christian, W.A. (1972). *Person and God in a Spanish Valley*. Princeton: Princeton University Press.

Christie, D. J. (1997). Reducing Direct and Structural Violence: The Human Needs Theory. *Peace and Conflict: Journal of Peace Psychology 3* (4), pp. 315-332.

CIA: Central Intelligence Agency (2008). *The World Fact Book: Bolivia.* www.cia.gov/library/publications/the-world-factbook/geos/bl.html

CLADEM: Comité de América Latina y el Caribe para la Defensa de los Derechos de la Mujer (2005). *Dossier sobre Violencia Domestica en América Latina y el Caribe*. Lima: Forma & Imagen.

Clark-Ibáñez, M. (2004). Framing the Social World with Photo-Elicitation Interviews. *American Behavioral Scientist 47* (12), pp. 1507-1527.

Clifford, J. (1986). Introduction: Partial Truths. In: J. Clifford & G. E. Marcus (Eds.), *Writing Culture: The Poetics and Politics of Ethnography*. Berkeley, Los Angeles, London: University of California Press.

Coleman, S. (2002). Do You Believe in Pilgrimage? Communitas, Contestation and Beyond. *Anthropological Theory 2* (3), pp. 355-368.

Coleman, S. (2006). Pilgrimage. In: R.A. Segal (Ed.), *The Blackwell Companion to the Study of Religion* (pp. 385-396). Malden: Blackwell Publishing.

Coleman, S. & Eade, J. (2004). Introduction: Reframing Pilgrimage. In: S. Coleman & J. Eade (Eds.), *Reframing Pilgrimage: Cultures in Motion*. London, New York: Routledge.

Collier, J. F. (1986). From Mary to Modern Woman: The Material Basis of Marianismo and its Transformation in a Spanish Village. *American Ethnologist 13* (1), pp. 100-107.

Crandon-Malamud, L. (1993). Blessings of the Virgin in Capitalist Society: The Transformation of a Rural Bolivian Fiesta. *American Anthropologist 95* (3), pp. 574-596.

Crompton, R. (1998). *Class and Stratification: An Introduction to Current Debates*. Cambridge: Polity Press.

Cuentas, E. (1984). El 'Equeqo' y las 'Alasitas': Manifestaciones de Aculturación Religiosa. *Boletín de Lima 11* (33), pp. 65-70.

Cutcliffe, J. R. (1999). Methodological Issues in Grounded Theory. *Journal of Advanced Nursing 31* (6), pp. 1476-1488.

Daarte, J. & Doerge, S. (1992). *Violencia Contra la Mujer*: Panama: Instituto Cooperativo Interamericano.

Davids, T. & Willemse, K. (1999). In het Lichaam Gegrift: Feministische Antropologen op de Grens van Kennisoverdracht en Representatie. *Tijdschrift voor Genderstudies 2* (1), pp. 3-13.

Defensor del Pueblo. (2006). *Miradas a la Realidad: Estudio de Violencia Intrafamiliar en Contextos de Violencia Generalizada: Trópico Cochabambino*. La Paz: Grupo Impresor.

De Haardt, M. (1999). "Kom, Eet mijn Brood..." Exemplarische Verkenningen naar het Goddelijke in het Alledaagse. Radboud Universiteit Nijmegen: Oration.

De Haardt, M. (2008). Maria, meer dan een dubbelzinnig en gevaarlijk symbool. In: S. El Bouayadi- Van de Wetering & H. Vroom (Eds.), *In het Spoor van Jezus en Mohammed. Op Zoek naar God en Hoe te Leven* (pp. 169-186). Zoetermeer, Kapellen: Meinema.

Delamont, S. (2007). Ethnography and Participant Observation. In: C. Seale, C. Gobo, J. F. Gubrium & D. Silverman (Eds.), *Qualitative Research Practice* (pp. 205-217). London, Thousand Oaks, New Delhi: Sage Publications.

Delgado Morales, S. (1990). Templo San Ildefonso: Corolario de Mons. Mencía. In: R. Peredo Antezana (Ed.), *El Milagro de Urcupiña: Antología de las Manifestaciones del Folklore de Urcupiña*. Cochabamba: Cueto.

Delgado Morales, E. (1999). *Etnografía y Folklore Uru-Valluna: 'Supaykuna chayamusk'an...' - Carnavales de Oruro; 'Muyuj huyrapi muyuririspa...' -Urcupiña de Cochabamba*. Cochabamba: Talleres Gráficos Kipus.

Denzin, N. & Lincoln, Y. S. (2005). Introduction: The Discipline and Practice of Qualitative Research. In: N. Denzin & Y. S. Lincoln (Eds.), *The Sage Handbook of Qualitative Research: Third Edition* (pp. 1-32). Thousand Oaks, London, New Delhi: Sage Publications.

Desmond, J. (1999). Introduction: Touring the Essential. In J. Desmond (Ed.), *Staging Tourism: Bodies on Display from Waikiki to Sea World* (pp. xii-xxv). Chicago: University of Chicago Press.

Dijck, van P. (1998). *The Bolivian Experiment: Structural Adjustment and Poverty Alleviation*. Amsterdam: CEDLA.

Driessen, H. & De Jonge, H. (1994). *In de Ban van Betekenis: Proeven van Symbolische Antropologie*. Nijmegen: SUN.

Droogers, A. (1980). Symbols of Marginality in the Biographies of Religious and Secular Innovators. *Numen 27* (1), pp. 105-121.

Droogers, A. (2001). Joana's Story: Syncretism at the Actor's Level. In: S.M. Greenfield & A. Droogers (Eds.), *Reinventing Religions: Syncretism and Transformation in Africa and the Americas*. Lanham, Boulder, New York, Oxford: Rowman & Littlefield Publishers.

Dubisch, J. (1995). *In a Different Place: Pilgrimage, Gender and Politics at a Greek*

Island Shrine. New Jersey: Princeton University Press.

Durrans, B. (2000). (Not) Religion in Museums. In: C. Paine (Ed.), *Godly Things: Museums, Objects and Religion* (pp. 57-79). London, New York: Leicester University Press.

Eade, J. & Sallnow, M. J. (1991). Introduction. In: J. Eade & M. J. Sallnow (Eds.), *Contesting the Sacred: The Anthropology of Christian Pilgrimage*. Chicago: University of Illinois Press.

Ebron, P. A. (2000). Tourists as Pilgrims: Commercial Fashioning of Transatlantic Politics. *American Ethnologist 26* (4), pp. 910-932.

Elliott, J. (2005). *Using Narrative in Social Research: Qualitative and Quantitative Approaches*. London, Thousand Oaks, New Delhi: Sage.

Ellsberg, M., Peña, R., Herrera, A., Liljestrand, J. & Winkvist, A. (2000). Candies in Hell: Women's Experiences of Violence in Nicaragua. *Social Sciences & Medicine 51* (11), pp. 1595-1610.

Emerson, R. M., Fretz, R. I. & Shaw, L. L. (1995). *Writing Ethnographic Fieldnotes*. Chicago, London: The University of Chicago Press.

Emmerij, L. (1998). Bolivia: Permanent Revolution and Permanent Failure. In: P. van Dijck (Ed.), *The Bolivian Experiment: Structural Adjustment and Poverty Alleviation* (pp. 7-15). Amsterdam: CEDLA.

Eróstegui R, C. (2003). El Repartimiento de Sipe Sipe: Apuntes para la Histórica Colonial Temprana de Cochabamba. *Yachay 20* (37), pp. 85-94.

Estermann, J. (1993). Filosofía Andina: Elementos para la Reivindicación del Pensamiento Colonizado. *Stromato 2*, pp. 203-228.

Farmer, P. (1997). On Suffering and Structural Violence: A View from Below. In: A. Kleinman, V. Das & M. Lock (Eds.), *Social Suffering* (pp. 261-283). Berkeley, Los Angeles, London: University of California Press.

Farmer, P. (2004). An Anthropology of Structural Violence. *Current Anthropology 45* (3), pp. 305-326.

Farmer, P. (2005). *Pathologies of Power: Health, Human Rights, and the New War on the Poor*. Berkeley, London: University of California Press.

Favret-Saada, J. (1980). *Deadly Words: Witchcraft in the Bocage*. Cambridge: Cambridge University Press.

Felix Arias, J. (1993). El Modelo Neoliberal en Bolivia y su Impacto en los Aymaras Urbanos. *Presencia*, pp. 14-15.

Field, L. W. (1994). Who are the Indians? Reconceptualizing Indigenous Identity, Resistance, and the Role of Social Science in Latin America. *Latin American Research Review 29* (3), pp. 237-248.

Flake, D. F. & Forste, R. (2006). Fighting Families: Family Characteristics Associated with Domestic Violence in Five Latin American Countries. *Journal of Family Violence 21* (1), pp.19-28.

Foucault, M. (1977). *Power/Knowledge: Selected Interviews and Other Writings 1972-1977*. New York: Pantheon Books.

Foucault, M. (1982). The Subject and Power. *Critical Inquiry 8*, pp. 777-796.

Freedberg, D. (1989). *The Power of Images: Studies in the History and Theory of Response*. Chicago, London: The University of Chicago Press.

Friedman-Rudovsky, J. (2008). A Brewing Civil War in Bolivia? *Time* (17-8).

Friedson, S. M. (2005). Where Divine Horsemen Ride: Trance Dancing in West Africa. In: A. Hobart & B. Kapferer (Eds.), *Aesthetics in Performance: Formations of Symbolic Construction and Experience* (pp. 109-128). New York, Oxford: Berghahn Books.

Frey, N. L. (2004). Stories of the Return: Pilgrimage and its Aftermaths. In: E. Badone & S. R. Roseman (Eds.), *Intersecting Journeys: The Anthropology of Pilgrimage and Tourism* (pp. 89-109). Urbana Chicago: University of Illinois Press.

Frijhoff, W. (1993). Cultuur op Termijn: Een Verkenning van Identiteit in de Tijd. In: C. Bouw, & B. Kruithof (eds), *De Kern van het Verschil: Culturen & Identiteiten* (pp. 17-40).

Garcia Mérida, W. (2001). En los Umbrales del Horizonte Utópico. In: W. G. Valdivia & W. Garcia Mérida (Eds.), *Historia del Milagro: Antología de Urqupiña* (pp. 21-58). Cochabamba: Los Tiempos.

Garcia Mérida, W. (2001). ¿UrKupiña, UrCupiña o UrQupiña? In: W. G. Valdivia & W. Garcia Mérida (Eds.), *Historia del Milagro: Antología de Urqupiña* (pp. 77-82). Cochabamba: Los Tiempos.

Gavanas, A. (2008). Grasping Communitas. *Ethnos 73* (1), 127-133.

Gebara, I. & Bingener, M. (1989). *Mary: Mother of God, Mother of the Poor*. Maryknoll: Orbis Books.

Gemzöe, L. (2000). *Feminine Matters: Women's Religious Practices in a Portugese Town*. Stockholm: Almqvist & Wiksell International.

Gill, L. (1993). 'Proper Women' and City Pleasures: Gender, Class, and Contested Meanings in La Paz. *American Ethnologist 20* (1), 72-88.

Gill, L. (1997). Relocating Class: Ex-miners and Neoliberalism in Bolivia. *Critique of Anthropology 17* (3), pp. 293-312.

Giorgis, M. (2001). Con sus Santos se fueron Rumbo a Córdoba. In: W. G. Valdivia & W. G. Mérida (Eds.), *Historia del Milagro: Antología de Urqupiña* (pp. 271-286). Cochabamba: Los Tiempos.

Giorgis, M. (2004). *La Virgen Prestamista: La Fiesta de la Virgen de Urkupiña en el Boliviano Gran Córdoba*. Buenos Aires: Antropofagia.

Goldstein, D. M. (2004). *The Spectacular City: Violence and Performance in Urban Bolivia*. Durham & London: Duke University Press.

Goldstein, D. M. (2005). Flexible Justice: Neoliberal Violence and 'Self-help' Security in Bolivia. *Critique of Anthropology 25* (4), pp. 389-411.

Golombok, S. & Fivush, R. (1994). *Gender Development*. Cambridge: Cambridge University Press.

Goodall, H. L. (2000). *Writing the New Ethnography*. Lanham: AltaMira.

Grodzins Gold, A. (1994). Gender, Violence and Power: Rajasthani Stories of Shakti. In: Kumar, N. (ed), *Women as Subjects: South Asian Histories* (pp. 26-43). Charlottesville, London: University Press of Virginia.

Grimes, R. (2000). *Deeply into the Bone: Reinventing Rites of Passage*. Berkeley: University of California Press.

Guerrero Jimenez, B. (2004). Bailar, Jugar y Desfilar: La Identidad Cultural de los Nortinos. *Revista de Siencias Sociales: Universidad Arturo Prat 14*, pp. 89-104.

Gumucio Hinojosa, W. (2005). *Legislación Familiar y otras Leyes por Analogía*. Cochabamba: Grafix Impresores.

Guss, D. M. (2000). *The Festive State: Race, Ethnicity and Nationalism as Cultural Performance*. Berkeley, Los Angeles, London: University of California Press.

Gutmann, M. (1996). *The Meanings of Macho: Being a Man in Mexico City*. Berkeley, Los Angeles: University of California Press.

Hall, D.D. (1997). Introduction. In: D.D. Hall, (Ed) *Lived Religion in America: Toward a History of Practice*. Princeton: Princeton University Press.

Hamington, M.(1995). *Hail Mary? The Struggle for Ultimate Womanhood in Catholicism*. New York, London: Routledge.

Hammersley, M. (1990). *Reading Ethnographic Research: A Critical Guide*. London, New York: Longman.

Hanna, J. L. (1988). The Representation and Reality of Religion in Dance. *Journal of the American Academy of Religion 56* (2), pp. 281-306.

Hardin, M. (2002). Altering Masculinities: The Spanish Conquest and the Evolution of the Latin American Machismo. *International Journal of Sexuality and Gender Studies* 7 (1), pp. 1-22.

Harris, M. (1976). History and Significance of the Emic Etic Distinction. *Annual Review of Anthropology 5*, pp. 329-350.

Harris, O. (2000). *The Mythological Figure of the Earth Mother*. London: Institute of Latin American Studies.

Harris, O. (2000). The Sources and Meanings of Money: Beyond the Market Paradigma. In O. Harris (Ed.), *To Make the Earth Bear Fruit: Essays on Fertility, Work and Gender in Highland Bolivia*. London: Institute of Latin American Studies.

Harskamp van, A.(2006). Introduction: On Play, Imagination, and the Study of Religion. In A. van Harskamp, M. Klaver, J. Roeland & P. Versteeg (Eds.), *Playful Religion: Challenges for the Study of Religion* (pp. 1-8). Delft: Eburon.

Hastrup, K. (1995). The Ethnographic Present: On Starting in Time. In K. Hastrup (Ed.), *A Passage to Anthropology: Between Experience and Theory* (pp. 9-25). London, New York: Routledge.

Heessels, M. (2005). *De Vele Gedaantes van Guadalupe in het Dagelijkse Leven in Mexico*. Radboud Universiteit Nijmegen: MA-thesis.

Henriquez Rojas, P. (1996). *Por que Bailando? Estudio de los Bailes Religiosos del Norte Grande de Chile*. Santiago de Chile: Printext Ltda.

Hermkens, A.-K. (2005). *Engendering Objects: Barkcloth and the Dynamics of Identity in Papua New Guinea*. Radboud University Nijmegen: Ph.D. thesis.

Hermkens, A.K. (2007). The Power of Mary in Papua New Guinea. *Anthropology Today 23* (2), pp. 4-8.

Hermkens, A.K. (2008). Josephine's Journey: Gender-based Violence and Marian Devotion in Urban Papua New Guinea. *Oceania 78* (2), pp. 151-167.

Hermkens, A.K. (2008). Religion in War and Peace: Unravelling Mary's Intervention in the Bougainville Crisis. *Culture and Religion 8* (3), pp. 271-289.

Hermkens, A.K. (forthcoming). Journeys of Violence and Peace: Marian Pilgrimages in Bougainville: In: A.K. Hermkens, C. Notermans & W. Jansen (Eds.), *Moved by Mary: The Power of Pilgrimage in the Modern World*. Hampshire: Ashgate.

Hermkens, A.K., Notermans C. & Jansen, W. (forthcoming). Introduction. In: A.K. Hermkens, C. Notermans & W. Jansen (Eds.), *Moved by Mary: The Power of Pilgrimage in the Modern World*. Hampshire: Ashgate.

Herrera-Sobek, M. (1990). *The Mexican Corrido: A Feminist Analysis*. Bloomington & Indianapolis: Indiana University Press.

Hobsbawn, E. (1983). Introduction: Inventing Traditions. In: E. Hobsbawm & T. Ranger (Eds.), *The Invention of Tradition* (pp. 1-14). Cambridge: Cambridge University Press.

Holden, P. (1983). *Women's Religious Experience*. Kent: Croom Helm.

Hornberger, N. H. & Coronel-Molina, S. F. (2004). Quechua Language Shift, Maintenance, and Revitalization in the Andes: The Case for Language Planning. *International Journal of Social Languages 167*, pp. 9-67.

Hoskins, J. (1998). *Biographical Objects: How Things Tell the Stories of People's Lives*. London: Routledge.

Hubbell, L. J. (1993). Values under Siege in Mexico: Strategies for Sheltering Traditional Values from Change. *Journal of Anthropological Research 49* (1), pp. 1-16.

INE (2003). *Bolivia: Características de la Población con Enfoque de Género*. La Paz: Instituto Nacional de Estadística.

INE (2004). *Anuario Estadístico 2003*. La Paz: Instituto Nacional de Estadística.

INE (2007). *Anuario Estadístico 2006*. La Paz: Instituto Nacional de Estadística.

Jackson, M. (2002). *The Politics of Storytelling: Violence, Transgression, and Intersubjectivity*. Copenhagen: Museum Tusculanum Press.

James, S. E., Johnson, J., Raghavan, C., Lemos, T., Barakett, M., & Woolis, D. (2003). The Violent Matrix: A Study of Structural, Interpersonal and Intrapersonal Violence among a Sample of Poor Women. *American Journal of Community Psychology 31* (1/2), pp. 129-141.

Jansen, W. (1987). *Women without Men: Gender and Marginality in an Algerian Town*. Leiden: Brill.

Jansen, W. (1991). Dansen voor de Geesten: Bezetenheid in Multidisciplinair Perspectief. In: W. Jansen & C. Brinkgreve (Eds.), *Waanzin en Vrouwen* (pp. 191-222). Amsterdam: Zwets & Zeitlinger.

Jansen, W. (1997). Gender Identity and the Rituals of Food in a Jordanian Community. *Food and Foodways* 7 (2), pp. 87-117.

Jansen, W. (2005). Visions of Mary in the Middle East: Gender and the Power of a Symbol. In: I.M. Okkenhaug, & I. Flaskerud (Eds). *Gender, Religion and Change in the Middle East: Two Hundred Years of History* (pp.137-154). Oxford, New York: Berg.

Jansen, W. & H. de Jonge (1991). *Islamitische Pelgrimstochten*. Muiderberg: Coutinho.

Janssen, J. (2002). *Aan de onbekende God: Reiken naar Religie in een Geseculariseerde Cultuur*. Amsterdam: SUN.

Janssen, J. (2009). *The Disappearing Object Phenomenon: Over Religie en Cultuur in Kunst en Wetenschap*. Radboud University Nijmegen: Farewell speech.

Janssens, D. (2001). *De Cosmovisión van de Aymara's: Analyse van hun Kosmocentrische Ecologische visie*. Katholieke Universiteit Leuven: MA thesis.

Jenkins, R. (1997). *Rethinking Ethnicity: Arguments and Explorations*. London, Thousand Oaks, New Delhi: Sage Publications.

Jolly, M. (1992). Specters of Inauthenticity. *The Contemporary Pacific 4* (1), pp. 49-62.

Katyal, A. (2001). Performing the Goddess: Sacred Ritual into Professional Performance. *The Drama Review 45* (1), pp. 96-107.

Kerfoot, D. & Knights, D. (1994). Into the Realm of the Fearful: Power, Identity and the Gender Problematic. In L. H. Radtke & H. J. Stam (Eds.), *Power/Gender: Social Relations in Theory and Practice*. London, Thousand Oaks, New Delhi: Sage Publications.

Kessel van, J. (1992). Virgen Pachamama: El Mito de la Fundación. *Boletín del Instituto de Estudios Aymaras 2* (41), pp. 69-92.

Kessel van, J. (1992). Faith Healing in the North Chilean Andes of Pilgrimage. *Exchange*, 21 (1), pp. 62-83.

King, U. (1997). Religion and Gender. In: J. R. Hinnells (Ed.), *The New Penguin Handbook of Living Religions* (pp. 647-666). London: Penguin Books.

Kleinman, A., Das, V. & Lock, M. (1997). Introduction. In: A. Kleinman, V. Das and M. Lock (Eds.), *Social Suffering* (ix-xxvii). Berkeley, London: University of California Press.

Kohl, B. (2006). Challenges to Neoliberal Hegemony in Bolivia. *Antipode 38* (2), pp. 304-326.

Kohl, B. & Farthing, L. (2007). *El Bumerán Boliviano: Hegemonía y Resistencia Social*. La Paz: Plural.

Kolig, E. (2005). The Politics of Indigenous -or Ingenious- Tradition: Some Thoughts on the Australian and New Zealand Situation. In: T. Otto & P. Pedersen (Eds.), *Tradition and Agency: Tracing Cultural Continuity and Invention* (pp. 292-326). Aarhus: Aarhus University Press.

Koopman, E. (2008, 27-9-2008). Kritiek op de Goede Indiaan. *Trouw*.

Kopytoff, I. (1986). The Cultural Biography of Things: Commoditization as Process. In: A. Appadurai (Ed.), *The Social Life of Things: Commodities in Cultural Perspective* (pp. 64-91). Cambridge, New York, Melbourne: Cambridge University Press.

Laan, E. (1993). *Bailar para Sanar: Estudio de la Praxis de la Peregrinación de los Bailes Religiosos del Norte de Chile*. Iquique: Centro de Investigación de la Realidad del Norte/Crear.

Lagos, M. L. (1993). 'We Have to Learn to Ask': Hegemony, Diverse Experiences, and Antagonistic Meanings in Bolivia. *American Ethnologist 20* (1), pp. 52-71.

Lagos, M. L. (1997). *Autonomía y Poder: Dinámica de Clase y Cultura en Cochabamba*. La Paz: Centro de Información para el Desarrollo.

Lagos, M. L. (2001). La Virgen y los Indios. In: W. G. Valdivia & W. Garcia Mérida (Eds.), *Historia del Milagro: Antología de Urqupiña* (pp. 107-114). Cochabamba: Los Tiempos.

Las Brigadas de Protección a la Familia. (2005-2007). *Police Reports Cochabamba: Statistics on Domestic Violence*. Cochabamba: Las Brigadas de Protección a la Familia.

Lautaro Nuñez, A. (1989). *La Tirana*. Antofagasta, Chile: Norprint.

Levine, S. (1993). *Dolor y Alegría: Women and Social Change in Urban Mexico*. Wisconsin: The University of Wisconsin Press.

Ley 2536. (2003). *Reglamento de la Ley no 25 36: Declaración de Patrimonio Cultural de Bolivia a la 'Festividad Religiosa de la Virgen Nuestra Señora de Urqupña'*. Quillacollo: Unpublished Manuscript.

Los Tiempos (1977, 14-8-1977). Hoy se Realiza la Tradicional Entrada de la Virgen de Urkupiña. Cochabamba: *Los Tiempos*.

Los Tiempos (2005, (15-8-2005). 10 Mil Personas Lucen su Danza de Fe y Alegría. Cochabamba: *Los Tiempos*.

Los Tiempos (2005, 17-8-2005). La Fe Mueve Montañas. *Los Tiempos*.

Los Tiempos (2007, 22-7-2007). Cochabamba Tiene las Zonas mas Pobres del Pais. Cochabamba: *Los Tiempos*.

Los Tiempos (2008, 14-8-2008). 15 Mil Bailarines Hoy en Tribute a la Virgen. Cochabamba: *Los Tiempos*.

Los Tiempos (2008, 12-8-2008). Quillacollo Alista Semana de Folclore, Fe y Riesgo. Cochabamba: *Los Tiempos*.

Los Tiempos (2008, 13-9-2008). Gobierno Confirma 16 Muertos en el Conflicto del Norte del País. Cochabamba: *Los Tiempos*.

Luke (1: 46-55). In: (1990). *The Holy Bible: Containing the Old and New Testaments with the Apocryphal/Deuterocanonical Books*, New Revised Standard Version. Nashville: Thomas Nelson Publishers.

MacCannell, D. (1973). Staged Authenticity: Arrangements of Social Space in Tourist Settings. *The American Journal of Sociology* 79 (3), pp. 589-603.

Madison, S. (2005). *Critical Ethnography: Method, Ethics, and Performance*. Thousand Oaks, London, New Delhi: Sage Publications.

Maduro, O. (1982). *Religion and Social Conflicts*. Maryknoll, New York: Orbis Books.

Maeckelberghe, E. (1991). *Desperately Seeking Mary: A Feminist Appropriation of a Traditional Religious Symbol*. Kampen: Kok.

Malešević, S. (2004). *The Sociology of Ethnicity*. London, Thousand Oaks, New Delhi: Sage Publications.

Manzanera, M. (1993). Critica Filosófica del Neoliberalismo. *Yachay: Revista de Cultura, Filosofia y Teologia 10* (18), pp. 13-62.

Margolis, M. (2008, 29-8-2008). The Battle of Bolivia. *Newsweek*.

Margry, P.J. (2003). Persoonlijke Altaren en Private Heiligdommen: De Creatie van Sacrale Materiële Cultuur als Resultante van Geïndividualiseerde Religiositeit. In: A.L. Molendijk, (Ed.), *Materieel Christendom: Religie en Materiële Cultuur in West-Europa* (pp. 51- 78). Hilversum: Verloren.

Margry, P.J. (2008). Secular Pilgrimage: A Contradiction in Terms? In: P.J. Margry (Ed.), *Shrines and Pilgrimage in the Modern World. New Itineraries into the Sacred*. Amsterdam: Amsterdam University Press.

Martinez Espinoza, N. W. (1995). La Feria de Alasitas: Un Fenómeno de la Cultura Urbana Moderna: Aproximación a la Semiótica de la Miniatura. *Reunión Anual de Etnología II*, pp. 135-142.

Matter, E. A. (2001). Apparitions of the Virgin Mary in the Late Twentieth Century: Apocalyptic, Representation, Politics. *Religion 31*, pp. 125-153.

Mauss, M. 1990. *The Gift: Forms and Functions of Exchange in Archaic Societies*. London: Routledge.

McCarthy Brown, K. (2001). *Mama Lola: A Vodou Priestess in Brooklyn*. Berkeley, Calif, London: University of California Press.

Mc Dannell, C. (1995). *Material Christianity: Religion and Popular Culture in America*. New Haven & London: Yale University Press.

Mcguire, M. B. (2003). Why Bodies Matter: A Sociological Reflection on Spirituality and Materiality. *Spiritus 3*, pp. 1-18.

Mendoza, Z. S. (1998). Defining Folklore: Mestizo and Indigenous Identities on the Move. *Bulletin of Latin American Research* 17 (2), pp. 165-183.

Mendoza, Z.S. (1999). Genuine but Marginal: Exploring and Reworking Social Contradictions through Ritual Dance Performance. *Journal of Latin American Anthropology 3* (2), pp. 86-117.

Mendoza, Z.S. (2008). *Creating Our Own: Folklore, Performance, and Identity in Cuzco, Peru*. Durham & London: Duke University Press.

Mendoza Flores, J. (1996). La Tradicional Entrada Folklórica de Urkupiña. *aquipacha 1* (1), pp. 31-45.

Ministerio de Salud y Deportes, Bolivia (2004). *Prevención y Atención de Violencias: Plan Nacional 2004 - 2007*. La Paz: Ministerio de Salud y Deportes.

Ministerio del Trabajo, Bolivia (2008). Salario Minimo. www.mintrabajo.gov.bo.

Montaño Aragón, M. (2006). Breve Estudio Toponímico de Quillacollo. In: R. Peredo Antezana (Ed.), *María de Urqupiña* (pp. 17-28). Cochabamba: Aliaga.

Moore, H. L. (1988). *Feminism and Anthropology*. Cambridge: Polity Press.

Moore, H. L. (1994). 'Divided we Stand': Sex, Gender and Sexual Difference. *Feminist Review 47*, pp. 78-95.

Morales Basadre, R. (2000). Educación, Valores y Derechos Humanos en Tiempos de Neoliberalismo. *Allpanchis 55*, pp. 11-30.

Morales-Gorecki, V. (1988). Cultural Variations on Gender: Latin American Marianismo/Machismo in Australia. *Mankind 18* (1), pp. 26-38.

Morgan, D. (1998). *Visual Piety: A History and Theory of Popular Religious Images*. Berkeley, Los Angeles, London: University of California Press.

Morgan, D. (2005). *The Sacred Gaze: Religious Visual Culture in Theory and Practice* Berkeley and Los Angeles: University of California Press.

Morgan, D. (forthcoming). Aura and the Inversion of Marian Pilgrimage: Fatima and her Statues. In: A.K. Hermkens, C. Notermans & W. Jansen (forthcoming). *Moved by Mary: The Power of Pilgrimage in the Modern World*. Hampshire: Ashgate.

Morgan, D., & Wilkinson, I. (2001). The Problem of Suffering and the Sociological Task of Theodicy. *European Journal of Social Theory 4* (2), pp. 199-214.

Morinis, A. (1992). *Sacred Journeys: The Anthropology of Pilgrimage*. Westport: Greenwood Press.

Morphy, H. & Banks, M. (1997). Introduction: Rethinking Visual Anthropology. In: H. Morphy & M. Banks (Eds.), *Rethinking Visual Anthropology* (pp. 1-35). New Haven, London: Yale University Press.

Movisie (2007). *Factsheet. Huiselijk Geweld: Feiten en Cijfers*. www.movisie.nl.

Myerhoff, B. (1984). Rites and Signs of Ripening: The Intertwining of Ritual, Time, and Growing Older. In: D. Kertzer & J. Keith (Eds.), *Age and Anthropological Theory* (pp. 305-330). London, Ithaca: Cornell University Press.

Myers, F. R. (2001). Introduction: The Empire of Things. In: F. R. Myers (Ed.), *The Empire of Things: Regimes of Value and Material Culture* (pp. 3-61). Santa Fe: School of American Research Press.

Nagel, J. (1994). Constructing Ethnicity: Creating and Recreating Ethnic Identity and Culture. *Social Problems 41* (1), pp. 152-176.

Navarro, M. (2002). Against Marianismo. In: R. Montoya, L. J. Frazier & J. Hurtig (Eds.), *Gender's Place: Feminist Anthropologies of Latin America* (pp. 257-272). New York: Palgrave MacMillan.

Nijhoff, G. (1993). Cultuur op Termijn: Een Verkenning van Identiteit in de Tijd. In: C. Bouw & B. Kruithof (Eds.), *De Kern van het Verschil: Culturen en Identiteiten* (pp.17-39). Amsterdam: University Press.

Nijhof, G. (2000). *Levensverhalen: De Methode van Autobiografisch Onderzoek in de Sociologie*. Amsterdam: Boom.

Nolan, M. L. (1991). The European Roots of Latin American Pilgrimage. In: A. Morinis & N. R. Crumrine (Eds.), *Pilgrimage in Latin America* (pp. 19-47). New York, London: Greenwood Press.

Notermans, C. (1999). *Verhalen in Veelvoud: Vrouwen in Kameroen over Polygamie en Christendom*. Nijmegen: Valkhof Pers.

Notermans, C. (2008). Local and Global Icons of Mary: An Ethnographic Study of a Powerful Symbol. *Anthropos 103* (2), pp. 471-481.

Notermans, C. (2007). The Healing of Loss: A Marian Pilgrimage in Secular Dutch Society. *Ethnology 46* (3), pp. 217-234.

Obando Stemberg, J. R. (2007). *Guía Turística de Quillacollo*. Quillacollo: Editorial Rogos.

Oldersma, J. & Davis, K. (1991). Introduction. In: K. Davis, M. Leijenaar & J. Oldersma (Eds.), *The Gender of Power* (pp. 1-18). London, Newbury Park, New Delhi: Sage Publications.

Ontiveros, E. (2001). La Devoción Llego hasta California. In: W. G. Valdivia & W. Garcia Mérida (Eds.), *Historia del Milagro: Antología de Urqupiña* (pp. 287-292). Cochabamba: Los Tiempos.

Orsi, R. A. (1996). *Thank You, St. Jude*. New Haven: Yale University Press.

Orsi, R. A. (1997). Everyday Miracles: The Study of Lived Religion. In: D. Hall (Ed.), *Lived Religion in America: Towards a History of Practice* (pp. 3-21). Princeton: Princeton University Press.

Orsi, R. A. (2002). Is the Study of Lived Religion Irrelevant to the World We Live in? Special Presidential Plenary Address, Society for the Scientific Study of Religion, Salt Lake City, November 2, 2002. *Journal for the Scientific Study of Religion, 42* (2), 169-174.

Orsi, R. A. (2002). *The Madonna of 115th Street*. New Haven, London: Yale University Press.

Orsi, R. A. (2005). *Between Heaven and Earth: The Religious Worlds People Make and the Scholars Who Study Them*. Princeton, Oxford: Princeton University Press.

Orsini, J. (2000). *Mary: Images of the Holy Mother*. San Francisco: Chronicle Books.

Ortner, S. B. (1996). *Making Gender: The Politics and Erotics of Culture*. Boston: Beacon Press.

Padilla, M.R. (1993). *Danzas Folklóricas del Beni*. Trinidad: Unpublished Manuscript.

Pargament, K. I. (1997). *The Psychology of Religion and Coping: Theory, Research, Practice*. New York: Guilfort Press.

Parker, C. (1996). *Popular Religion and Modernization in Latin America: A Different Logic*. New York: Orbis Books.

Paulson, S. & Calla, P. (2000). Gender and Ethnicity in Bolivian Politics: Transformation or Paternalism? *The Journal of Latin American Anthropology 5* (2), pp. 112-149.

Peelen, J. & Jansen, W. (2007). Emotive Movement on the Road to Santiago de Compostella. *Etnofoor 20* (1), pp. 75-96.

Peredo Antezana, R. (1990). Origen de la Festividad de la Virgen de Urqupiña. In: R. Peredo Antezana (Ed.), *El Milagro de Urcupiña: Antología de las Manifestaciones del Folklore de Urcupiña*. Cochabamba: Cueto.

Peredo Antezana, R. (2001). El Mundo Colonial de Quillacollo. In: W. G. Valdivia & W. Garcia Mérida (Eds.), *Historia del Milagro: Antología de Urqupiña* (pp. 85-97). Cochabamba: Los Tiempos.

Peredo Antezana, R. (2006). Leyendas de la Virgen de Urqupiña. In: R. Peredo Antezana (Ed.), *María de Urqupiña* (pp. 54-60). Cochabamba: Aliaga.

Pereira Herrera, D. M. (1994). Las Qollqas Incaicas de Cotapachi - Quillacollo. *Analisis Cultural 2*, pp. 69-73.

Pilar Aquino, M. (1992). *Nuestro Clamor por la Vida. Teología Latinoamericana Desde la Perspectiva de la Mujer*. San José: Departamento Ecuménico de Investigaciones.

Plate, S. B. (2002). Introduction. In: S. B. Plate (Ed.), *Religion, Art and Visual Culture: A Cross-cultural Reader* (pp. 1-18). New York: Palgrave.

Poole, D. A. (1990). Accommodation and Resistance in Andean Ritual Dance. *The Drama Review 34* (2), pp. 98-125.

Poole, D. A. (1991). Rituals of Movement, Rites of Transformation: Pilgrimage and Dance in the Highlands of Cuzco, Peru. In: N. R. Crumrine & A. Morinis (Eds.), *Pilgrimage in Latin America* (pp. 307-357). New York, Westport, London: Greenwood Press.

Psacharopoulos, G. & Patrinos, H. A. (1994). *Indigenous People and Poverty in Latin America*. Washington: The World Bank.

Quiroga Flores, M. A. (2006). Estudio del Vocablo Quechua 'Urkupiña'. In: R. Peredo Antezana (Ed.), *María de Urqupiña* (pp. 15-16). Cochabamba: Aliaga.

Radcliffe, S. A. (1997). The Geographies of Indigenous Self-Representation in Ecuador: Hybridity, Gender and Resistance. *Revista Europea de Estudios Latinoamericanos y del Caribe 63*, pp. 167-172.

Radtke, L. H. & Stam, H. J. (1994). Introduction. In: L. H. Radtke & H. J. Stam (Eds.), *Power/Gender: Social Relations in Theory and Practice*. London,

Thousand Oaks, New Delhi: Sage Publications.
Reader, I. (2007). Pilgrimage Growth in the Modern World: Meanings and Implications. *Religion* 37 (3), pp. 210-229.
Reader, I. & Walter, T. (2001). *Pilgrimage in Popular Culture*. New York: Palgrave.
Reid, B. V. & Whitehead, T. L. (1992). Introduction. In: B. V. Reid & T. L. Whitehead (Eds.), *Gender Constructs and Social Issues* (pp. 1-9). Urbana, Chicago: University of Illinois Press.
Revollo Quiroga, M. (1995). *Violencia Domestica Registrada en Bolivia*. La Paz: Grupo Design.
Rey, T. (1999). *Our Lady of Class Struggle: The Cult of the Virgin Mary in Haiti*. Trenton: Africa World Press.
Reynolds, B. & Stott, M. A. (1987). *Material Anthropology: Contemporary Approaches to Material Culture*. Lanham: University Press of America.
Rockefeller, S. A. (1999). 'There is a Culture Here': Spectacle and the Inculcation of Folklore in Highland Bolivia. *Journal of Latin American Anthropology* 3 (2), pp. 118-149.
Rodriguez, J. (1994). *Our Lady of Guadalupe: Faith and Empowerment among Mexican-American women*. Austin: University of Texas Press.
Rostas, S. & Droogers, A. (1993). *The Popular Use of Popular Religion in Latin America*. Amsterdam: CEDLA.
Rothman, R. A. (1999). *Inequality and Stratification: Race, Class, and Gender*. New Jersey: Prentice Hall.
Rowland, C. (1999). *The Cambridge Companion to Liberation Theology*. Cambridge: Cambridge University Press.
Rowlands, J. (1997). *Questioning Empowerment: Working with Women in Honduras*. Oxford: Oxfam.
Ruiz Martinez, G. (2007). *Etnias, Culturas y Lenguas de Bolivia*. La Paz: Graf-Uno.
Sagot, M. (2005). The Critical Path of Women Affected by Family Violence in Latin America. *Violence Against Women 11* (10), pp. 1293-1318.
Salles Reese (1992). Buscando Armonía en Dos Universos Religiosos. In: S. Arzo, R. Barragán, L. Escobari, & M. Medinaceli (Eds.). *Etnicidad, Economía y Simbolismo en los Andes* (pp. 255-265). La Paz: Hisbol.
Sallnow, M. J. (1982). A Trinity of Christs: Cultic Processes in Andean Catholicism. *American Ethnologist 9* (4), pp. 730-749.
Sallnow, M. J. (2000). Pilgrimage and Cultural Fracture in the Andes. In J. Eade & M. J. Sallnow (Eds.), *Contesting the Sacred: The Anthropology of Pilgrimage* (pp. 137-153). London, New York: Routledge.
Salman, T. (2006). The Jammed Democracy: Bolivia's Troubled Political Learning Process. *Bulletin of Latin American Research 25* (2), pp. 163-182.
Salyers Bull, S. (1998). Machismo/Marianismo Attitudes, Employment, Education, and Sexual Behavior Among Women in Ecuador and the Dominican Republic. *Journal of Gender, Culture, and Health 3* (1), pp. 1-27.

Samuels, J. (2004). Breaking the Ethnographer's Frames. Reflections on the Use of Photo Elicitation in Understanding Sri Lankan Monastic Culture. *American Behavioral Scientist 47* (12), pp. 1528-1550.

Sanabria, H. (2001). Exploring Kinship in Anthropology and History: Surnames and Social Transformations in the Bolivian Andes. *Latin American Research Review 36* (2), pp. 137- 155.

Sánchez, W. C. (1992). La Fiesta en la Entrada de Urkupiña: Música, Identidad y Conflicto Social Alrededor de una Virgen. In *Reunión Anual de Etnología 2*, pp. 141-165.

Scarborough, I. M. (2005). Construyendo Identidad Cultural y Patrimonio en la Festividad de la Virgen de Urkupina de Quillacollo. In: N. A. Robins (Ed.), *Cambio y Continuidad en Bolivia: Etnicidad, Cultura e Identidad* (pp. 119-132). La Paz: Plural.

Scarry, E. (1985). *The Body in Pain: The Making and Unmaking of the World*. Oxford: Oxford University Press.

Scheper-Hughes, N. (1992). *Death Without Weeping: The Violence of Everyday Life in Brazil*. Berkeley, Los Angeles: University of California Press.

Schillebeeckx, E. & Halkes, C. (1993). *Mary: Yesterday, Today, Tomorrow*. New York: Crossroad.

Schneider, F. (2007). Shadow Economies and Corruption All Over the World: New Estimates for 145 Countries. *Ejournal: Economics 9*, pp. 1-47.

Schramm, K. (2004). Coming Home to the Motherland: Pilgrimage Tourism in Ghana. In: S. Coleman & J. Eade (Eds.), *Reframing Pilgrimage: Cultures in Motion* (pp. 133-149). London, New York: Routledge.

Seligmann, L. J. (1989). To Be in Between: The *Cholas* as Market Women. *Comparative Studies in Society and History 31* (4), pp. 694-721.

Sills, D. L. (1979). *International Encyclopaedia of the Social Sciences* (Vol. 18). New York: Macmillan.

Sklar, D. (2001). *Dancing with the Virgin: Body and Faith in the Fiesta of Tortugas*. New Mexico, Berkeley and Los Angeles: University of California Press

Social Watch (2005). *Social Watch Report: Roars and Whispers: Gender and Poverty*. Montevideo: Social Watch.

Spooner, B. (1986). Weavers and Dealers: The Authenticity of an Oriental Carpet. In: A. Appadurai (Ed.) *The Social Life of Things* (pp. 195-235). Cambridge: Cambridge University Press.

Spradley, J. P. (1980). *Participant Observation*. Wadsworth: Thomson Learning.

Steegstra, M. (2004). *Resilient Rituals: Krobo Initiation and the Politics of Culture in Ghana*. Münster: LIT.

Steenbeek, G. (1986). Macht en Mystificatie in Man-Vrouw Relaties. Het Machismo-Marianismo Complex in Mexico. *Antropologische Verkenningen 5* (2), pp. 62-75.

Steenbeek, G. (1995). *Vrouwen op de Drempel: Gender en Moraliteit in een*

Mexicaanse Provinciestad. Amsterdam: Thela Publishers.
Stevens, E. P. (1973). Marianismo: The Other Face of Machismo in Latin America. In: A. Pesciatello (Ed.), *Female and Male in Latin America*. Pittsburgh, Oxford: Princeton University Press.
Stocking, G. W. (1985). *Objects and Others: Essays on Museums and Material Culture*. Madison: The University of Wisconsin Press.
Stoller, P. (1986). *The Taste of Ethnographic Things: The Senses in Anthropology*. Philadelphia: University of Pennsylvania Press.
Sweetinburgh, S. (2004). *The Role of the Hospital in Medieval England: Gift-Giving and the Spiritual Economy*. Dublin: Four Courts.
Taboada Teran, N. (1999). *Urqupiña por Siempre*. Cochabamba: Editora H&P.
Tamisari, F. (2006). The Responsibility of Performance: The Interweaving of Politics and Aesthetics in Intercultural Contexts. *Visual Anthropology Review 21* (1), pp. 47-62.
Tapia Vargas, G. (2005). *Realidad Nacional*. La Paz: Génesis Publicidad e Impresión.
Taussig, M. T. (1977). The Genesis of Capitalism among a South American Peasantry: Devil's Labor and the Baptism of Money. *Comparative Studies in Society and History 19* (2), pp. 130-155.
Taussig, M. T. (1980). *The Devil and Commodity Fetishism in South America*. Chapel Hill: The University of North Carolina Press.
Taward, G. H. (1996). *The Thousand Faces of the Virgin Mary*. Collegeville: The Liturgical Press.
Taylor, M. C. (1999). *About Religion: Economies of Faith in Virtual Culture*. Chicago, London: The University of Chicago Press.
Taylor, P. (2004). *Goddess on the Rise: Pilgrimage and Popular Religion in Vietnam*. Honolulu: University of Hawai'i Press.
Thomas, H. R. (1995). Las Piedras Sagradas de los Aymaras. *Fuentes Etológicas 5* (5), pp. 3-11.
Tombs, D. (2002). *Latin American Liberation Theology*. Boston, Leiden: Brill.
Tweed, T. A. (1997). *Our Lady of the Exile: Diasporic Religion at a Cuban Catholic Shrine in Miami*. Oxford, New York: Oxford University Press.
Turner, V. & Turner, E. (1978). *Image and Pilgrimage in Christian Culture: Anthropological Perspectives*. Oxford: Blackwell.
Turner, V. (1979). *Process, Performance and Pilgrimage*. New Delhi: Concept Publishing Company.
Twinam, A. (1989). Honor, Sexuality, and Illegitimacy in Colonial Spanish America. In: Lavrin, A. (Ed). *Sexuality and Marriage in Colonial Latin America*. London: University of Nebraska Press.
United Nations (2006). *Human Development Report 2006*. www.undp.org.
United Nations. (2006). *In-depth Study on All Forms of Violence Against Women. Report of the Secretary-General*. New York: United Nations.

Upchurch, C. S., Aneshengel, S., & Mudgal, J. (2001). Sociocultural Contexts of Time to First Sex among Hispanic Adolescents. *Journal of Marriage and Family 63* (4), pp. 1158-1169.

USAID United States Agency for International Development (2007). *Latin America and The Caribbean: Selected Economic and Social Data*. Washington: United States Agency for International Development.

Valdivia, W. G. (2001). El Devenir de la Fiesta Mediática. In: W. G. Valdivia & W. Garcia Mérida (Eds.), *Historia del Milagro: Antología de Urqupiña* (pp. 59-76). Cochabamba: Los Tiempos.

Vanlangenacker, M. (1990). *Pachamama in de Religie van de Aymara en Quechua: Achtergrond en Betekenis binnen het Eigen Religieuze Systeem en Confrontatie met Hedendaagse Missiologische Inzichten*. Katholieke Universiteit Leuven: Ph.D. thesis.

Venbrux E. (2007). *Ongelooflijk! Religieus Handelen, Verhalen en Vormgeven in het Dagelijks Leven*. Radboud Universiteit Nijmegen: Oration.

Venbrux, E., Heessels, M. & Bolt, S. (2008). *Rituele Creativiteit: Actuele Veranderingen in de Uitvaart en Rouwcultuur in Nederland*. Zoetermeer: Meinema.

Villarreal, M. (1994). *Wielding and Yielding: Power, Subordination and Gender Identity in the Context of a Mexican Development Project*. Landbouw Universiteit Wageningen: Ph.D. thesis.

Villarreal, M. (1996). Power and Self-Identity: The Beekeepers of Ayuquila. In: M. Melhuus & K. A. Stolen (Eds.), *Machos, Mistresses, Madonnas: Contesting the Power of Latin American Gender Imagery* (pp. 184-206). London: Verso Press.

Vleet van, K. E. (2008). *Performing Kinship: Narrative, Gender, and the Intimacies of Power in the Andes*. Austin: University of Texas Press.

Vuola, E. (2006). Seriously Harmful for your Health? Religion, Feminism and Sexuality in Latin America. In: M. Althaus-Reid (Ed.), *Liberation Theology and Sexuality* (pp. 137-162). Hamsshire UK, Burlington, USA: Ashgate Publishing Company.

Walsh, D. (2000). Doing Ethnography. In: C. Seale (Ed.), *Researching Society and Culture* (pp. 217-232). London: Sage.

Wang, N. (1999). Rethinking Authenticity in Tourism Experience. *Annals of Tourism Research* 25 (2), pp. 349-370.

Warner, M. (1976). *Alone of All her Sex: The Myth and Cult of the Virgin Mary*. London: Weidenfeld and Nichelson.

Webber, J. (2005). Left-Indigenous Struggles in Bolivia: Searching for Revolutionary Democracy. *Monthly Review 57* (4), pp. 1-15.

Weiss Ozorak, E. (1996). The Power, but Not the Glory: How Women Empower Themselves Through Religion. *Journal for the Scientific Study of Religion* 35 (1), pp. 17-29.

Wester, F. & Peters, V. (2004). *Kwalitatieve Analyse: Uitgangspunten en Procedures*. Bussem: Coutinho.

Westmore, P. (2006, 18-2-2006). Tide Turns for Global Capitalism. *News Weekly*.

Wiley, E. (2005). Romani Performance and Heritage Tourism. *The Drama Review 49* (2), pp. 135-158.

Wilson, F. (2000). Indians and Mestizos: Identity and Urban Popular Culture in Andean Peru. *Journal of Southern African Studies* 26 (2), pp. 239-253.

Wolf, E. (1969). *Peasant Wars of the Twentieth Century*. New York, Evanston, London: Harper & Row Publishers.

Womankind Worldwide (2008). *Bolivia Fact File*. www.womankind.org.uk.

Woodhead, L. (1996). Religious Representations of Women. In: T. Cosslett, A. Easton & P. Summerfield (Eds.), *Women, Power and Resistance: An Introduction to Women's Studies* (pp. 125-135). Buckingham, Philadelphia: Open University Press.

World Health Organization (2002). *World Report on Violence and Health*. Geneva: World Health Organization.

www.apparitions.org

Yamane, D. (2000). Narrative and Religious Experience. *Sociology of Religion 61* (2), pp. 171-189.

Young, J. (2005). On Insiders (Emic) and Outsiders (Etic): Views of Self, and Othering. *Systemic Practice and Action Research 18* (2), pp. 151-162.

NEDERLANDSE SAMENVATTING

Virginia, een arme, inmiddels 59-jarige, Quechua vrouw die tegen betaling gebeden en zegeningen aanbood aan bezoekers van het bedevaartsoord van de Maagd van Urkupiña in Bolivia, verzuchtte regelmatig: 'Deze pelgrimage is een lijdensweg'. Met deze woorden verwees zij naar haar eigen economische lijden, omdat het verkopen van zegeningen haar enige bron van inkomsten was, waarvan ze nauwelijks in haar basisbehoeften kon voorzien. Tegelijkertijd verwees de verzuchting naar het lijden van pelgrims, omdat Virginia in haar gesprekken met pelgrims dagelijks werd geconfronteerd met hun problemen.

In deze studie werd pelgrimage onderzocht als een verschijnsel waarin verschillende soorten sociale ongelijkheden tot uidrukking komen. Het houden van een bedevaart geeft pelgrims ruimte om huiselijke, sociale, economische en politieke problemen te uiten, en tegelijkertijd beïnvloedt pelgrimage de percepties en mogelijkheden van gelovigen om met deze problemen om te gaan. Onderzoek van de religieuze praktijken op een pelgrimsoord kan zo inzicht geven in de manier waarop mensen in het alledaagse leven met machtsongelijkheden omgaan. In het bijzonder kwamen problemen gerelateerd aan klasse (zoals armoede), aan gender (hoofdzakelijk huiselijk geweld) en aan etniciteit (met name het spanningsveld tussen het waarderen van Indiaanse identiteiten en het tegelijkertijd marginaliseren van deze groepen in de samenleving) naar voren op het pelgrimsoord. Dit leidde tot de formulering van de hoofdvraag: Hoe gaan Boliviaanse gelovigen om met klasse, gender en etnische ongelijkheid op het pelgrimsoord van de Maagd van Urkupiña?

Deze antropologische studie gaat in op de ervaringen van gelovigen in een Boliviaans Maria-bedevaartsoord. Dit pelgrimsoord ligt in Quillacollo, een marktplaats in de centrale provincie Cochabamba. Tot de jaren zeventig van de vorige eeuw was de verering van de Maagd van Urkupiña een lokale verering die met name Quechua-Indianen aantrok uit de bergdorpen die Quillacollo omringen. Vervolgens raakten pelgrims uit het bloeiende handelsdistrict van Santa Cruz geïnteresseerd in deze Mariaverering en begonnen zij de Maagd van Urkupiña te benaderen met verzoeken om economische verbetering. Sindsdien geniet het oord nationale bekendheid en tegenwoordig komen pelgrims uit het gehele land - en zelfs daarbuiten - met allerlei verschillende achtergronden naar Quillacollo om hun jaarlijkse bedevaart naar Maria te maken.

De meeste pelgrims brengen zowel een bezoek aan de kerk in het dorp als aan 'het Calvario', een heuvel twee kilometer buiten het dorp waar zij hun verzoeken doen en de meeste rituelen uitvoeren. Hoewel er elke dag pelgrims komen, wordt het oord het drukst bezocht in de maand augustus, wanneer het feest van Urkupiña plaatsvindt. Het feest voor Maria vindt plaats van 13 tot en met 16 augustus. De eerste drie dagen worden er dansprocessies gehouden waarbij ter verering van Maria dansgroepen in kleurrijke kostuums door de straten van Quillacollo dansen. De meeste dansen verwijzen naar de hedendaagse variëteit van etnische identiteiten als ook naar gebeurtenissen en culturele gebruiken van de verschillende etnische groepen in het verleden. De laatste dag staat in het teken van het Calvario en gaan de pelgrims massaal naar de berg buiten het dorp om te offeren en ritueel hun verzoeken uit te voeren. Voor en na het feest worden er diverse processies gehouden waarbij het beeld van Maria door zingende en biddende bewoners door verschillende wijken van het dorp wordt gedragen.

Mijn benadering van het concept pelgrimage is gebaseerd op het idee van Eade & Sallnow (1991) over pelgrimage: een arena waar een veelheid aan vaak concurrerende betekenissen samenkomen. Op een bedevaartsplaats zijn verschillende betekenissen aanwezig omdat mensen met diverse achtergronden en belangen samenkomen. Ik heb gekeken naar de manier waarop ervaringen van sociale ongelijkheid de interpretaties van Maria, de pelgrimage en het leven van de gelovigen beïnvloed hebben. Tevens heb ik gekeken naar de manieren waarop mensen uiting geven aan deze interpretaties. Verschillende groepen mensen, zoals kerkelijke autoriteiten, verkopers en pelgrims hebben verschillende belangen, en deze belangen kunnen veranderen afhankelijk van de context en machtspositie. Ik ga uit van Foucaults (1977: 98) visie op het concept macht, waarbij mensen worden gezien als 'altijd in de positie om gelijktijdig zowel macht te ondergaan als uit te oefenen'. Ik kijk dus naar de 'macht' van de gelovigen om betekenis te geven aan Maria, de pelgrimage en de ervaringen van sociale ongelijkheid in het dagelijkse leven. De nadruk op de verschillende betekenissen bracht mij ertoe pelgrimage te zien als een manier om macht uit te oefenen, omdat de gemarginaliseerden de betekenissen beïnvloeden en veranderen. Tevens leidde de focus op de dagelijkse ervaringen van klasse, gender en etniciteit in het Maria-oord tot een herziening van het begrip pelgrimage. Pelgrimage is niet alleen een gebeurtenis die mensen losmaakt van hun alledaagse bestaan, maar wordt hier vooral gezien als wezenlijk verbonden met het alledaagse, als een vorm van 'geleefde religie'. Geleefde religie richt zich immers op de manier waarop religie wordt ervaren in de context van het dagelijks leven.

Om de hoofdvraag te beantwoorden is elf maanden veldwerk uitgevoerd in Quillacollo en Cochabamba in het jaar 2005 en drie maanden in 2007. Data werden verzameld door een combinatie van verschillende onderzoeksmethoden. Deze bestonden uit participerende observatie op verschillende plaatsen en tijdens verschillende gebeurtenissen in combinatie met informele conversaties met ongeveer 200 Bolivianen, en etnografische diepte-interviews met ongeveer 25 personen. Vijf van hen heb ik intensief gevolgd in hun dagelijkse bezigheden. Tevens heb ik de levensverhalen van deze vijf personen verzameld. Daarnaast heb ik methoden van foto-elicitatie gebruikt waarbij afbeeldingen van 25 verschillende Maria-presentaties van over de hele wereld aan de geïnterviewden werden getoond om de betekenis van Maria te achterhalen. Ook gebruikte ik bij de etnografische interviews foto's die ik maakte tijdens het veldwerk. Vervolgens heb ik drie soorten surveys afgenomen. Deze korte vragenlijsten hadden tot doel inzicht te krijgen in de sociaaleconomische achtergrond van de pelgrims en hun motieven voor bedevaart. Een vragenlijst is afgenomen bij 43 huishoudens in drie districten van Quillacollo en richtte zich op de gezinssamenstelling en inkomsten van de bewoners. Een tweede survey is afgenomen bij 86 bezoekers van het bedevaartsoord om inzicht te krijgen in de motivaties en praktijken van pelgrims. Een laatste vragenlijst is voorgelegd aan 62 leden van een dansgroep die deelnamen aan de religieuze dansprocessies tijdens het feest van Urkupiña om kennis en ervaringen van dansers te bestuderen. Verder zijn er semi-gestructureerde interviews afgenomen bij 22 Boliviaanse religiespecialisten, zoals antropologen en kerkelijke autoriteiten.

Om te begrijpen hoe pelgrimage gerelateerd is aan ongelijkheid heb ik speciale nadruk gelegd op het bestuderen van objecten, rituelen en verhalen, omdat mensen hiermee uitdrukking geven aan hun religie. Door de objecten, rituelen en verhalen te volgen, richtte mijn aandacht zich ook op de religieuze ervaringen buiten het terrein van de officiële kerk. In het bijzonder heb ik veel informatie verzameld op het Calvario. Het was moeilijk om een vertrouwelijke relatie op te bouwen met pelgrims. Zij brachten meestal maar een kort bezoek aan het pelgrimsoord en dit maakte het onmogelijk om lange tijd stil te staan bij de motivaties voor de pelgrimage en de ervaringen van machtsongelijkheid. Ik heb me daarom voornamelijk gericht op de verkoopsters van offermateriaal en heb in de loop der tijd een hechte band met hen opgebouwd. Hun levens zijn verweven met de pelgrimage naar de Maagd van Urkupiña, omdat ze elke dag aanwezig zijn bij het heiligdom en bovendien als actieve gelovigen ook zelf het oord bezoeken. Een andere belangrijke groep respondenten bestond uit de deelnemers aan de dansprocessies. Door samen met hen de bijdrage aan de dansprocessie voor te bereiden en mee te dansen in de dansprocessies tijdens het feest van de Maagd van Urkupiña in 2005 en 2007 kreeg ik veel zicht op hun Mariadevotie en de betekenis die ze daaraan gaven.

De pelgrimage naar de Maagd van Urkupiña kan gezien worden als een materialistische pelgrimage. Verzoeken voor economische verbetering zijn zeer prominent aanwezig op dit pelgrimsoord. Pelgrims doen niet alleen verbaal economische verzoeken, maar uiten deze ook visueel, materieel en publiekelijk in objecten en rituelen. De eerste vorm van ongelijkheid die naar voren kwam tijdens deze pelgrimage, was dan ook klassenongelijkheid. Deze vorm van ongelijkheid is geanalyseerd op macro- en op microniveau.

Hoofdstuk vier gaat in op het macroniveau en richt zich op de neoliberale politiek in Bolivia en hoe de sociaaleconomische structuren tot uiting gebracht worden op de pelgrimsplek van de Maagd van Urkupiña, met name op het Calvario. Veel Bolivianen zien als oorzaak van de toegenomen ongelijkheid en armoede in hun land het neoliberale beleid van de regering gedurende de afgelopen decennia. Om beter met de gevolgen van dit beleid in hun persoonlijk leven om te kunnen gaan bezoeken de pelgrims het bedevaartsoord. In hun behoefte aan bescherming en sociale zekerheid die de overheid hen niet geeft, wenden de pelgrims zich tot de Maagd van Urkupiña. De pelgrimage biedt dus ruimte, symbolen en woorden om uiting te geven aan klassengerelateerde problemen die op staatsniveau gegenereerd worden.

Op hetzelfde moment echter eigenen de gelovigen zich het neoliberale model toe en reproduceren het op de pelgrimsplek in de rituelen en in economisch gedrag. Zij passen zowel in hun hoedanigheid van pelgrims als van verkopers zelf de regels van de vrije markt toe. Deze paradox is vooral zichtbaar in het ritueel van het hakken van stenen, waarbij pelgrims met een hamer stukken steen van de rotsen beitelen die symbool staan voor de wensen die ze hebben. De gelovigen gebruiken een kapitalistisch jargon waarin de berg vergeleken wordt met een financiële bank. Zo spreken de pelgrims over de stenen als 'geld', ze spreken over 'kapitaal' dat met 'rente' moet worden terugbetaald. De rente wordt betaald door de stenen na een jaar terug te brengen en door te investeren in offers. Ook de commercie rondom de pelgrimsplek wordt gestructureerd door de neoliberale regels van competitie, zelfverantwoordelijkheid en het recht van de sterkste. Ondanks politiek en sociaal verzet tegen het neoliberale model wordt het in feite gereproduceerd tijdens de pelgrimage. In de pogingen om met de consequenties van de gewelddadige neoliberale structuren in de maatschappij om te gaan raken de pelgrims verwikkeld in een conditionele uitwisselingsrelatie met de Maagd van Urkupiña. Volgens de gelovigen kan zij gewelddadig ingrijpen in het hier en nu en gemene straffen uitdelen. In deze relatie onderwerpen de gelovigen zich dus aan een ander gewelddadig regime.

Hoofdstuk vijf gaat in op het microniveau van klassenongelijkheid en zoomt in op de wederkerige uitwisselingsrelatie die pelgrims opbouwen met Maria. Centraal staat het microniveau waarop de economische verzoeken gedaan worden en hoe deze vertaald worden in bovengenoemde stenen en in miniaturen. De miniaturen, door gelovigen gekocht en ter zegening aangeboden, zijn letterlijke representaties van de verzoeken die ze doen aan Maria, zoals auto's en huizen. De miniaturen worden net als de stenen na de zegening meegenomen naar huis, waar ze zorgvuldig worden opgeborgen of uitgestald op huisaltaren.

Het bestuderen van het sociale leven van de stenen en miniaturen draagt bij aan de kennis over hoe deze materiële religieuze objecten deel uitmaken van de symbolische uitwisseling en hoe ze functioneren in de geleefde religie van de pelgrims. Pelgrims bouwen een 'spirituele economie' op, een term die ik, in navolging van David Morgan, gebruik om te verwijzen naar de economische uitwisselingsrelatie die wordt opgebouwd tussen Maria en de pelgrims.

De wederkerige relatie omvat zowel de bovennatuurlijke wereld van Maria als het alledaagse leven van de pelgrims. Geloften en offers worden ingeruild tegen Maria's steun. Opnieuw komt de economische manier waarop pelgrims onderhandelen met Maria naar voren. Mijn studie laat echter zien dat de spirituele economie geen automatische uitwisseling is waarin pelgrims gebeden en geloof ruilen voor Maria's hulp. Integendeel, de miniaturen herinneren gelovigen aan de investering die ze zelf moeten doen. De stenen en miniaturen functioneren als de tastbare en krachtige herinnering aan de relatie tussen de pelgrims en Maria. De biografie van de objecten onthult dat de pelgrims een relatie van samenwerking met Maria opbouwen waarin pelgrims geloven dat Maria de nodige condities schept voor de verwezenlijking van de verzoeken en hen bemoedigt om hun eigen stappen te zetten om hun economische aspiraties te realiseren. Pelgrims verwachten geen directe hulp van Maria, maar doen hun verzoeken in het bijzonder om zichzelf te motiveren om aan hun doelen te werken. Pelgrimage verschaft niet alleen de ruimte om op het leven te reflecteren en de doelen te benoemen of te herzien, maar heeft ook materiële effecten in het dagelijkse leven. De spirituele uitwisseling heeft daadwerkelijk consequenties omdat de pelgrims hard werken om hun doelen te bereiken. Mijn studie geeft inzicht in deze motiverende kracht van religie. Bovendien daagt deze studie de dichotomie tussen het spirituele en materiële uit door te laten zien hoe deze samenkomen in de religieuze ervaring van mensen.

Naast deze materiële verzoeken benaderen pelgrims de Maagd van Urkupiña voor problemen inzake gender-ongelijkheid. Huiselijk geweld, ervaren door talloze Boliviaanse vrouwen, kwam naar voren als een dominante vorm van genderongelijkheid. Veel vrouwelijke gelovigen verwezen hiernaar, met name op het Calvario. Wetenschappelijke literatuur over huiselijk geweld in Latijns-Amerika verklaart de hoge cijfers van huiselijk geweld en het lijden van vrouwen die hiervan slachtoffer zijn vanuit de dominante genderstereotypen *machismo* en *marianismo*. Het *machismo* gaat uit van een agressieve houding van mannen ten opzichte van vrouwen, terwijl het *marianismo*, de notie van vrouwelijkheid, ervan uit gaat dat vrouwen de Maagd Maria als passief en onderdanig rolmodel omhelzen. In studies die gebruikmaken van het concept *marianismo*, wordt veelal verondersteld dat mishandelde Latijns-Amerikaanse vrouwen een passieve en lijdzame houding aannemen ten opzichte van hun gewelddadige partners. Impliciet lijken deze studies te veronderstellen dat vrouwen de Maagd Maria als voorbeeld nemen, vandaar de naam *marianismo*. Er wordt echter zelden aandacht besteed aan de daadwerkelijke interpretaties die de vrouwen geven aan Maria. Verschillende studies hebben inmiddels aangetoond dat het *machismo-marianismo*complex een te simpele duale voorstelling geeft van genderverhoudingen in Latijns-Amerika. Hoofdstuk zes draagt daarom vanuit een nieuwe invalshoek bij aan de kritieken op het concept *marianismo* door te analyseren hoe de vrouwelijke gelovigen die in een gewelddadige relatie verkeren of hebben verkeerd, zelf tegen Maria aankijken. Mijn studie laat zien dat het lijden onder huiselijk geweld niet zo passief en eendimensionaal is als gesuggereerd wordt in studies die gebruikmaken van het concept *marianismo*. Hoewel het lijden duidelijk naar voren komt in de verhalen van de Boliviaanse vrouwen, accepteren zij dit lijden niet in marianistische termen. Een diepe woede, ook wel *rabia* genoemd, kwam naar voren als een sleutelconcept in de verhalen van de geïnterviewde Boliviaanse vrouwen. Deze strijdlustige emotie van woede is een reactie die niet samengaat met de notie van *marianismo*, die uitgaat van opofferingsgezindheid. Tevens benadrukken de mishandelde vrouwen dat de Maagd van Urkupiña ook zowel een lijdende als een woedende kant heeft. Deze Maria wordt ook vereerd omwille van haar wraakzuchtige karakter en haar talent om gewelddadig in te grijpen in het leven van de echtgenoten. Vrouwen dragen hun woede over aan Maria, die wordt ervaren als een wraakgodin. De Maagd van Urkupiña kan haar woede over het geweld inzetten tegen de gewelddadige man om zijn vrouw te wreken.

Etnische ongelijkheid kwam tot uitdrukking in de religieuze dansprocessies die jaarlijks worden gehouden in augustus. Tijdens het feest van Urkupiña voeren folkloristische urbane groepen hun spectaculaire dansen op in de straten van Quillacollo tijdens een vier kilometer lange dansprocessie, de *Entrada Folklórica*. Sinds 1999 wordt er een *Entrada Autóctona* gehouden, een dag eerder dan de reeds lang bestaande *Entrada Folklórica*, met als hoofddoel de Indiaanse mensen bij het feest te betrekken. De introductie van deze dansprocessie versterkt het debat over 'authenticiteit' waardoor de vraag rijst welke vormen van etnische identiteit geconstrueerd worden in de twee *Entradas*. Mijn analyse laat zien dat deze identiteiten verschillen, omdat de stedelijke *mestizos* die dansen in de *Folklórica,* etnische authenticiteit claimen op basis van een overkoepelend inheems Boliviaans verleden, terwijl de dansers van de *Autóctona* authenticiteit claimen door de actuele etnische regionale variëteiten te laten zien in hun dansen. Bij beide *Entradas* wordt gebruikgemaakt van het concept authenticiteit om hun link met etniciteit te rechtvaardigen. Omdat 'authenticiteit' een claim is en geen feit, is er sprake van politiek waarin groepen worden onderscheiden die verschillende belangen hebben. In de dansprocessie wordt niet alleen etnische identiteit, maar ook etnische ongelijkheid tot uiting gebracht. Zo komt er minder publiek kijken naar de *Autóctona* (ook omdat het een minder spectaculaire processie is), heeft de organisatie minder geld en keuren de kerkelijke autoriteiten de *Autóctona* af, omdat de dansers volgens hen niet dansen uit de juiste religieuze overwegingen. Paradoxaal genoeg wordt de *Folklórica* meer gewaardeerd, terwijl deze over het algemeen wordt geïnterpreteerd als minder authentiek. In feite wordt de bestaande etnische hiërarchie in Bolivia gereproduceerd in de dansprocessies. Ook laat ik zien dat de door de dansers ervaren gevoelens van 'communitas' alleen gelden voor de eigen groep en juist de verschillen tussen de groepen onderling en tussen de *Entradas* versterken. Gevoelens van gemeenschapszin en broederlijkheid worden versterkt binnen de groepen, waardoor een groepsidentiteit wordt gecreëerd waarin de onderlinge verschillen tussen de leden tijdelijk worden opgeheven. Tegelijkertijd verscherpt deze groepsidentiteit de verschillen met andere groepen. Dit hoofdstuk laat zien dat de theorieën van de Turners (1978) over communitas in pelgrimage en van Eade & Sallnow (1991) over de met elkaar concurrerende discoursen elkaar niet uitsluiten. Mijns inziens maakt communitas deel uit van de concurrerende discoursen: communitas binnen de dansgroepen draagt bij tot de constructie van etnische ongelijkheid tussen de groepen en *Entradas* onderling.

Tijdens de pelgrimage worden gelovigen zowel bemoedigd - *empowered*, als ontmoedigd - *disempowered*. Pelgrimage verschaft een ruimte waar zij worden aangemoedigd te reflecteren op hun leven en waar ze worden geactiveerd stappen te ondernemen om hun doelen te bereiken. Zoals de mishandelde Boliviaanse vrouwen aangemoedigd worden om zich tegen het geweld te verzetten door hun woede over te dragen aan Maria, zo worden in de dansprocessie de gemarginaliseerden aangemoedigd hun etnische identiteit publiekelijk te demonstreren. Tegelijkertijd is er in de pelgrimage ook sprake van ontmoediging. Zo komt naar voren in het hoofdstuk over het neoliberale model dat pelgrims ondanks hun kritiek hierop het model reproduceren. Ook onderwerpen zij zich aan het gewelddadige regime van de Maagd van Urkupiña door de regels van offeren, bidden en investering toe te passen. Op deze manier zijn ze overgeleverd aan Maria's straffende krachten. Ook de mishandelde vrouwen laten zien dat zij, door hun woede aan Maria over te geven, ontmoedigd worden de situaties zelf te veranderen. Bovendien neemt Maria de sociale ongelijkheden niet weg. Dansprocessies laten ook ontmoediging zien, omdat de ruimte om etnische identiteit uit te drukken begrensd is. De gemarginaliseerde etnische minderheden krijgen ruimte om hun etniciteit te tonen in de *Autóctona*, maar tegelijkertijd wordt hun opvoering gemarginaliseerd in vergelijking met de *Folklórica*. Samengevat kan religie dus bemoedigende persoonlijke tactieken verschaffen voor het omgaan met sociale ongelijkheden, maar heft het de structurele ongelijkheden niet op.

RESUMEN EN ESPAÑOL

El peregrinaje revela mucho acerca de las estructuras de poder de una sociedad, ya que a través de este medio los creyentes expresan sus problemas cotidianos en un discurso religioso. En el presente estudio veremos el peregrinaje como una lente a través de la cual podemos investigar varios tipos de desigualdades sociales. Las peregrinaciones dan a los peregrinos la oportunidad de expresar problemas personales, sociales, económicos y políticos, y a la vez influyen en su percepción y en la posibilidad de creyentes de afrontar estos problemas. El presente estudio antropológico se basa en las experiencias de creyentes en un lugar de peregrinación mariana en Bolivia. Este lugar de peregrinación se encuentra en Quillacollo, una pequeña ciudad mercantil en la provincia central de Cochabamba. La veneración de la Virgen de Urkupiña era, hasta los años setenta del pasado siglo, una veneración local que atraía a los indígenas Quechua de las aldeas de las montañas que rodean Quillacollo. A continuación se interesaron los peregrinos del floreciente distrito mercantil de Santa Cruz en esta representación mariana y empezaron a relacionar a la Virgen de Urkupiña con cuestiones económicas. Este lugar goza desde entonces de popularidad a nivel nacional y en la actualidad llegan peregrinos de todo el territorio nacional –e incluso de fuera- y de todo tipo de entornos para su peregrinación anual.

La mayoría de los peregrinos visitan tanto la iglesia del pueblo como el "Calvario", una colina a dos kilómetros del pueblo donde hacen sus peticiones y realizan sus rituales. Aunque llegan peregrinos todos los días, agosto es el mes en el que más visitas se reciben, que es cuando se celebra la festividad de Urkupiña. Las peticiones de la gente reflejan las desigualdades sociales que sufren en su día a día. En el lugar de peregrinación se escuchan sobre todo problemas relacionados con la clase social, como la pobreza, el género, sobre todo violencia doméstica, y la etnicidad. Esto llevó a la formulación de la pregunta clave: ¿Cómo tratan los creyentes bolivianos con las desigualdades de clase, de género y de etnicidad en el lugar de peregrinación de la Virgen de Urkupiña?

Mi enfoque del concepto de peregrinación se basa en la idea de Eade & Sallnow (1991) de la peregrinación como una arena en la que convergen varios significados y compiten entre ellos. He visto cómo los significados que los peregrinos dan a la Virgen María, la peregrinación y sus vidas se basan en sus experiencias de clases, género y etnicidad, y cómo las personas expresan, resisten o reproducen estos significados. Aquí parto del punto de vista de Foucault (1977:98) acerca del concepto poder, según el cual las personas son consideradas 'siempre en la posición de a la vez padecer como ejercer poder'. El enfoque sobre la multitud de significados llevó a la idea de ver el peregrinaje como una forma de ejercer poder. El enfoque de las experiencias cotidianas de clase, género y etnicidad en el lugar de peregrinaje llevó a la revisión del concepto peregrinaje. El peregrinaje no es sólo un acto que libera a la gente de su existencia cotidiana, sino que aquí es sobre todo considerado como una conexión fundamental con lo cotidiano, como una forma de 'religión vivida'. La religión vivida se basa de hecho en la manera en que se vive la religión en el contexto de la vida diaria.

Para contestar a la pregunta clave se han realizado 11 meses de trabajo de campo en Quillacollo y Cochabamba en el año 2005 y 3 meses en 2007. Se recopilaron datos mediante una combinación de diferentes métodos de investigación. Estos se basaron en la observación participativa en diferentes lugares y durante diferentes sucesos en combinación con conversaciones informales con aproximadamente 200 bolivianos, y minuciosas entrevistas etnográficas en profundidad con más o menos 25 personas. Cinco de ellas fueron seguidas de forma intensiva en sus quehaceres cotidianos. A la vez se recopilaron los relatos biográficos de estas cinco personas. De forma paralela se utilizaron métodos de foto-elicitación, en los que se enseñaban 25 imágenes marianas distintas de todo el mundo a los entrevistados para descubrir el significado de la Virgen María. También se utilizaron imágenes tomadas durante el trabajo de campo en las entrevistas etnográficas. A continuación se realizaron encuestas (43 encuestas acerca de la composición de las familias en tres distritos de Quillacollo; 86 encuestas a peregrinos acerca de las motivaciones, significados y practicas en su peregrinaje y 62 encuestas a miembros de un grupo de baile que participaba a la procesión religiosa de baile durante la festividad de Urkupiña) para poder comprender el entorno socio-económico de los peregrinos en el lugar de peregrinación. Por último se realizaron entrevistas semi-estructuradas a 22 especialistas en religión de origen boliviano, como antropólogos y autoridades eclesiásticas.

Para comprender cómo está vinculado el peregrinaje a las desigualdades se puso especial énfasis en el estudio de objetos, rituales y relatos, porque eran considerados como instrumentos para expresar la religiosidad. Este enfoque llevó a estudiar las experiencias religiosas fuera del reino de la iglesia oficial. Aquí se recopiló mucha información en el Calvario. Crear relaciones intersubjetivas con los peregrinos era difícil, porque en la mayoría de los casos realizaban visitas muy cortas al lugar de peregrinación por lo que era imposible comprender el contexto entero de sus vidas. Por eso me dirigí sobre todo a los comerciantes de material de ofrenda y estreché lazos con ellos. Sus vidas se entrelazan con la peregrinación a la Virgen de Urkupiña porque están presentes todos los días y además son todos creyentes practicantes y hacen su peregrinación anual. Un segundo grupo importante eran los bailarines. Al preparar junto a ellos su aportación a la procesión de baile y bailar con ellos durante la festividad de la Virgen de Urkupiña en 2005 y 2007 pude comprender muy bien su devoción a la Virgen y el significado que le otorgan.

El peregrinaje a la Virgen de Urkupiña podría ser considerado un peregrinaje materialista. Las peticiones para una mejora económica predominan mucho en este lugar de peregrinación. Los peregrinos no sólo hacen peticiones económicas, también las expresan de forma visual, material y pública a través de objetos, rituales y relatos. La primera forma de desigualdad que salió a la luz durante esta peregrinación era entonces la desigualdad entre clases. Esta forma de desigualdad ha sido analizada a nivel micro y macro.

El capítulo cuatro se centra en el nivel marco y se basa en la política neoliberal en Bolivia y en cómo las estructuras socio-económicas son manifestadas en el lugar de peregrinación a la Virgen de Urkupiña. Muchos Bolivianos culpan al gobierno neoliberal de las últimas décadas del aumento de la desigualdad y pobreza de su país. Para poder abordar las consecuencias del modelo neoliberal sobre sus vidas personales, los peregrinos se acercan a la Virgen de Urkupiña en busca de la protección y seguridad social que el estado no les proporciona. La peregrinación ofrece por lo tanto espacio, símbolos y palabras para expresar problemas relacionados con clase y que son creados a nivel de estado. Sin embargo, los creyentes se apropian al mismo tiempo el modelo neoliberal y lo reproducen en el lugar de peregrinación en los rituales y en su comportamiento económico, tanto como comerciantes como peregrinos, al aplicar las reglas del mercado libre. Esta paradoja es sobre todo visible en el ritual de sacar piedras, en el que los peregrinos pican trozos de piedra de las rocas que simbolizan los deseos que tienen. Los creyentes utilizan una jerga capitalista en la que el cerro es comparado con el banco financiero. De esta manera, los peregrinos hablan de las piedras como de "dinero", hablan de "capital" que ha de ser devuelto con "intereses". Estos intereses se pagan devolviendo las piedras el año siguiente e invirtiendo en ofrendas. Incluso el comercio alrededor del lugar de peregrinación se rige según las reglas neoliberales de competencia, sentido de responsabilidad y la ley del más fuerte. No obstante la oposición política y social al modelo neoliberal, este es en realidad reproducido durante la peregrinación. En los intentos por abordar las consecuencias de las violentas estructuras neoliberales en la sociedad, los peregrinos acaban involucrados en una relación de intercambio condicional con la Virgen de Urkupiña. Según los creyentes ella puede intervenir de forma violenta en el aquí y ahora y repartir castigos severos. En esta relación, los creyentes se someten por lo tanto a otro régimen violento.

El capítulo cinco estudia en profundidad la relación de intercambio recíproca que los peregrinos crean con la Virgen María. Investiga sobre todo el nivel micro en el que se realizan las peticiones económicas que se traducen en las piedras mencionadas anteriormente y en miniaturas. Las miniaturas son compradas por los creyentes y entregadas como ofrenda y literalmente representan las peticiones que hacen a la Virgen María, como coches y casas. Las miniaturas son bendecidas al igual que las piedras y se llevan a casa, donde son guardadas cuidadosamente o expuestas sobre un altar. El estudio de la vida social de las piedras y las miniaturas consigue ampliar el conocimiento acerca de cómo estos objetos religiosos materiales forman parte del intercambio simbólico y cómo funcionan en la religión vivida de los peregrinos. Los peregrinos construyen una "economía espiritual", un término que, al igual que David Morgan, empleo para referirme a la relación de intercambio económico que se crea entre la Virgen María y los peregrinos. La relación recíproca abarca tanto el mundo sobrenatural de la Virgen María como la vida cotidiana del peregrino. Se intercambian promesas y ofrendas por apoyo de la Virgen. Otra vez más vuelve a destacar la forma económica en la que los peregrinos negocian con la Virgen María. Sin embargo, mi estudio demuestra que la economía espiritual no consiste en un intercambio automático en el que los peregrinos cambian oraciones y fe por ayuda de la Virgen María. Es más, las miniaturas sirven de recordatorio para los creyentes de la inversión que todavía tienen que hacer. Las piedras y las miniaturas representan el recuerdo tangible y poderoso de la relación entre los peregrinos y la Virgen. La biografía de los objetos revela que los peregrinos construyen una relación de colaboración con la Virgen María en la que los peregrinos creen que la Virgen María aporta las condiciones necesarias para el cumplimiento de las peticiones y los anima a dar sus propios pasos para alcanzar sus aspiraciones económicas. Los peregrinos no esperan una ayuda directa de la Virgen María, pero hacen sus peticiones sobre todo para animarse a sí mismos a intentar cumplir a sus metas. La peregrinación no sólo facilita el espacio para reflexionar acerca de la vida y para nombrar y revisar las metas, sino que también tiene efectos materiales sobre la vida cotidiana. El intercambio espiritual se transforma en consecuencias reales. El presente estudio por tanto explica el poder motivador de la religión. Además desafía la dicotomía entre espiritual y material al explicar cómo ambos convergen en la experiencia religiosa de la gente.

También se aproximan los peregrinos a la Virgen de Urkupiña por problemas de desigualdad de género. La violencia doméstica, sufrida por incontables mujeres bolivianas, destacó como una forma dominante de desigualdad de género expresada en el lugar de peregrinación. Escritos científicos sobre violencia doméstica en América Latina aclaran las altas cifras de violencia doméstica y el sufrimiento de las mujeres víctimas de violencia doméstica desde los estereotipos dominantes de género *machismo* y *marianismo*. El *machismo* parte de una postura agresiva del hombre hacia la mujer, mientras el *marianismo*, concepto de feminidad, parte del hecho de que la mujer se aplica los valores de la Virgen María como modelo pasivo y de supresión. Esos estudios por lo tanto dan por hecho que la mujer latinoamericana adopta una postura pasiva, sumisa y sufridora ante la violencia porque toma a la Virgen María como modelo de comportamiento. Diferentes estudios han mostrado mientras tanto que el complejo *machismo-marianismo* ofrece una representación dual demasiado simplificada de las relaciones de género en América Latina. El capítulo seis es una aportación a las existentes críticas del concepto de estereotipo de *marianismo*. Mi estudio demuestra que el sufrimiento de violencia doméstica no es tan pasivo o unidimensional como sugieren los estudios que utilizan el concepto *marianismo*. Aunque el sufrimiento destaca claramente en los relatos de las mujeres bolivianas, no aceptan dicho sufrimiento en términos marianísticos. Una profunda rabia aparecía como concepto clave en las historias de las mujeres bolivianas entrevistadas. Este sentimiento agresivo de rabia es una reacción que no encaja con el concepto de *marianismo*, basado en el sacrificio. Además mi estudio amplía la crítica del *marianismo* desde una nueva perspectiva. En los estudios que utilizan el concepto *marianismo* sencillamente se da por hecho que las maltratadas mujeres latinoamericanas veneran a la Virgen María por su sumisión, sufrimiento y pasividad. Sin embargo, a penas dan importancia a las interpretaciones reales que las mujeres puedan tener de la Virgen María. Mi estudio muestra las interpretaciones reales que las mujeres bolivianas maltratadas tienen de la Virgen de Urkupiña. Ellas subrayan que esta Virgen tiene tanto un lado sufridor como un lado agresivo. La Virgen de Urkupiña también es venerada por su carácter vengativo y su capacidad de intervenir de forma agresiva en la vida de los maridos. Las mujeres traspasan su rabia a la Virgen María, a la que perciben como una diosa de venganza. La Virgen de Urkupiña puede desplegar su rabia sobre la violencia en contra del marido violento para así vengar a su esposa.

La desigualdad étnica salió sobre todo a la superficie en las procesiones religiosas de baile que se celebran todos los años en agosto. Grupos folklóricos urbanos realizan durante la festividad de Urkupiña sus espectaculares bailes por las calles de Quillacollo en una procesión de baile de cuatro kilómetros, la Entrada Folklórica. Desde 1999 se celebra una Entrada Autóctona, un día antes de la Entrada Folklórica, que existe desde hace más tiempo, con como meta principal incluir a los indígenas en la fiesta. La introducción de esta procesión de baile refuerza el debate sobre la "autenticidad" por lo que surge la pregunta de qué formas de identidad étnica se crean en las dos Entradas. Mi análisis deja entrever que estas identidades difieren, porque los mestizos urbanos que bailan en la Folklórica reivindican autenticidad étnica en el marco de un pasado indígena boliviano general, mientras los bailarines de la Autóctona reivindican autenticidad enseñando las variedades étnicas regionales actuales en sus bailes. Ambos utilizan el concepto autenticidad para justificar su vínculo con la etnicidad. Porque "autenticidad" es una reivindicación en lugar de un hecho, se trata de un proyecto político en el que se distinguen grupos con intereses distintos. En la procesión de baile no sólo se expresa identidad étnica sino también desigualdad étnica. Así hay menos público que sigue la Autóctona (y también porque es una procesión menos espectacular), su organización dispone de menos dinero y las autoridades eclesiásticas desaprueban la Autóctona porque según ellos los bailarines no bailan inspirados por las motivaciones religiosas correctas. Paradójicamente, se valora más la Folklórica, mientras generalmente se la considera menos auténtica. En realidad en las procesiones de baile se refleja la jerarquía étnica existente en Bolivia. Luego muestro cómo los sentimientos de la "communitas" experimentados por los bailarines sólo valen para el grupo en sí y lo que hacen es reforzar las diferencias entre los grupos y entre las Entradas. Los sentimientos de comunidad y fraternidad se refuerzan dentro de los grupos, por lo que se crea una identidad de grupo en el que las diferencias entre los miembros son omitidas temporalmente. Dicha identidad de grupo al mismo tiempo agudiza las diferencias con otros grupos. Este capítulo demuestra por lo tanto que las teorías de los Turner (1978) acerca de la communitas en la peregrinación y las de Eade & Sallnow (1991) acerca de los discursos que compiten entre ellos no se excluyen. Desde mi punto de vista, la communitas forma parte de discursos que contienden: la communitas en un nivel aporta a la construcción de desigualdad étnica en un nivel superior.

Durante la peregrinación, los peregrinos son animados y desanimados a la vez. La peregrinación facilita un espacio donde son animados a reflexionar acerca de sus vidas y donde son motivados a dar pasos para alcanzar sus metas. También las mujeres bolivianas maltratadas entrevistadas son animadas a oponerse a la violencia mediante el traspaso de su rabia a la Virgen de Urkupiña. En la procesión de baile aparece la animación, porque los marginados son animados a demostrar públicamente su identidad étnica. Al mismo tiempo podemos vincular la peregrinación a la desanimación. Así muestra el capítulo sobre el modelo neoliberal cómo los peregrinos lo reproducen no obstante las críticas. También se someten al violento régimen de la Virgen de Urkupiña al adoptar las reglas de hacer ofrendas, rezar e invertir. De esta manera se ven desanimados, porque son sometidos a los poderes de castigo de la Virgen María. También las mujeres maltratadas muestran cómo, al traspasar su rabia a la Virgen María, son desanimadas a ser ellas mismas quienes cambian la situación. Encima la Virgen María no hace desaparecer las desigualdades sociales. Luego las procesiones de baile muestran desanimación porque el espacio para expresar la identidad étnica es limitado. Los grupos étnicos minoritarios marginados obtienen espacio para mostrar su etnicidad en la *Autóctona*, pero su representación es a la vez marginada en comparación con la *Folklórica*. En resumen, la religión puede facilitar tácticas personales confortantes para abordar las desigualdades sociales, pero no las cambia ni tampoco suprime las desigualdades estructurales.